The Other Side of Success

Advance Praise For
The Other Side of Success

"An often-insightful look back on one man's pursuit of the American dream . . . throughout his memoir, Sawa paints a vivid portrait of a diverse and vibrant California."

—*KIRKUS REVIEWS*

"America's melting pot melds cultures and characters before your eyes in this wild ride of real estate developer Martin Sawa's life. This saga of sales, seances, and successes shows the magic of self-invention in America. It's a page-turner, and while clinging to the sides of the real estate roller-coaster, reveals core values of goodness that make it all worthwhile."

—PHILIP K. HOWARD, award-winning author, attorney, and founder of Common Good

"You won't read many memoirs like this one . . . a financially successful son of immigrant parents who crosses racial boundaries in search of love, creating a fulfilling life."

—CHERYL Y. JUDICE, author, sociologist, and researcher on race, class, and gender

The Other Side of Success

Money and Meaning in the Golden State

A MEMOIR

Martin Sawa

STEEPLE
PRESS

Published by Steeple Press, Oakland, California

Edited and designed by Girl Friday Productions
www.girlfridayproductions.com
Cover design: Paul Barrett
Project management: Alexander Rigby

Image credits: cover © Shutterstock/ IM_photo

ISBN (hardcover): 978-1-7350469-0-7
ISBN (paperback): 978-1-7350469-1-4
ISBN (ebook): 978-1-7350469-2-1

Library of Congress Control Number: 2020913664

The following names are pseudonyms: Daniel, Don,
Ihor, Ivan, Mohamed, Mr. Mitsui, and Tina.

Contents

Prologue

Life is short, its possible experiences many . . .
—William Zeckendorf Sr., legendary
American commercial real estate
developer, speculator, and broker

For where your treasure is, there will your heart be also.
—Matthew 6:21 KJV

In the distance, a car speeds westward on Interstate 10 through the Mojave Desert, slicing through the heat shimmer emanating from the scorched pavement. A closer inspection reveals a gold 1970 Pontiac GTO convertible and its occupants: the driver, a woman well into her 50s with a platinum beehive hairdo and outrageous cat-eye sunglasses, and the passenger, a scrawny young man barely 20, dressed in a brown leather vest over a white tee and jeans.

The woman fiddles with the radio dial and picks up "Big Yellow Taxi" by Joni Mitchell, barely audible over the wind rush. She lights a joint and takes a long toke, then offers it to the young man, who obliges her generosity. Both stare ahead in stoned silence.

The scene dissolves to the Santa Monica Pier at sunset as the ocean slowly swallows the red and orange wafer in a stunning display. The GTO screeches to the curb on Ocean Avenue, whereupon the young man climbs out and grabs a tan duffel bag from the back seat. He prepares to speak, possibly to thank the woman, but it is too late. She has already sped off.

He wends through the rollicking crowd clomping on the wooden deck amid the aroma of churros mixed with sea air, past the carousel and food stands and novelty shops and Ferris wheel to the very end of the pier—and the continent. He leans against the metal railing, surveying the immeasurable Pacific, and nods.

From the end of World War II to the millennium, the population of California tripled, from roughly 10 million to 33 million residents, accounting for nearly 20 percent of the total net population growth of the United States. Immigrants streamed in from other states as well as from foreign countries, resulting in the oft-repeated observation that if you tipped the country on its side, everything loose would slide into California. They jostled for position in communities of increasing racial and ethnic diversity.

To house these people and their activities, real estate developers leveled hillsides, orchards, pastureland, and desert and built vast subdivisions, apartment blocks, shopping malls, industrial parks, and office buildings. The inhabitants obsessed over real estate, which became the conversation staple of every cocktail party and of most casual discourse.

At one point, the number of real estate licensees in California exceeded the individual population of all but the twenty-five largest American cities.

Bold men such as Walter Shorenstein and John Sobrato in the San Francisco Bay Area and Rob Maguire and Donald Bren in Southern California altered the landscape with prodigious commercial real estate developments. As the millennium turned, the trading price of trophy properties and portfolios routinely exceeded nine figures. The most coveted assets were the skyscrapers of downtown San Francisco: tangible and unequivocal symbols of wealth, which lured investor capital from around the world.

Yet, unlike the more transparent transactions in the financial markets or the dissected celebrity purchases in residential real estate, the megadeals of California commercial real estate remained remarkably opaque. Developers, investors, brokers, and politicians charmed and schemed, wheeled and dealed, in a fierce game played for the highest of stakes. How these deals were arranged and executed remained a mystery to all but the inner circles.

I wasn't born with a passion for real estate. Conceived overseas to immigrant parents and birthed on US soil in the Midwest, I was just happy to be here. After starting college, I decided to solo hitchhike across the country, inspired by the adventures of Kerouac and Kesey. I sought to bear witness to a sprawling yet shrinking America in its twilight moments of innocence rather than discover it years later in books.

As I stood on Santa Monica Pier, the California dream seared my memory: total freedom to do as I pleased. I thumbed my way up the coast through the lush orchards of San Jose and disembarked in the San Francisco Financial District, where I wandered among the high-rises and craned my neck at the just completed Bank of America Center, then the tallest building west of the Mississippi. I returned home satisfied that I had seen what needed to be seen.

Years later, I turned to commercial real estate not out of ardor but necessity and for the first time tasted the "juice," the adrenaline rush derived from conceiving and closing a major deal. Through direct experience, I absorbed the fundamentals of this peculiar industry, like a sensor spinning atop an autonomous vehicle. The numbers got bigger and the competition more intense; I found myself at the table with the property magnates—and winning.

In retrospect, an interesting tale to be sure. However, memoir demands honesty under penalty of artistic perjury. For myself, this means not only a truthful accounting of time, events, and outcomes as best as I can recall but the admittance of my personal failings, hurtful acts, and repressed memories that lurked behind a business persona worn as a suit of armor. And so, I must also speak of love and death, of faith and family, of the search for meaning and the meaning of true success.

For this, I ask your indulgence.

PART I

CHAPTER 1

Birth of a Salesman

"Ah, Marty, ready to get rich?"

Flashing a practiced grin, Irv leaned forward and presented beefy fingers, recently manicured. Slightly overweight in a good way, he wore a perfectly cut navy pinstripe suit. Flecks of gray peppered his abundant dark hair, carefully combed in gentle waves. The scent of Old Spice clung to his jowls.

"Yes, sir," I said, presenting a heavily bandaged hand in return.

I had arrived in Chicago by train barely a week before, escaping a small town in rural Wisconsin on the day of my high school graduation. I immediately found work at a bottling plant where I promptly gashed myself on a massive shard. The owner, a surly Pole, refused to take me to emergency until I signed a waiver relieving him of liability, causing me to quit in disgust.

I scanned the classifieds in the Chicago Tribune, braking at an ad that screamed "Unlimited Income!" The next day, I caught the subway to a cheap hotel in the Loop to learn more. Jammed into a sweaty conference room, I listened to a hunched sales manager extol the virtues of the Fuller Brush Company and door-to-door sales, the revelation of which caused most of the twenty or so attendees to flee. I remained steadfast and was assigned to their top hitter for training.

Irv reached over to a table stacked with promotional material and grabbed the Fuller Brush Catalog. Glossy in four-color print, it illustrated the full range of household and personal care products—from the Bristlecomb, the famed boar-bristle hairbrush; to the Debutante cosmetics line, to the powerful oven cleaner—along with a brief description and the suggested retail price. He stuffed two catalogs into a handsome faux-leather black demo case replete with samples of the most popular products.

"We'll meet tomorrow, 10:00 a.m. sharp, Belmont and Kimball," Irv directed, all business. "Take the case and study the products."

"Great," I replied and turned to leave.

"By the way, I'd like you to do one more thing," Irv said, almost as an afterthought.

"What's that, Irv?"

"Erase all the prices in the catalog."

"But how will I know what to ask?"

For an instant, he regarded me with pity and then smiled. "See how bad they want it."

That night, I sat at the wobbly desk in my rented room furnished in Goodwill contemporary. Under the inadequate illumination offered by the naked ceiling light, I spit on the eraser of a No. 2 pencil and methodically erased prices. I regarded the seeming stupidity of the exercise as a barometer of my desperation. I needed to make money to pay the bills and save for college in the fall, a mere three months away. Higher education would fulfill my immigrant father's dream and enable me to be a productive cog in the American economy.

I periodically checked the prices in the second catalog and tried to at least gauge the orders of magnitude. Eyes blurry, I glimpsed the hard-shell Samsonite suitcase opened on the floor. Among the tossed clothes was a plastic bag filled with dimes and quarters, a gift from Mom to ensure I phoned at least twice a week. She had implored me to attend a nearby community college and never leave. The thought of having to return home in disgrace jolted me awake. Eighteen and scared, I erased furiously.

The "L" train was crammed at peak morning commute. From my abode on the West Side, I could simply have taken a bus north for a few miles, rather than take the subway east into downtown, transfer, and take another train back to the northwest side. But what the crumpled Rand McNally map failed to disclose was that two months earlier, in the aftermath of the assassination of Martin Luther King Jr. on April 4, 1968, the area along West Madison Street had erupted in violence and flames: eleven dead, more than 2,000 arrested, and over 200 buildings destroyed.

And more shit could break out at any minute. Hippies and anarchists were already streaming into Chicago for the Democratic National Convention in August, and the cops, "Chicago's Finest," were buttressing the defenses. The only rational response was to adopt a siege mentality. Shielding my demo case as if it held atomic bomb diagrams, I quizzed myself on the price of hair spray.

"Whatcha lookin' at, Opie?"

A militant woman, street-lean with an immense Afro, glowered at me. My contact with black folks growing up had been limited to televised images of them getting pummeled in the South, and more recently, doing some pummeling of their own in the North. Caught off guard and with no concrete experience to draw on, I winced and stared out the window. Perhaps I should have mastered the city dweller's ability to avert a gaze and so disguise fear.

But a sliver of memory suggests I also felt frustration at not having been adroit enough to ignore stereotype and engage her at eye level, without regard for our differences, perhaps with a smile and even the hint of flirtation, playing the rube and, against long odds, making her laugh. Such deftness and wisdom, akin to a Zen monk disarming a samurai, would need to be developed.

I emerged from the subway station and scanned the intersection. An arm extended through the open window of a parked Cadillac DeVille and beckoned me. I hopped in with Irv, who drove to a nearby neighborhood of modest, well-maintained homes while dispensing general instructions on how to write up an order. He pulled to the curb, told me to meet back here at two o'clock, and ejected me like a pinball as he sped away to ply his trade in the more prosperous zip codes.

The first house loomed before me. I pressed the doorbell but heard no ring, so I moved down the block. What followed was a montage of misery. A furtive shadow in the window drawing the curtain. An angry dog biting through the screen. A refrigerator-sized guy in a wife beater regarding me quizzically and then speaking in a foreign tongue (I apologized and left). And my favorite, the voice of an annoyed housewife emanating from somewhere inside the shuttered premises: "There's no one home!"

By 2:00 p.m., I had not made it inside even one house. Disheveled and humiliated, I waited on the corner until Irv's Caddy materialized curbside. I reluctantly opened the door and slid into the air-conditioned oasis.

"Irv, I can't do this."

He took my measure, probably knowing me better than I knew myself, and simply stated, "This is a business for men." Pausing a beat, Irv continued, "Half of the trainees don't even wait to meet with me—they're gone by noon. Most of the others wash out in the first week or two. I've seen big guys break down, bawl, and go back to their real job."

"But I'm only 18. I've never . . . "

"'But, but, but.' It doesn't matter. Too young? It doesn't matter. Don't know enough? It doesn't matter. Can't stand rejection? No one can, but it doesn't matter. You must want this so badly that nothing else matters. So, kid, what'll it be?"

My thoughts swirled. I had to make a defining life choice, on the spot and under duress. We sat in silence for a long time. Finally, I whispered, "Okay."

For the next hour, Irv taught me how to sell. As he drove off, I stood exactly where I had earlier that morning. Pulling back my shoulders, I strode purposefully to the front door of the first home I had tried earlier, knocked, paused, and then knocked again.

"Who is it?" a feminine voice inquired.

"Good afternoon, ma'am . . . it's Fuller Brush."

"I don't want any."

"I have a little gift for you."

The door opened a crack, as much as the security chain would allow. I espied a mass of unkempt hair and a worn housecoat.

"We have a nice spatula or pastry brush," I stammered. Irv revealed that these two items were selected not only for their utility in the kitchen but precisely because they could fit in the narrow gap formed by the jamb and a door clutched by a suspicious homemaker.

"Maybe I'll take the spatula." With that, she snatched the gift from my hand, sized me up, and then reluctantly let me in.

I entered the foyer and then the living room, decorated in the Old World style with legions of tchotchkes. She offered me a soft-cushioned chair and remained mute. Irv cautioned that I only had precious minutes to gain trust. I complimented her on the beauty of all the family members whose likenesses hung on the wall. Trembling, I opened the case, considered the contents, and extracted the lemon-scented furniture polish and a soft cloth. Begging indulgence with my eyes, I secured tacit approval and shined the coffee table.

"We have a special . . . today only!" I blurted, straining to summon Irv's basic prompts for creating a sense of urgency. "Buy three and get one free."

She eyed the spray can like radioactive waste. "How much?"

At a total loss, I squeaked, "$1.99 for all four?" She remained impassive, a Sphinx.

I slowly lifted out the toilet bowl cleaner. "Your neighbors really like this product." I beamed, recalling Irv's dictum for spurring envy. I peered down the hallway. "May I demonstrate?"

Intrigued, she led me to the bathroom. I lifted the lid and instantly recoiled from the grotesqueries I beheld within. Flushing several times, I proceeded to do wonders on the head. As we hovered over the sink, I held up the bottle and stammered, "Are th-three enough . . . Are s-six too many?" Irv had instructed me to offer six or even twelve units if the customer displayed a hint of interest. I had asked him incredulously why anyone would want that many, to which of course he replied with measured restraint that it didn't matter.

Fifteen minutes later, she opened the front door to let me out. I had sold six bowl cleaners, four cans of furniture polish, and a hairbrush that she had caressed longingly and for which I quoted a favorable price. With a flourish worthy of Caesar at Gaul, I declared, "Thank you, ma'am. My name is Martin, and I'm your Fuller Brush Man."

By the end of July, I had hit my stride, cherishing every secret I learned from Irv. Erasing the prices was simply Irv's way of teaching me that pricing was fluid . . . elastic! Of course, the Company didn't endorse this stratagem, just as it forbade selling non–Fuller Brush merchandise from the case. But Irv would stuff in whatever he could pick up at a deep discount as he plied the affluent suburbs of Chicago's North Side. This month featured women's leather gloves courtesy of a relative in Skokie.

Irv's maxims etched my brain like a laser. Upon receiving a customer's order, the company required a week or more for fulfillment, and it was up to the individual salesman to personally deliver the products, receive payment, and pay back the house. After a customer sweet-talked me into canceling her order, Irv thundered, "We're not in the business of selling, we're in the business of selling *and collecting!*"

Unlike me, Irv could afford to pay an old guy who couldn't be argued with to deliver his orders. In the rare event that he had to do it himself, Irv would arrive in a rusted ten-year-old Chevy Impala, sporting J.C. Penney garb and occasionally accompanied by his son disguised as a waif. Irv's knowledge of the human animal left me breathless.

I had by now missed Sunday Mass three weeks in a row. One side of my brain argued with the other that I had justifiably been too busy with self-survival and that the Big Guy would understand. I regretted most missing the previous Sunday because I had something legitimate to pray for. The following day, I was scheduled for my military physical; the reward for being in decent health was a card marked "1-A" and an all-expenses-paid vacation in Vietnam.

My wisps of memory of that day: gaping at the roiling clouds amid stifling humidity that surely portended thunderstorms; riding the L with all the windows open (most of the antiquated rolling stock still lacked A/C) and thus trading the risk of heat stroke for hearing loss as the train executed the ninety-degree turn below Jackson Street, the wheels flanging at probably 110 decibels; approaching the drab induction center in a drab neighborhood, picketed by anti-war demonstrators whose numbers that day required the presence of a couple of cops, appearing even burlier in riot gear.

As I wended through the demonstrators, a tough Italian-looking lad took a mock punch at an emaciated hippie who stumbled over himself. The kid laughed and proceeded into the building. A cute flower girl with pleading eyes—dressed in Levi's, tie-dyed tee, and indigenous paraphernalia—cut me off.

"You don't have to go in there. Do you want to napalm innocent women and children and then die yourself?"

My silence hinted no.

"We can help you. Show you how to beat the physical."

A confederate chimed, "Yeah, sneak in some bad pee-pee and tell them you like boys."

The girl continued, "Or you can become a conscientious objector. Worst case, we have friends in Canada."

When I started high school, the word Vietnam barely registered on people's radar screens. Four years later, young men were coming home in body bags, even in tiny Prairie du Chien. While many of the townspeople still expressed loyalty to the government, the mood had shifted. In Chicago in the summer of 1968, I found myself in the eye of the storm. All the anti-war and anti-everything forces of the cosmos were converging on Grant Park, to be unleashed like the Furies at the International Amphitheatre the following month.

The hippies' arguments were not novel to me, but their swelling numbers represented an influential voice that argued it was right to not do your duty, serving as a sort of summation argument for the jury in the court of public opinion, a ready response I could give my children and my children's children and all the others who would, for the rest of my life, ask me why I didn't go. I hesitated, then took a deep breath and stepped around the girl.

The specific details of the examination process elude me. I undressed to my shorts and stood in line with young men of all shapes and colors, startled not at how different people are but how similar when confronted with the same fate. Apart from occasional outbursts of fake bravado, the prospective inductees remained mute, most likely reflecting on how the dice would be rolled half a world away. As the day wore on, I passed more and more tests.

The windows on the L were closed on the ride home in deference to the rain whipping off Lake Michigan. Nauseated by the BO, I nonetheless crystalized my thinking. Ho Chi Minh, the top dog of the North Vietnamese communists, had been pals with Stalin—enough said. Whatever the morality or "justness" of the war, I reasoned that more communism would make the world a worse place. Also, as a first-generation immigrant, I hadn't yet forgotten the value of what I had, marveling at the hypocrisy of the so-called activists, unemployed by choice and unwilling to support the greatest country on earth. Eventually, all this soul searching was reduced to its essence, like cooking sherry for a glaze. My inner voice simply said: Be a man. I resolved to attend college until called to serve.

With only three days left in August, I stoically endured the mob of protesters squashing me on the L. Tomorrow, I would board the Greyhound Bus bound for the University of Detroit, located smack-dab in the middle of another racial cauldron. I needed to meet with Irv for the last time to return the demo case and square accounts.

Like a hurricane crossing the Atlantic, the weeklong protests gained momentum, and today was landfall: The Democrats would nominate their candidate for president on the last night of the convention. The train stopped shy of downtown due to the riots in progress and everybody piled out. I decided to leg it across the Loop to the transfer station and broke out in a quick walk—Irv didn't countenance lateness even if attributable to epic social unrest. I was quickly met by an onrush of protesters chanting:

"Hell, no! We won't go!"

"Hey! Hey! LBJ! How many boys did you kill today?"

They hurled expletives and solid objects at the cops, who responded with a vengeance, wielding billy clubs, chucking tear gas grenades, and scooping up the less mobile, writhing and kicking, into paddy wagons. I suddenly realized that there were no innocent bystanders from the cops' POV; in fact, they might mistake my sample case for something more sinister. I broke out in a dead run, slaloming through the chaos, and finally reached the transfer station.

Half an hour later, I spotted Irv at a back booth in the coffee shop. Ignoring me as I slid in, he continued to scribble calculations.

"Top it off, Irv?"

As Irv nodded imperceptibly, the waitress refreshed his coffee. "Here, hon," she said, pouring me a cup. I sat patiently until Irv finished his arithmetic. He reached into an attaché and produced a handful of checks, which he slid toward me.

"This covers the orders from last week. My delivery-man will take care of the open orders and I'll mail you the remaining checks."

"Thanks, Irv." I handed over the demo case. "Just seem to be short a bottle of lotion."

Irv shot the cuff and glanced at his watch. "From the look of the August numbers, you'll be the number one rookie and ahead of most of the pros."

"Irv, I can't thank you—"

"Ah, Marty, gotta go."

Smiling that Irv smile, he rose, fumbled in his pocket for a money clip, and proceeded to liberate a Benjamin, which he stuffed into my pocket. Gathering his attaché and my case, Irv moved toward the doorway with the grace of a big cat. The waitress opened the door and patted his butt on the way out, then resumed watching the riots on the diminutive black-and-white TV suspended in the ceiling corner.

I neatly folded the checks and tucked them in my wallet.

CHAPTER 2

The Call

Undoing the bindings of the papoose board, I gently transferred my infant daughter to her crib. Earlier that evening, my wife and I had proudly shown off Natalie at the Intertribal Friendship House, the gathering place for Native Americans in Oakland, California. During the potluck dinner, we referred to Natalie as "Precious" and endured relentless teasing.

After cooing her to sleep, I trudged to the dining room and beheld the monthly bills littering the table, which I hoped would have disappeared but which unfortunately loomed even larger than the day before. Ten years had passed since I'd left Chicago, and now I found myself married with children—my step kids, David and Alice, happened to be

visiting with their dad tonight—and striving to live the
California dream while confronting fiscal realities.

As I lifted the pen to sign a check, my wife breezed
past, pausing to squeeze my shoulder sympathetically, then
flipped on the TV and snuggled into the sofa.

I inhaled and set the pen down.

"Wanda, we need to talk."

"Can you believe this? All three channels are still showing nothing but Jonestown."

Two days earlier, the world discovered that cult leader
Jim Jones had induced his 900-plus followers, mostly from
the Bay Area, to commit mass suicide in a makeshift commune in a South American jungle. I had heard the politically
connected Jones speak once at a fundraiser and left stunned
by his dark charisma.

"I've been doing a lot of thinking," I said.

"Cronkite says they're still finding bodies. He says babies
were given Kool-Aid laced with cyanide."

I rose, turned off the TV, and faced my wife.

"I'm going to quit my job."

I had fulfilled, in theory, the dream of my Ukrainian parents,
which could be condensed to the then-popular bromide, "To
get a good job, get a good education." Starting college, I had
nervously waited to be called into military service. To my
amazement, Congress, influenced by the mounting anti-
war protests, authorized the first draft lottery since 1942 as
a more equitable means of maintaining troop strength in
Vietnam.

In the inaugural lottery year of 1969, the order of call was determined by the sequential drawing of small plastic capsules (each containing a date of the year) from a glass jar; all men of draft age who shared the birth date would then be called to serve as a group. The quota was met two dates short of my number. I was home free. More than feeling relief, I marveled at the operation of Fate in such a heavy-handed fashion.

I matriculated through three midwestern universities before finally graduating with more credits than I knew what to do with and no keen desire to do anything in particular. My worldview had been shaped as much by a series of cross-country hitchhiking and auto drive-away trips as by scholastic pursuits in college.

In October 1973, after college graduation and a brief stint toiling for the US Postal Service (and discovering why people went postal), I stuffed everything I owned into my weather-beaten '65 Ford Fairlane, stopped by my hometown to kiss Mom and Dad goodbye, and headed west. I calculated that my classes in architecture, economics (Marxist, but hey), and urban studies might lend themselves to employment in the expanding field of city planning.

I filled out job applications in Los Angeles and then proceeded up Highway 101 to the San Francisco Bay Area, sleeping in the car and occasionally splurging for a cheap motel. Four weeks later and drained of capital, I faced the dreaded prospect of returning to the Midwest like a whipped dog when the owner of a planning consultant firm in Berkeley invited me for an interview. A prim Scot with two middle initials, he intensely studied my resume and strained to muster enthusiasm.

"Ahem . . . as I mentioned, Mr. Sawa, we can only hire you on a part-time basis."

"That's fine," I said.

"And we . . . hmm . . . typically like our people to have an advanced degree in—"

"I plan on applying to grad school next semester."

"—urban planning or a related field. And the pay . . . well . . . I wish I could offer you more, but our circumstances are such that—"

"I understand."

Now employed, albeit at a poverty-level wage, I hastened to put down roots. If one could not stomach the Berkeley vibe or bear a long commute, then that left Oakland, the underappreciated stepchild of debauched San Francisco across the Bay. The mere mention of the word Oakland to a San Francisco native would trigger the de rigueur response, "There is no there there," reflexively quoting Gertrude Stein and her dubious syntax.

Oakland had recently undergone a transformative demographic shift, whereby in the span of two decades, the black population doubled as the white population was halved. Perhaps due to clement weather, generally less circumscribed neighborhoods, a low-density housing stock, and the absence of immense public housing projects, Oakland avoided the race riots of the '60s and picked up a rep as a "melting pot." In truth, it was both a vibrant and violent city, but after Chicago and Detroit, I could deal with that.

The city's social life centered around Jack London Square, a cluster of waterfront restaurants and bars at the foot of Broadway sporting names like the Sea Wolf, Elegant Farmer, and Uppy's, the latter owned by Gene Upshaw, an All-Pro lineman for the Oakland Raiders. One Saturday night, with nothing to do and dateless for months, I repaired to Uppy's and reflected on my romantic past.

I met the first love of my life in college when I dated a wealthy Jewish girl from the Upper East Side of New York City. Politically progressive and trained as a modern dancer, she attended Broadway plays in her youth while I drank beer in cornfields. She was beautiful and worldly and everything I wasn't. The relationship lasted for a year before she left me . . . bewitched, bothered, and bewildered. I later dated a sweet Wisconsin girl who cared for me deeply. Wary of being tied down, I broke it off but harbored regret in hindsight.

Having completed my pre-game warm-up at Uppy's, I crossed the street to the Square Apple, which had recently adopted a disco format. I entered to a packed house, squeezed into position at the corner of the bar, yelled "Budweiser!" to the barman, and inhaled the scene. The DJ cut to "Disco Inferno" and the crowd surged to the dance floor and coalesced in a writhing mass under the disco ball, which rotated phlegmatically, casting myriad points of reflected light.

I noticed a woman—dark and slender, perhaps Hispanic?—at a table with her girlfriend. She brushed off a jerk with a wave of her cigarette, without looking up or interrupting her conversation. Admiring her moxie, I glanced over from time to time until I caught her eye, and when she did not discourage me, took a swig to steady myself and sauntered over.

"Care to dance?"

Without a word, she rose and straightened her short, simple, sexy dress and headed to the dance floor as her girlfriend smiled mischievously. I set down my beer and rushed to catch up. We danced energetically, without talk or eye contact, and then returned to the table. I managed to pull out her chair in the nick of time and leaned over.

"You gals like a drink?"

"I'm Wanda," she said while moving her hand over the glass to decline.

"I'm Martin."

"Marty Mart," her friend giggled. She reached up and straightened the lapel of my brown leather blazer. "You interested in my homegirl?"

As Donna Summer moaned through the speakers, I grinned. "Sure, why not?"

Wanda, a full-blooded Choctaw, lived in a bungalow on 38th Avenue with her children, David and Alice, 8 and 6, and her mother, also Alice.[1] Her father—mean, alcoholic, and gone— was not talked about. Wanda had divorced acrimoniously several years earlier from a Pomo man and had toiled as a line worker at the Owens Illinois glass factory before landing a job with Bay Area Rapid Transit (BART), the recently built subway and elevated train system. Wanda was a station agent and the perfect point-of-contact with patrons as they entered the system: She took shit from no one.

On the surface, in laid-back California with its pillars of hedonism—hot tubs in Marin, gay bathhouses in San Francisco, and the Playboy Mansion in LA—interracial love seemed like no big deal. The reality was that it was still a big deal. For all their reputed tolerance, Bay Area residents harbored racial prejudice like the rest of the world, except that, in the words of one local, "they were sneakier about it." Freewheeling cohabitation and experimental sex were one thing, marriage and family—skin in the game—quite another.

The heavy lifting by mixed couples had been accomplished by the prior generation, culminating in *Loving v. Virginia*, the Supreme Court decision published ten years earlier in 1967, which invalidated any remaining state laws prohibiting interracial marriage. The threat of being thrown in the pokey for crossing racial lines had finally been eliminated, but societal opprobrium remained.

Nonetheless, the promise of love cut through social differences and racial history like a knife through butter, and Wanda and I became an item. As an added bonus, when I got Wanda, I also got her extended family, which accepted me instantly. Numbering over a hundred strong at holiday picnics, the clan embodied the spirit of friendship that Wanda's mother had instilled at the community center and the assurance that no matter what path an individual chose to pursue, he or she would always be welcomed back and embraced by family.

I was also impressed by the pay and benefits Wanda earned at BART and evaluated my own circumstances. I deduced that I could do better financially in the employ of a government agency than at a cash-strapped consulting firm and so applied to a number of municipal planning departments in the Bay Area. The City of San Jose offered me a job, and since I was already schlepping to San Jose State University from Oakland in part-time pursuit of a master's degree, I reasoned it was worth the commute and would enable Wanda and me to upgrade our lifestyle.

Firmly situated, I proposed marriage. Wanda joyously accepted the engagement ring and our talk turned to the wedding.

"Let's get married in Death Valley!" I said.

In the two years following my arrival in California, I traveled throughout the state and visited virtually every scenic landmark, from the coast redwood forests to the giant sequoias of the interior, from majestic Yosemite to the crystalline, alpine Lake Tahoe, from the dormant volcano Mount Shasta to the mythic allure of Big Sur. Yet none moved me more than Death Valley National Park.

Death Valley holds the record for the highest registered air temperature on earth, 134.1 degrees Fahrenheit, recorded in 1913. I was impressed not only by the heat but also by the desolate beauty: salt flats, sand dunes, and rugged canyons. I loved the clarity of the desert: You could clearly measure the resiliency of the plants and animals, competing ferociously for moisture, surviving under the harshest of conditions. I thought it ideal for our ceremony.[2]

Wanda's elation evaporated like the vestige of water in one of those salt flats.

"Are you crazy?" she said with her now characteristic temper.

"It's really beautiful, better than Yosemite," I said. "There's an overlook called Dante's View—"

"Stop it!"

"—and in the late fall, the weather will be perfect!"

I admitted that it was a tad distant (450 road miles), which would likely suppress attendance, but we could splurge on a reception back in Oakland. It was unlikely my parents would come in any event, the logistics being too overwhelming.

Wanda stormed off and brooded and eventually reconsidered and we set a date in November of 1977.

Wanda and I drove to Death Valley tailed by her sister Gloria, the maid of honor, and Gloria's husband. For best man, I selected Gordon, my college roommate. Viking-like in visage, he flew out from Wisconsin with his wife, rented a car in Las Vegas, and zigzagged through the Mojave Desert. We converged at the Furnace Creek Inn, a hideaway of a few dozen rooms with palm trees and a spring-fed pool. Built in the '20s and frequented by movie stars during Hollywood's Golden Age, it now appeared a touch faded.

We ate and drank too much and slept late into the morning and frolicked some more and then dressed and caravanned twenty-five miles to our destination.

"So what did you most remember about that day?" I asked Gordon many years later.

"It was so cold," he said. "Dante's View was about a mile above the valley floor. We were all dressed for 90 degrees."

There was a photograph—probably taken with a Kodak Instamatic and long since lost—of the six of us tilted against the wind, shivering and eking out smiles, Wanda resplendent in a lacy white dress, I in a cream polyester suit with a chocolate-brown shirt, sporting a mustache and resembling an old-world gangster. The photograph must surely have been taken by the United Methodist minister (no Catholic clergy were available) who allowed me to recruit her from Trona (a derelict mining town named for the mineral) and braved the drive over the Panamints (the abutting mountain range) to officiate our wedding, for verily there were no other inhabitants for miles around.

"You timed it for around sunset, and it was dramatic. The streaks of color in the mountains," Gordon continued.

"What was the mood?"

"You were happy, eyes all lit up. You and Wanda joked around the whole time."

"Really?"

"You called Wanda your Choctaw Princess."

I had forgotten it all, a moment I wouldn't treasure enough.

A week later, as we determined retroactively, Wanda became pregnant, to our surprise and delight.

We consolidated our households and rented a home in the Trestle Glen neighborhood of Oakland at a substantial rent increase and sans mother-in-law, who elected to move in with another daughter. David and Alice attended Crocker Highlands Elementary School, along with their cousin Jennifer, who lived nearby. I harbored no sentiment that I had become their new "Dad." They were close to their father, who seemed a decent enough chap, despite Wanda's bitterness. I tried to care for them and improve their lives.

While dating Wanda, I observed that she was hard on the kids and attributed it to a strict disciplinarian approach. But as time passed, I found the corporal punishment disturbing and noticed an "edge" to Wanda that led to unprovoked anger. At times, she unleashed her animosity toward her ex on David and Alice. Increasingly, I intervened to protect them.

I was commuting daily to San Jose along "the Nimitz," now Interstate 880. Named after fleet admiral Chester

Nimitz, the freeway enjoyed a fearsome reputation as the worst stretch of highway in the Bay Area. Truck traffic had been banned on adjoining routes, so the drive was a nerve-shattering enterprise, with defenseless cars wedged between columns of eighteen-wheelers. The Nimitz spawned road rage before there was road rage. The bizarre was commonplace; I was not wholly surprised when a two-by-four fell from the sky and bounced off the hood of my '67 Mustang.

I found a carpool partner in Mohamed, a San Jose city architect responsible for code enforcement who also lived in Oakland. Rather than fostering tranquility, carpooling heightened the angst. My partner seethed with rage, daily proclaiming the government job was beneath him. The trigger was usually the sight of the Coliseum Arena, which featured an innovative suspended ceiling system. "That was my design," he groused, "and those bastards stole it." I would arrive exhausted.

Six months after the wedding, I finally secured a Master of Urban Planning Degree from San Jose State University. When I had first enrolled at the school four years earlier, my consulting firm was writing general plans, environmental impact reports, and other land-use regulations for small California cities that weren't staffed to do it themselves. We would appear like the Lone Ranger, empower cities to plan their future, and then ride away. While the pay sucked, the intangible rewards were satisfying.

But the transition to the planning department of a major city bred frustration and cynicism. The lofty goals of idealistic planners were chewed up and spit out by the politicians, who did what they pleased.[3] I soured on the profession even as I strived to earn my advanced degree. The final prerequisite consisted of writing a thesis. I considered various topics and eventually selected *"Land-Use Planning on California Indian Reservations."*

I initiated my research and discovered that unlike the sprawling reservations of, say, the Navajo or Sioux, California's seventy-seven reservations were "postage-stamp" rancherias with a few dozen residents, tucked away in remote locations unknown to the general public. I studied the historical antecedents and discovered more than I bargained for.[4]

With most of these rancherias lacking any meaningful resources and their residents suffering from high rates of poverty, unemployment, alcoholism, and social distress, the concern was not on planning the future but on day-to-day survival. A tribe near Palm Springs attempted to generate revenue by expanding their bingo operation—popular with area tourists—but the idea was encountering stiff legal opposition as a form of gambling. I gamely wrote my thesis prescribing the standard planning bromides for tribal governments as I had done for functioning cities.

After the thesis was accepted, I wrapped it in a protective envelope and stowed it away.

In August of 1978, Wanda felt the baby stirring and we rushed to Kaiser Hospital at Broadway and MacArthur. We had taken Lamaze classes, and I struggled to remember my responsibilities in the supporting role. The false contractions continued, and Wanda lay in pain for twenty-four, then thirty-six, hours. The obstetrician finally decided to induce labor and ordered an intravenous infusion of Pitocin. Sleepy, I took a time-out and stumbled to the cafeteria for coffee while the drug took hold on my wife.

I returned to Wanda's room to find the bed gone. Frantic, I raced down the hall, pleading for directions to the delivery room. Barred at the door until I outfitted myself with gown and booties, I burst in to find a nurse cleaning the newborn. She glanced at me with disappointment, and then resumed her business. Discomfited, I slunk to the bed, hugged mother and daughter, and retreated.

For restitution, I purchased a scarlet perambulator with fat whitewall tires and cushiony springs. On Sunday afternoons, I would push the buggy containing the precious cargo and lead the family around Lake Merritt,[5] and strangers would peer inside and exclaim that the baby already had a full head of hair. These idylls would occupy a special place in my memory.

Wanda and I agreed that Natalie should be properly baptized in a church, although neither of us displayed much religiosity. I had lost my faith (or, more correctly, the practice of my faith) in college, not through any protracted moral struggle or intellectual conversion to atheism but rather a gradual "falling away" spurred by the siren song of secularism. The discipline instilled by eight years of Catholic grade school and four years of Jesuit high school proved insufficient to maintain my interest in the ritual; it was simply easier not to do it. My practice had been reduced to showing up for Mass at Christmas and Easter, and even then, oft absent in spirit.

I located a Ukrainian church in San Francisco, which would serve the additional purpose of comforting my parents that Natalie would not only be "raised right" but would also remain mindful of her Ukrainian heritage. Mom had been understandably ambivalent about my marriage, as she had long ago identified a Ukrainian girl for me to marry, the daughter of immigrant friends who lived in the East Village in Manhattan. She had struggled to relate to Wanda as best she could but found it difficult to bridge the cultural gulf.

We arranged for my parents to fly out to California, a matter of consequence, since to my knowledge they had never boarded a plane. Zenon and Lydia Sawa had spent four years after World War II in an Austrian refugee camp before being approved for legal emigration to the United States. By my reckoning, they conceived me shortly before boarding a steamship in Bremerhaven, Germany, in 1949, and then arrived at Ellis Island with my 2-year-old sister, Charlotte, and a couple of suitcases. Absent was sister Oksana, who perished as an infant during the War.

My parents were resettled in Prairie du Chien, a town on the banks of the Mississippi River in southwestern Wisconsin, noteworthy as the second-oldest community in the state and for its astonishing ratio of taverns to population: forty-two bars for 5,249 men, women, and children. They labored for a farmer sponsor as basically indentured servants until a local family befriended them and helped them find paid work. My dad's parents arrived a year later, and the six of us nested in a small house; another ten years would pass before my brother, Greg, was born.

The Cold War with the Soviet Union had cast a pall of suspicion on many immigrants, particularly those from Eastern Europe, who might, for whatever reason, harbor sympathies for the Commies. Drills in anticipation of thermonuclear war reminded a bewildered populace that annihilation was but thirty minutes away, the travel time of a

Soviet ICBM. In his banquet speech for the Nobel Prize, William Faulkner mused, "There is only one question: When will I be blown up?" And the McCarthy hearings ratcheted up the tension. This caused the locals to wonder: "Who are these Sawas? What's a Ukrainian? Isn't that like a Russian?"

Yet this was home, and my parents never left that tiny town. What few trips they took, they took by train until rail service was discontinued in 1971. They had no desire to travel and see the world—they had seen more than enough during the War. To fly meant prevailing on friends—and thus incurring social debt—to drive them 230 miles to O'Hare in Chicago, help them negotiate the world's busiest airport, and then later pick them up.

However, after much resistance, Mom and Dad capitulated and flew to California for the christening. We all gathered at the Immaculate Conception Ukrainian Greek Catholic Church. Due to the meager population of church-going Ukrainians in the Bay Area, the building itself was hardly monumental: barely 50 by 80 feet and of concrete block construction. However, the interior exploded with the colors of the icons and two stained glass windows in the diminutive nave, which in turn accommodated perhaps twelve pews.

As the two families gathered amiably, Wanda's sister Gloria thought my father resembled a celebrity whose name eluded her until, after much interrogation, I elicited Ben Gazzara, a durable actor of stage, screen, and television. David and Alice bounded about, eventually finding space between the two grandmothers. The priest entered, and Wanda and I established our position in front of the small altar. She held our swaddled daughter and I a candle while the priest, clad in robes of blue and gold, chanted prayers from the fourth century:

"O Lord our God . . . O Master all-powerful, bless this infant that has been brought to appear before You, the Creator of all. Let her grow to do good works that please You."

He anointed Natalie with oil on her forehead and, invoking the Trinity, thrice poured water from a glass pitcher onto her head, to her increasing irritation. He admonished the gathered—"Wisdom! Let us be attentive!"—and read verses from a Pauline epistle before concluding with a prayer imploring that Natalie be sustained in faith all the days of her life.

After the service, I watched as my parents cradled Natalie, and whatever concerns they harbored melted away.

They would never visit California again.

As Thanksgiving approached, I handled the front counter at the San Jose Planning Department, doing what I did every day: dealing with the walk-in traffic and attempting to satisfy citizen requests for information on anything from constructing a fence to laying out a technology park.

At the head of the customer line stood Angry Man, a silver fox with an expensive white shirt unbuttoned to the sternum, exposing a medallion on a gold chain framed by tufts of chest hair. I knew him by reputation as one of the more aggressive developers in the Valley. He clutched a paper with Planning Department letterhead.

"I want to see the director," he fumed.

"Sorry, sir," I said. "He's out for lunch."

"Read this," he said, stabbing my midsection with the document.

I perused the letter, a standard form notifying the applicant that an Environmental Impact Report would be required in order for the approval process to proceed.

"Yes, sir, the planning staff has made the determination that your proposed office building will require a full EIR," I said. "It's close to a creek and will impact a wildlife habitat."

"Do you have any idea how long that will set me back?"

"I would guess six to twelve months."

"You would guess . . . by then I will have lost my option with the landowner. You gonna reimburse me 500 grand?"

I studied the medallion, probably equaling a month's salary for a Planner II.

"You damn paper pushers have no idea what it's like to work for a living," he said.

I pondered how in space and time I had wound up here, behind this counter.

"I don't know why I'm wasting my time with you," he continued unabated. "I'll take care of this with the mayor."

By now, his words floated past me like soap bubbles. He snatched the letter from my hand, twirled indignantly, and tramped away. As the next person in line stepped up, I pretended to listen but drifted farther and farther away to a land where dreams really do come true.

"Hello?" queried an engineer type with a roll of drawings under his arm.

"Excuse me," I said. Turning around, I mumbled to a colleague, "Not feeling well. Can you take the counter?" and walked out the door.

On the Nimitz, I punished myself for being a whiner. I had a lovely wife and family, stable employment, and two college degrees. So what if I hated the job and hated the commute? A man should suck it up and act responsibly. But I was also dead broke—the Bay Area cost of living consumed savings faster than that shark in *Jaws*. I couldn't envision how on a planner's salary I could stay afloat, much less get ahead. Even with Wanda and I both employed, the likelihood of amassing enough capital for a down payment on a decent house in a nice neighborhood with quality schools seemed hopelessly remote.

WAAAAAAH!

The air horn of a big rig advised me that I had drifted into the adjoining lane. I jerked back and glimpsed a stocky trucker in the rearview flash the one-finger salute.

And then I remembered Irv, dormant all these years, and his insistence that what really mattered, and the only thing that mattered, was the will to succeed. Ten years before, I had proven to myself and the world that I could sell, and if I could do it once, I could do it again. I was pushing 30 and already starting to ossify. I needed to take action—now.

Tonight, I would broach the matter with my wife.

"Huh?"

"I'm going to quit my job."

"Oh, you got something better," Wanda said. "Why didn't you tell me you were out interviewing?"

"I'm going into sales. I did it after high school, I was pretty good—"

"Selling what?"

"I'm thinking of real estate."

"What does it pay?" she asked.

"It's based on commissions . . . the more you sell, the more you make. It's a great system."

"So it doesn't pay anything?"

"Well, not right off the bat. But once you get going—"

"What about the benefits?"

"I'll be more like an independent contractor than . . . a worker bee."

Wanda rose and paced the room. "We can't even pay the bills and you're going to chase some dream?"

"If I stay stuck in this dead-end job, we'll never—"

She stopped at the table full of bills. "Oh, I see. I'll be stuck in MY dead-end job while you have your fun. And I'll be the sole support of our family. Oh, hell no!"

The discussion was not progressing as envisioned.

"I'll still provide like I have been until the commission checks start rolling in," I offered.

"Just how are you going to do that?" she asked.

"I'll . . . I'm . . . working out the details . . . but I promise."

In a fury that had become alarmingly common, she slapped the table, causing the bills to go airborne. "If you can't be the man I married and accept responsibility, then we will leave you—and that includes your daughter!"

Wanda fumbled with a cigarette and stepped out into the night, neglecting to shut the front door. I regarded her silhouette nervously puffing, and slowly moved behind her, hoarsely whispering, "Don't worry, we'll make it."

CHAPTER 3

Initiation

Had I known anything about the financial markets, I would have picked a better time to enter the sales profession. In 1979, the rate of inflation had climbed to 12 percent and the prime interest rate to 15 percent, numbers unprecedented in modern memory. But lacking any baseline, I merely accepted the statistics as the new normal.

In terms of the products I could sell, I chose real estate since it generated hefty commissions and I could dive right in, with no pesky barriers to entry. At the time, procuring a real estate license involved slightly more effort than fogging a mirror. I appeased Wanda by securing the license before quitting the San Jose Planning Department. Then I vowed never again to hold down a real job.

I perused the classifieds of the Oakland Tribune and was again enticed by the promise of unlimited income. With remarkable symmetry to a decade earlier, I found myself in a hotel conference room listening to the manager's pitch to recruit salespeople. In this case, the objects of desire were unimproved lots for vacation homes in remote subdivisions.

The premise appeared straightforward: Teams of salesmen would entertain middle-class couples at dinner presentations held at Bay Area restaurants with the aim of inducing them to travel to a proposed resort community in the hinterland. There, the couples would be met by other sales teams, who would tour them around the purported master-planned community and sell them one or more paper lots.

I was assigned to a dinner party at a Velvet Turtle restaurant to promote a California coastal community. Prohibited from eating, I sat at a table with three couples and salivated as they feasted on steak. As the speaker projected images of the surf lapping on a black sand beach, I assured the suburbanites that not only would the property make a spectacular site for a second home, it would also serve as a superb investment.

After the dinner, the salesmen congregated at the bar. One veteran nursing a highball pulled me aside.

"How many did you bag?" he asked.

"Two of the three promised to make the trip," I said. "They were impressed that we would fly them up in a chartered plane at our expense."

He grinned. "The developer would rather they didn't drive three hours and then find twenty-five more miles of rough road once they got off the highway. And the place is socked in by fog for ten months of the year. So we gotta sell it out in six weeks. You get 'em on the plane, we'll ply 'em with coffee and sugar doughnuts and do the rest."

Another veteran put me in a playful headlock. "It's got this fucking tiny airstrip. Did he mention eight years ago a DC-3 crammed with salesmen crashed while taking off?"

I laughed awkwardly, assuming it was a joke.

"Yeah, I lost a buddy on that one," the first said.

And so I was introduced to the fraternity of land salesmen, hired by developers to sell dirt and a dream. In retrospect, they were perhaps the greatest natural salesmen I'd ever met, and unfortunately, responsible for the enactment of much California real estate consumer protection law.

As I worked more dinner parties and then trekked to watch the closers *in situ*, I gleaned the intricacies of the craft and, consequently, developed pangs of conscience. The innocence of the couples was heightened by their lack of any real estate knowledge or street smarts. When faced with the boisterous marketeers, I likened them to sitting ducks.

Developers would acquire extensive tracts of land and create hundreds or even thousands of paper subdivision lots, which they would sell to unsuspecting buyers. The projects frequently lacked any basic services such as roads, water, sewer, and electricity; in some cases, the lots were unbuildable due to terrain or soil conditions. At the time, local jurisdictions required little in the way of developer commitments to actually build the infrastructure.

I was constantly pressed to invite qualified friends and relatives to the dinner parties, which I resisted until Mohamed called out of the blue, curious as to what I was up to since leaving the planning department. I confessed to selling land for second homes, which piqued his interest, compelling me to extoll the virtues of a new development I was promoting: a wilderness retreat nestled among the redwoods. A week later, Mohamed and his wife sat at my right hand at the Velvet Turtle; a week after that, they owned a lot.

I tried to assuage my guilt by rationalizing that, in comparison to other developments being marketed across the state, this one was superior: close to town with improved roads and even a few houses under construction. I was earning a decent commission income and keeping my word with Wanda, to her stated surprise. As Mohamed excitedly described his vision for their dream house, I congratulated him again and then exited land sales the following day.[6]

Skimming the yellow pages for real estate companies, I immediately eliminated all the residential brokerages. I innately discerned that I was unsuited to selling homes (too emotional and right-brain dependent), and so I targeted the sale of commercial investment properties, which also represented the highest value assets I could think of and therefore *really* big commissions.

I called the commercial brokerages in alphabetical order, which roundly rejected me on the spot since I lacked experience and had no idea how to vet an investment property or negotiate with a crafty client. I had nearly exhausted the alphabet when a company in downtown Oakland eagerly sought to recruit me. With some difficulty, I located their premises: a two-room windowless office at the rear of an old commercial building. I met the manager, a gregarious Aussie, who immediately cut to the chase.

"Matey, we just opened for business, and I'm offering you a ground-floor opportunity."

I glanced about and verified the accuracy of his statement, then reached into my briefcase and extracted my resume.

"I have a strong background in city planning and some recent land—"

"Did you bring your sales license?" he asked.

I nodded, and he led me to the back room, where I found nine cheap desks brooding under a flickering fluorescent ceiling light. Only one desk was occupied, and that by a burly, mustachioed, chain-smoking Englishman talking nonstop into a handset that he periodically struck on his palm to clear the static. The manager pointed to the desk next to the Brit.

"That's yours."

I hesitated. "When do I start?"

"There's the phone."

Commercial real estate at the time was not yet fully recognized as an investable asset class by institutional investors due to "lack of transparency" (translated: "I can't tell how you're cheating me"). The industry was dominated by wild and crazy developers, private syndicates, and idiosyncratic individuals, who in turn attracted brokers that matched their personalities. There were few rules, and for the newbie, no help of any kind. In return for half the action, the manager promised me not only the desk and phone but all the beer I could drink at the adjoining dive bar on Friday afternoon wind-downs. I quickly accepted.

And so I pounded the pavement and called on the owners of property in downtown Oakland and around Lake

Merritt. I discovered that, in many cases, potential sellers were also buyers, typically selling one property to purchase another via a tax-deferred exchange. I again channeled Irv and embraced rejection.

While dialing for dollars, I distilled the rudiments of the profession from the Englishman via occasional, gruff, one-minute lectures, probably motivated by his desire to let off steam coupled with a modicum of pity for me. I discovered that investment property transactions took months to put together and close, if they closed at all. I had been spoiled by the immediacy and quick commissions of land sales and now faced an existential problem: how to feed the family. Wanda had expressed pleasant surprise at my ability to segue so quickly into a new position and assumed that everything was just fine. I reasoned there was no need for her to see me sweat.

The American ideals of thrift and savings that my dad cherished were fast disappearing as the United States strove mightily to become a debtor nation. I pondered how to accomplish my civic duty, but being broke with no current income dampened the prospects for any conventional borrowing. I suddenly conjured up those solicitations in the mailbox that I had reflexively discarded: banks pleading with me to apply for a credit card. The plastic rectangles, originally conceived as instruments of convenience to be paid off in full every month, had recently morphed into vehicles for consumers to borrow money to buy more stuff.

Why not use the cash advance feature to pay for something truly important, such as a roof over the Sawa family's head? I read the fine print on the application and convulsed at the interest rate and accompanying fees, which would make a Mafia accountant blanch. I then recalled the words of Reverend Ike, a Harlem-based huckster, prosperity theologian, and early televangelist who had recently swung through the Bay Area: "If I owe you a thousand dollars and I can't pay you, I've got a problem; if I owe you a million dollars and I can't pay you, *you've* got a problem." That day, I applied for three credit cards.

The remaining desks in the brokerage office filled up gradually, creating a small boiler room and thus the opportunity to hear everyone's conversation, and for the unprincipled, the opportunity to steal leads. To protect myself, I honed the art of speaking in code (this was the pre-cellphone era), an essential skill perhaps only exceeded by the ability to read proprietary documents upside down.

One afternoon, the Brit accused the Aussie—who was himself a player-coach, doing his own deals while monitoring the deals of the salesmen and thus never above suspicion of being the fox in the henhouse—of some malfeasance, which degenerated into a shouting match between the rooms. As I endeavored to explain agency law to a prospective client on the phone, the Aussie burst in and screamed:

"Pommy bastard!"

He challenged the Brit to a fight to settle the score, whereupon they grappled and fell to the floor and nearly took me out as my colleagues wheeled back frantically in their swivel chairs. The Aussie soon pinned his top salesperson, dusted himself off, and while adjusting his tie, announced:

"Let's have an office meeting!"

We finished our calls and headed to the dive bar. The manager praised the Englishman for his position atop the leaderboard for the month and then encouraged us to share our background and sales strategies. One colleague confided he ate one meal a day, consisting of happy hour hors d'oeuvres, but was optimistic at his prospects. Another revealed that he was an associate member at an exclusive men's social club, responsible for producing their skits and plays, and then proceeded to quote Shakespeare. A third, who wore the same clothes every day and rarely spoke, didn't speak. The lone female associate shared her preparations for the initial meeting with a prospect, which included inserting her hand into her nether regions and dabbing her cheeks before the encounter. And so forth.

Hours later, I stepped outside into the emptiness—when the sun set, downtown Oakland transformed into a ghost town, devoid of restaurants, entertainment, and purpose, and frequented by hustlers, hookers, alcoholics, and other shadowy figures. I realized that my teammates were misfits of one sort or another and wondered if I was one of them.

Six months passed, and I had generated no income. I had, however, succeeded in fully drawing down ten credit cards, which were becoming harder to come by as the banks questioned why I needed *another* card. Wanda sensed my anxiety and pressed me for information, to which I would respond, "Am I not paying the bills?" I had secured listings and even placed two deals in escrow, but both fell apart after the buyers could not perform. Undeterred, I relentlessly continued to cold call.

One evening, I drove to the upscale Broadway Terrace neighborhood in Oakland. I had unsuccessfully tried to contact a property owner with an unlisted phone number, and rather than give up, decided to pay a home visit. I pulled up to a ranch-style house built over a small canyon. Checking the street number on the curb with a flashlight, I parked and then stumbled to the front door. I patiently rang four or five times and turned to leave when the porch light flicked on and the door opened.

A diminutive Asian woman, perhaps in her forties and with a beatific countenance, smiled politely. She wore a sky-blue silk robe resplendent with butterflies, birds, and other creatures.

"Good evening," I said. "Are you Mrs. Pang?"

She nodded.

"Do you own a vacant property near the Lake?"

She nodded again.

"My name is Martin Sawa. I'm a real estate agent, and I stopped by to see if you'd be interested in selling the property."

She regarded me for an almost uncomfortable duration and then said, "I am Edna. Please, come in."

The living room was comfortably appointed in a contemporary style but with a number of consequential Chinese artifacts. At that moment, a man—short and sturdy with horn-rimmed glasses—entered and immediately extended his hand.

Edna turned to her husband. "This is Sawa . . . the Buddha has sent him."

I discovered that Edna and her family were ethnic Chinese who had emigrated from the Philippines and found success in America by buying small apartment buildings and other properties. Edna negotiated the deals while her husband provided the management muscle. She also ran an import/export business and an acupuncture practice for her father, a practitioner of considerable renown.

She revealed her dream to build a Buddhist temple in Oakland, but unfortunately, the capital campaign had stalled. The profit from the sale of the vacant lot would put them over the top and allow construction to commence. Edna questioned me thoroughly over price and my ability to close the deal in the face of the volatile financial times. I assured her I would—what else could I say? The next day, she signed a listing agreement, and I immediately prepared marketing materials and crafted my sales strategy.

In less than a fortnight, I found a buyer who offered the asking price, and we negotiated a purchase contract and opened escrow. For the next two months, the buyer conducted due diligence and tried to line up the equity and debt for a residential development project—at any time, he could walk away. I shadowed him mercilessly, accompanied him to City Hall to review zoning documents, introduced him to lenders, nervously waited for the outcome of the soils investigation, and left nothing to chance.

In the meantime, Edna scheduled the groundbreaking for the temple with supreme confidence and took an interest in my personal development. She proved to be a shrewd businesswoman—I discovered that the Chinese dominated Filipino commerce despite their minority status—but always acted in a supremely principled manner. She lectured that there was the right way and the wrong way (I felt no duty to disclose my land sales exploits).

She predicted that I would do much business with Chinese investors and counseled me on how to gain their trust. For a graduation gift, she gave me an exquisite *chop*[7] carved from jade with my name spelled in hanzi. I would dab the chop in a red paste embedded within an intricately designed tin and then, with considerable flair, press it onto a paper as my signature. She also sensed my high level of stress and urged me to visit her father, a renowned acupuncturist. At first I declined but then reconsidered, deeming it impolite to spurn such a generous offer.

I located his office amid the bustle of Oakland's Chinatown, a land where cars and pedestrians choked the streets and double-parking was deemed a virtue. Before I could enter, a tiny woman scurried past me like a frightened rabbit. I hesitated—Edna had mentioned that her father spoke no English and was a little old-school. As I struggled to accept the premise of no pain, no gain, the doctor materialized, surprisingly taller than myself and lacking humor. I cringed as he pushed me into a dusky room lined with time-worn texts.

He gruffly motioned for me to undress and lie on the treatment table. I soon found myself naked except for my briefs. I espied him rummaging on his desk to produce massive needles thick as drill bits, which he proceeded to thrust into me with such vigor that I howled like a banshee. Obviously deeming me a wuss, he slapped my head and muttered in Mandarin, reducing my screams to pathetic whines. The procedure lasted an eternity. I watched in horror as the doctor lit several of the needles tipped with incense, the smoke and aroma enshrouding the room. I resembled a sacrificial offering.

While I later dressed, he scribbled characters on a scrap of paper that he pressed into my palm and then pushed me out the door. He pointed to a building across the street and commanded me thence with stern eyes. I discovered a Chinese pharmacy, where I surrendered the paper and left with a bag of herbs and roots, which I boiled and reduced to a horrible tea. I drank the repulsive mixture obediently, more fearful of the doctor than any contraindications.

The next day I felt terrific.

As the closing approached, my fortunes reversed. Other listings that had languished sprang to life. A developer with mysterious foreign money bought several adjoining lots overlooking Lake Merritt as a teardown. To appease the bureaucrats and preservationists, we moved four two-story houses that occupied the site to a replacement location on a Sunday morning, with streets blocked off and PG&E crews racing ahead to take down the power lines.

Another listing, a site zoned for forty apartments near Kaiser Hospital, was snapped up by an Oakland "entrepreneur." I tried to confirm his capacity to close, whereupon he wrapped his arm around my shoulder. "Marty, you're my main man . . . not to worry!" He assured me that he would purchase the property all cash, which he did . . . literally. Other deals fell into place as if orchestrated by an invisible hand, perhaps attributable to Fate or at least some Chinese magic.

The buyer finally closed on Edna's lot and construction could now commence. I attended the groundbreaking for the Light of Buddha Temple at 7th and Oak Streets and watched intently as a monk studied his compass and confirmed that the building's orientation was indeed auspicious. Edna and her family were lauded by the faithful as well as by

a sprinkling of dignitaries. The doctor playfully slapped my
head and we all ate red bean buns accompanied by a deli-
cious tea.

By the end of 1980, I had paid off all my credit cards
and even stashed some loot in a savings account and short-
term CDs, which were paying double-digit rates of interest.
I played hooky for a day and sauntered along the Oakland
estuary, waving to the skippers of the sailboats and thanking
God for smiling on me even though I prayed infrequently.
And I squinted west across the Bay to the skyscrapers of San
Francisco and dreamed of bigger deals.

CHAPTER 4

Estrangement

"Heah ya . . . weah ah . . . ah . . . ah . . . ye-ee! . . . ya . . . ya . . . "

Five stout men sang in unison as they mercilessly beat a barrel-sized rawhide drum with wooden sticks crowned with leather heads. Fifty feet away, a young man—bedecked with two enormous feather bustles, a brilliantly colored bodice, leggings adorned with bells, and supple moccasins— leapt and twirled around a grassy field. Spectators reclined on blankets and relaxed on lawn chairs in roughly concentric circles.

We arrived late for the 10th Annual Stanford Powwow on Mother's Day weekend in 1981, missing the Grand Entry but catching the men's fancy dance competition, the most energetic event on the program. This particular pow-wow[8] had grown into a major event, not only for Bay Area

Native Americans, but also for attendees from throughout California and other states. Trucks and campers jammed the parking lots near the Eucalyptus Grove on the Stanford University campus.

David and Alice ran ahead and quickly located Wanda's extended family, which occupied a sizable portion of the spectator pool, as Wanda and I, holding Natalie's hands, trucked behind. I hugged Wanda's mother, the undisputed clan matriarch, appreciative of how all the relatives had accepted me without question and integrated me into their community, ever expanding with marriages and a constant output of babies.

A distinctive aroma hooked my nostrils and pulled me around the perimeter to several booths with long lines. As fundamental to any powwow as drumming, singing, and dancing, fry bread beckoned me: a circular slab of fried dough, six inches or more in diameter, to be eaten as is or fashioned into tacos or dusted with powdered sugar or smothered with strawberries and other toppings. Fry bread's simple appearance belies the difficulty of its manufacture. I had watched the Carnes women relentlessly knead the dough and labor over crackling skillets of oil in search of perfection: chunky disks of golden brown with tender puffs and, most critically, equally done on both sides.

Thirty minutes later, I returned laden with the bounty.

"Mom, can we go see Dad?" David asked between bites. I surmised that Wanda's ex had cautiously selected a spot at the opposite end of the gathering. Wanda's eyes flashed, but she held her tongue and glared as David and Alice sprinted away.

The powwow MC, typically chosen for his ability to tell corny jokes, announced over the loudspeaker that the next dance on the program would be an intertribal, a non-competitive social dance open to all. He intoned, "Calling all dancers, calling all dancers, get on in here!" Many of the attendees rose, with the women draping shawls over their shoulders, and slowly danced in a clockwise movement around the arena. I elected to sit it out, but Natalie, almost 3, boldly participated, mimicking her mother's steps, softly hopping from one foot to the other.

All ages, all tribes, all families . . . moving as one. I held that image as we later packed up and left amid the haunting closing songs.

I did not grow up with a host of cousins and aunts and uncles. Since my parents both worked, Dad as a meat cutter and Mom in a school kitchen, I spent my days cloistered with Grandpa, who taught me academic lessons in Ukrainian, and Grandma, who fostered my religious instruction.

My sister, Charlotte, walked me to school when I started first grade and assisted me on other matters, such as: getting polio shots (ouch) as part of the national immunization campaign using the new Salk vaccine; properly executing duck-and-cover drills; and, of course, supervising the burning of raked leaves. We stood vigilant with sticks in hand, mesmerized by the smell—the quintessential childhood memory from 1950s rural America.

I would huddle with Dad around the Philco radio for Gillette's Friday Night Fights, but the aural excitement of the boxing matches was regularly exceeded by the main event: the fights between Zenon and Lydia. Dad drank too much and Mom recruited her children to hunt for his hidden bottles, which she promptly destroyed, enraging him when he arrived from work after a layover at the bar. They would yell in Ukrainian and chase each other around the kitchen table, under which I staked out a ringside seat.

We welcomed my brother to the family when I turned 11. Greg had been a "surprise," created in a moment of dormant passion on a summer vacation. And for me, an occasion for more chores. To spare Mom constant laundry, I pedaled to the coin-op on my red Schwinn bike, laden with Greg's soiled cloth diapers and surely resembling to passersby a street peddler in Shanghai.

A year later, a "family" pool hall opened in Prairie du Chien, which proved an ideal place to escape. I'd bike downtown after school and march through a gangway to the rear of a storefront and enter an indifferent world where I would shoot for hours. Soon I played for money against high schoolers and won most of the time, although collections posed a problem. A young tough, beaten and humiliated, would lead me outside to settle and then slam me against the wall in the gangway, sneering, "Whadya gonna do about it, you little prick?!"

Charlotte adapted less adroitly. In high school, her personality changed as she became more prone to fits of anger and antisocial behavior and entered into a running battle with Dad. On a humid summer evening, I heard a motorcycle revving outside our house. Zenon opened the front door and stared out aghast: A biker resembling Brando in *The*

Wild One lounged on his Harley hog, combing back greasy hair. He noticed my dad and smirked.

"Charlotte!" Dad stammered.

My sister appeared with too much makeup and a skirt shorter than what would be considered appropriate at the all-girls Catholic school she attended. Wordless, she advanced toward the door despite Lydia's efforts to restrain her.

"Who is *that*?" my dad mouthed, trembling.

"My date."

He reached to push her away, but she broke free, bursting through the defenseless screen door. She paused on the porch to straighten up and then marched defiantly to her new boyfriend and mounted the bike. They roared off into the night as half the neighbors watched enthralled from their front yards.

Charlotte graduated later that year and moved away. After I left home in 1968, I saw my family infrequently, and visits were rarer still after I moved to California. My grandparents passed, and Lydia's correspondence with distant relatives in Ukraine dwindled and then evaporated under constant Soviet censorship. Save for Natalie, the extant Sawas had now been reduced to five.

Urbane and prematurely gray, the sales manager leaned back in the oversized desk chair and grinned. "Welcome aboard, but know this: No brown in town."

Barely two weeks before the powwow, I had sat in a well-appointed suite in the Alcoa Building, a Skidmore, Owings & Merrill–designed high-rise in the San Francisco

Financial District. Rubloff, Inc., a Chicago-based commercial brokerage company, had embarked on a national expansion, recently opening seven offices in key cities. The manager offered me a position as an investment broker, despite the company's misgivings: I had flunked their "sales aptitude" test, spoke with an accent, and looked like a hick.

But the manager admitted he had also failed the psychological test ("it's all horseshit"), and we bonded over our shared experience. The fact that I had closed deals impressed him, but not as much as my tenacity in meeting Edna: "You actually went to her house—in Oakland—at night?" he gaped. He sensed potential, and while unable to change my elocution, he could alter my dress. He commanded me to adopt IBM attire and never wear a brown suit again.

As he led me around the office for introductions, I sensed I had entered a different world. While the leasing brokers were principally frat boys two years out of college with names like Chip and Drew, the investment brokers were serious men who had seen a thing or two. At 31, I was the youngest of the lot. I gravitated toward Gary, the only investment broker who had an interest in talking to me.

A former shopping center developer from the Central Valley, Gary spoke with a twang and affected Western attire for social occasions. He had borrowed too much and lost his properties; undeterred, he now reattacked business with a vengeance. In terms of the bricks and mortar, Gary knew more about retail properties than anyone I have ever met, before or since. He needed someone who would sniff out deals and grab the bone and not let go. I needed someone to show me the ropes—negotiating $10–50 million deals was a tad more challenging than selling lots around Lake Merritt.

"We got some good ole boys back in Chicago who are itchin' to buy a little real estate out here," he remarked casually. "Why don't you dig us up a nice shopping center or two in LA?"

"It will be hard to get a listing since I don't know that market," I countered, feeling a sense of déjà vu reminiscent of an Irv conversation.

"Hell, we aren't going to beg for a listing. That'd be a waste of time; those sharpies on the Westside think all brokers are stupid."

"So how do—"

"Just find us a deal."

Gary patiently explained the theory of the case. Ronald Reagan, newly elected president, was hell-bent on deregulation, which meant a freewheeling investment environment. Already, crafty operators with company names such as JMB and VMS (honoring the initials of the founding partners) were putting together public limited partnerships, raising beaucoup dollars by promising investors massive tax write-offs. They would outbid other buyers, so why run with anyone else? We merely had to find the right properties to adorn the covers of their prospectuses.

I flew to LA and sleuthed the landscape for the best community shopping centers, smaller than regional malls but larger than the neighborhood food-and-drug. Upon identifying a suitable candidate, I would create an investment package with floor plans obtained from a municipality's planning department, rent and sales numbers derived from surreptitious interviews with tenants, operating expenses gleaned from lunches with property managers, and any other relevant information I could cobble together, without any contact whatsoever with the owner.

My partner, in turn, would present the package to the tax syndicator, who would eagerly write up an offer, which we, in turn, would present to the owner, always in person so as to read the body language. Initially miffed at our gall for peddling his center without permission, the owner would invariably acquiesce to greed and counter at a ridiculous number, and soon we had a transaction in escrow.

Gary was utterly fearless. At times, *he* would make the offer as the buyer and then later flip the contract to the syndicator and profit from the spread. I watched in awe and discerned that deals were made not by the intellectually brilliant or the technically proficient but by those who could calculate risk and impose their will.

And I realized that there was always "hot" money coming from somewhere, certain investors who would simply pay more. For the individuals who controlled this money, there was only one unforgivable offense—not, as you might think, making a bad deal, but rather, not spending the money.

In the weeks following the powwow, Wanda's aggression toward David and Alice—and me—escalated. I can't recall the details of major blowups, although I know they happened. Try as I might, I seem to have deleted the worst from conscious memory.

Recently, I asked Alice what she remembered.

"Mom used to beat the crap out of us, and she never forgave our dad for walking out," Alice told me. "When he met his new wife, Wanda drove up to the rez and walloped her." How could I have forgotten? I certainly believed Alice, especially since David later corroborated the story.

"One day David and I called 911," Alice continued. "You were holding Natalie and had scratches all over you, and Mom was threatening to kill you."

That resulted in the cops coming and Wanda subsequently muting her behavior.

"The day David and I left for good, I had gotten my ears pierced and David forgot to do the yard work, which infuriated Mom," Alice said. "She called Dad and demanded he come and take us away, which he did." This moment I did recall, along with the resolve of David and Alice to escape their mother. Wanda called her ex the very next day and contritely asked him to return the children. But the die had been cast. David and Alice opted to live with him, and in the subsequent court hearing, the judge agreed.

Barely a month later in December 1981, the phone rang vehemently on the bedside table. As Wanda sleepily reached for the handset, I glanced at the alarm clock: barely 6:00 a.m.

"Who is it?" I asked as Wanda sat up.

I watched her face darken and contort, whereupon she screamed, "Oh God, no!" and dropped the phone, leaping out of bed and running out of the room. I picked up the handset and listened, stunned, as Gloria revealed between sobs that their sister Betty Jo had been murdered and had passed away minutes ago at Highland Hospital despite the heroic efforts of trauma specialists.

The horrific killing was splashed across the pages of the Oakland Tribune: Betty Jo Grunzweig, 37, stabbed some twenty-five times in a home invasion, discovered by her daughter, Jennifer, who frantically called 911 and then rushed to a neighbor for help. In the ensuing investigation, the lead detective very publicly named her estranged husband, Ken, as the primary suspect, reasoning that this was "a crime of passion."

However, the police could not muster sufficient evidence, and no charges were filed. With his reputation ruined, Ken later moved out of state with Jennifer and cut off all ties with Wanda's extended family, resulting in more turmoil as Jennifer lost all contact with her cousins.

This nightmare tore the family apart, and our marriage never recovered. I found more and more reasons to stay late at the office and avoid Wanda. And then, only months after the murder, my own sister simply disappeared.

Charlotte's life had grown increasingly grim, plagued by vehement and aberrant behavior, which had cost her two marriages and the custody of two sons. Greg happened to be working for the summer in Prairie du Chien between semesters at college and related what happened on that last week.

"She just showed up alone, unannounced," Greg said. "Charlotte looked like a wreck. She basically moved herself in and immediately started fighting with Dad." As Greg described it, the behavior was eerily similar to Wanda's: a hair-trigger temper and a propensity for unprovoked fits of rage, which had intensified over the years.

"She spent her days hanging out at the bars," he continued, "until about a week later, Dad got the call." A patron from the Prairie Schooner—a country bar with a life-sized replica of a horse-drawn covered wagon suspended over the entrance—informed Zenon that his daughter was getting out of hand. Embarrassed and infuriated, my father stormed out with Greg in tow and drove to the tavern.

"Dad grabbed her and shoved her out the door," Greg said, "with both of them cursing. When they got home, he told her to pack up and leave. That's the last we saw of her."

We all expected her to resurface in the ensuing weeks, then months, then years. But she didn't. Mom had lost one daughter during the War and now another.

My marriage to Wanda remained a stalemate, and we tolerated the situation for Natalie's welfare. Finally, in October 1985, after a particularly vehement argument with my wife that could find no end, I threw several suits and an armful of casual clothes in a suitcase and stormed out.

Of immediate concern was our daughter, not in terms of any potential abuse—for unlike with David and Alice, Wanda never laid a hand on Natalie—but from the shock of a divorce. We had recently bought a house in the family-friendly community of Alameda, and Natalie had just started first grade at a highly regarded elementary school; I could not violate her sense of rootedness.

I consulted several family law practitioners and deduced that their primary interest was to foster ill will and maximize legal fees. And so I proposed to Wanda a state of de facto rather than de jure divorce: We would share custody, I would pay the mortgage and other expenses, and Natalie's home and school life would not be disrupted. Wanda agreed to what promised to be a temporary accommodation but which would last for seven years.

The timing of our separation was less than opportune. In one of the more incomprehensible moves in the annals of commercial brokerage, Rubloff hired a consultant (perhaps the same one who had suggested the psychological tests) to advise them on employee compensation. These experts, untethered to the real world, recommended that all the brokers be put on salary rather than staying on commission. In a business where top brokers made more money than the senior executives and even the president, I imagined the company's motivation was to keep more money for the house. But the practical effect of cutting the brokers' income was to destroy their incentive. Dazed, I wandered into Gary's office.

"You heard?" I said.

"Yeah."

"I guess it's been a nice run."

"Time to move on, pardner."

"What are your plans?"

"Our syndicator buddies are pulling back—tax laws are changing," Gary said. "But some of these savings and loans are runnin' into a little trouble. I'll help them out, take some properties off their hands."

I stood silently.

"You've got some nice deals under your belt," Gary said. "You can hang your shingle pretty much anywhere. Go get 'em, tiger."

We looked each other in the eye and shook hands. Eventually, all the top hitters quit, and Rubloff's commercial brokerage business folded.

Without significant downtime, I joined Cushman & Wakefield, a highly regarded commercial real estate services firm, in their San Francisco office. Founded in 1917 in Manhattan and later acquired by the Rockefeller Group, the firm had brought New York know-how to the West Coast twenty years earlier, offering not only leasing and sales brokerage but also property management, appraisal, and other services.

I found myself in a private office in the Bank of America Center, the most prestigious office building in the city, gazing down on the imposing plaza dominated by a 200-ton, black granite, liver-shaped sculpture officially named *Transcendence* but known affectionately as "The Banker's Heart."

Once again, I didn't fit the mold. Most of the senior brokers belonged to one of San Francisco's private men's clubs. With names such as the Bohemian, Pacific Union, and Olympic, and founded in the nineteenth century with counterparts in the major American centers of commerce, the clubs reeked of old money. Notwithstanding strict admonitions about mixing business with pleasure—most famously the Bohemian's motto, "Weaving Spiders Come Not Here"—I sensed this was where things got done; allegedly, aspects of the Manhattan Project were conceived at the Bohemian Grove.

Nonetheless, I lacked not only the social graces but also the desire to join fraternal organizations. I found golf stupid (hit a ball and walk after it?), cocktail parties boring, and social networking a waste of time. During the interview process, I confessed to Cushman & Wakefield's upper management that I was only interested in doing deals and making money. Since my production could not be denied, they crossed their fingers and offered me a desk.

I studied the markets and pondered what to do next. A broker does not sell real estate but rather time, and the crucial decision is where to apply it. The looming savings and loan crisis might produce a cornucopia of deals, but for the most part these would be marginal, low-value assets whose sale would be subject to bureaucratic red tape. At the other end of the spectrum, money was pouring into US real estate from around the world, with international investors seeking the absolutely best properties as a safe haven for their capital. And the most prolific buyers were the Japanese.

The behemoth Japanese banks and real estate companies had already closed megadeals in New York City and were eyeing other markets. Through the Rockefeller Group's relationships, Cushman & Wakefield had a leg up in accessing Japanese investor capital—but how could I benefit? My most direct competitors were not investment brokers at other firms but the men who sat around me and had seniority and were thinking the same thoughts.

I discovered that the strongest Japanese connections on the West Coast passed through Cushman & Wakefield's Los Angeles office and reasoned that if I found the right colleague who could control the buyer, then I could find the right deals in San Francisco and significantly enhance the odds of closing. For merely knowing whom a buyer *is* leads nowhere; I or any other broker could phone Tokyo until the cows came home.

I flew to LA and first met with the office manager and stated that I came in peace. I assured him that I had no intentions of poaching, the practice of a broker doing deals outside of his or her home territory and siphoning off commission dollars from the local manager. Au contraire, I vowed to enhance his revenue stream. He eagerly filled me in on the background of the individual investment specialists, and I quickly identified the most promising accomplice.

Adrian not only enjoyed the trust of a key executive of a notable Japanese bank but also lived by his wits. He had emigrated from London at 20 years of age and drove a cab to make ends meet, offering a Thomas Brothers map book to patrons to help set the course. With charm and chutzpah, he graduated to selling real estate in the shark-infested waters of Los Angeles. I later learned he was nominally Jewish but considering becoming observant, which I respected.

The manager ushered me into Adrian's office.

"Yo, Adrian," I said, extending my hand. (After four *Rocky* movies, the greeting had entered the vernacular.)

"What's on your mind, boychik?" he said with a grin.

I proceeded to explain my plan to turn the spigot up on the flow of yen into San Francisco.

"So what do you bring to the table?" he asked.

"'Sawa' is a fairly common Japanese surname," I said. "They'll be excited that you're collaborating with a Japanese broker."

Adrian laughed.

"And with your insufferable British accent, how can we go wrong?" I said.

He proceeded to explain their rigorous financial underwriting standards. When I entered the business, investors priced buildings using the traditional "cigar box" approach: Collect the rents, pay the expenses, and count up what's left, the net income. Then divide the little number (net income) by the big number (price), and the result is the so-called "cap rate."

But with the increased flow of institutional capital into commercial real estate, the investment community began to adopt Wall Street shenanigans, such as the discounted cash flow pricing model, which projected net income and cash flow ten or more years into the future and then discounted it back to a present value, most typically expressed as the internal rate of return (IRR). I had studied the intricacies of the IRR calculation and its dependency on a host of assumptions and thought the metric absurd—akin to forecasting the weather a decade out—but vowed to master it.

"My client has an IRR hurdle rate of 10.0 percent," Adrian warned. "Can you get to that?" As with cap rates, IRRs were typically expressed to one decimal place.

Appreciating the Japanese penchant for precision, I countered, "Adrian, I can not only get to 10.0 percent, I can get to 10.00 percent!"

He chuckled and we shook hands and proceeded to iron out the details of our arrangement.

After the "divorce" from Wanda, I lived modestly, renting an apartment in downtown San Francisco, driving a sensible car, and incurring no debt, although I still rotated my credit cards and increased their limits, not knowing when I might need to bring them out of retirement.

Natalie stayed with me every weekend. I attended the powwows and family picnics and maintained contact with David and Alice; why should the end of one relationship mean the end of others? And it was these times that I felt the most fortunate—to be able to experience the breadth of what life had to offer.

During the 1980s, Oakland's racial composition continued to diversify. The Asian population doubled, swollen by Vietnam War refugees, and the Hispanic population multiplied as a result of legal and illegal immigration from Mexico. Most significantly, for the first time, the black population exceeded the white population. Thus, social life in Oakland was an interracial smorgasbord for those who did not feel compelled to stick with their own kind.

My life became more and more compartmentalized, best described as circles of activity that rarely intersected. Business was one circle, which demanded total focus and 110 percent commitment. The life of a salesman is all or nothing, requiring the mindset of predation: to steal out on the savannah in the early light and limp back at dusk empty-handed, only to venture out again tomorrow. Half the effort does not produce half the income; it merely produces no income. Each year, the counter is reset to zero.

The time I spent with my daughter was another circle—it was her time and her time alone. To achieve this goal meant not only words of love but also the dedication of personal time and the subordination of ego. When asked at school what her father did, she replied, "He says he sits in an office and talks on the phone." During the week, we would do homework nightly over the telephone (I had procured copies of her textbooks). Of course, weekends were hers.

My social life became a third circle. I dated cautiously, in no hurry to remarry. If I met a nice lady, great, and if I didn't, fine. I rarely chased. Wanda and I entered into an unspoken pact that we would not bring dates home when Natalie was present.

And through these dissociative identities, I thought I had achieved . . . balance.

CHAPTER 5

Metamorphosis

I preened in front of the bathroom mirror.

Several months earlier, the movie *Wall Street* had been released for the 1987 holiday calendar, causing an immediate impact on the financial and investment communities. Michael Douglas portrayed a fictitious corporate raider named Gordon Gekko, a role for which he won the Academy Award for best actor. The superbly crafted script captured the tenor of the times, when nefarious financiers were busted for insider trading and other misconduct. Through his dress, speech, and mannerisms, Gekko embodied the essence of Manhattan dealmaking.[9]

I had decided to up my game within Cushman & Wakefield and demonstrate a commitment to the changing times. The days of the cowboy broker had waned, and the profession now demanded sophistication. I had pondered how to effectuate this transition when I saw *Wall Street,* and in an aha moment, resolved to become Gordon Gekko.

And then came the day of the unveiling. I had not only shaved my mustache, paid for a pricey salon cut, and slicked my hair back with heavy-duty gel, but I also bought an expensive custom suit and a baby-blue shirt with a white cutaway collar, all accompanied by a power tie and the pièce de résistance: red suspenders.

I gently patted down a recalcitrant hair, pulled my shoulders back, and headed to the office. The brisk walk through the San Francisco fog quelled my nerves. I entered the office at precisely 10:00 a.m., when everyone was sure to be there.

The receptionist chatted idly into her headset and then looked up, agape.

"Martin, is that *you?*"

I smiled nonchalantly and proceeded down the aisle, in a gauntlet formed by the bullpen and the private offices.

A leasing broker did a double take and then bowed repeatedly with raised arms in mock respect.

An investment colleague stepped out of his office, and when confronted with my makeover, convulsed in laughter. Setting me up perfectly, he stammered, "Mr. Gekko, are you free for lunch today?" To which I replied to all within earshot, "Lunch? Aw, you gotta be kidding, lunch is for wimps!"—one of the signature lines from the movie.

A manager entered and, nodding approvingly, wrapped his arm around my shoulder. "Your production should increase by 50 percent," he predicted confidently.

I basked in the attention and palm-slapped my way around the cubicles, but then glanced at the wall clock. I was

scheduled to meet a new contingent of Japanese businessmen in ten minutes.

Waving to all present, I rushed out, admonishing a
rookie on the way: "Money never sleeps, pal."

The limo driver picked me up curbside at the Bank of
America Plaza, and I directed him to the newly opened
Hotel Nikko. I strode confidently into the lobby where three
gentlemen stood patiently, one stifling a yawn. Adrian had
persuaded the clients—in this case, the representatives of a
major Japanese bank—to get on a plane, and now it was my
responsibility to close them. I had prepared a tour of prospective investment properties and needed to secure a purchase commitment by the end of the day or risk losing face,
not to mention a sizable commission.

"Mitsui-san?" I asked, approaching the oldest and most
dignified man.

He eyed me quizzically. "Sawa-san?"

"Hai." I beamed.

Mr. Mitsui was the senior bank officer accompanied
by two subordinates, best described as "salarymen." Japan's
amazing transformation after the War—from a humiliated country in the eyes of the Allies to an economic
superpower—had been built on the backs of the salarymen,
those white-collar employees who joined a company out of
high school and stayed to retirement in a remarkable display
of loyalty. They worked crazy hours and then entertained
clients into the night, boarded a train for a one- or two-
hour ride into the suburbs, kissed the wife and kids in a tiny

apartment, slept for a couple of hours, and then caught the train back to Tokyo. Salarymen appeared perpetually tired and prone to *karoshi*, or death by overwork. I proceeded to explain to Mr. Mitsui that I was in fact Ukrainian and had no idea of how I wound up with a Japanese surname except perhaps it could have been the milkman. Mr. Mitsui, fluent in English and its idioms, understood the joke and translated it to his colleagues, who paused and then exploded with laughter. "Ah . . . mirkman!"

We piled into the limo and proceeded down Highway 101 toward Silicon Valley. As we passed a twelve-story office building with "Hitachi" emblazoned above the top floor, I casually mentioned that I had recently sold this property to the Japanese conglomerate, eliciting impressed nods. I showed them several technology buildings in Mountain View leased to Japanese companies, but which they declined—Mr. Mitsui felt that low-density real estate like a one-story tech building was a waste of land, and besides, if they liked the company, they would buy its stock.

They rejected several other opportunities on the return to San Francisco, and I grew increasingly apprehensive. However, I had saved the best for last. The limo deposited us at Union Square, San Francisco's famed public plaza and park, surrounded by elite department stores and world-class luxury retailers, all packed with Japanese tourists.

I ushered my clients into an older office building that faced the Square. A signature retailer occupied the ground floor while local tenants leased the upper floors. We rode a creaky elevator to the vacant penthouse suite, which offered an unobstructed view of the Square. One of the salarymen gazed through the window and frowned—"Grass . . .

no good"—commenting on the antiquated glass that had warped a bit. I tried to explain to Mr. Mitsui that the tenants didn't mind, and in any event, we could replace the windows. But he demurred; they didn't crave the headaches and intensive management of an older building.

We quietly rode the elevator down. Forlorn, I led them outside and searched for the limo. As I turned the corner and spotted our driver, Mr. Mitsui stopped abruptly, taken by a building across the street. Known in the industry as a "jewel box," the building had been exquisitely modernized and entirely leased to an international designer brand.

"Nice property," he said.

"Uh, it's not for sale," I muttered as the limo pulled up. I opened the door and paused . . . and then told the driver to trail us. Like the Pied Piper, I led them to the nearby Hyatt Hotel, which faced the Square. Inside the lobby, I excused myself with a flurry of bows and beelined for the pay phone.[10]

I knew the owner of the jewel box, a suave, soft-spoken developer and unyielding negotiator. Flipping through the phone book, I located his business, deposited a quarter, punched the number, and prayed. After convincing the secretary that I needed to discuss a matter of supreme urgency, I extracted an HP-12C calculator from my pocket and fumbled with the hotel pen and notepad.

Among San Francisco brokers, I was one of the few who dedicated himself to understanding the world of High Street Retail, those tony shops that lined Fifth Avenue, Rodeo Drive, and Union Square. The stores paid astronomical rents, which translated into astronomical sales prices, which even the most aggressive of buyers were loath to pay. Moreover, a location could be a mere fifty feet off a corner yet produce only half the rent, a mystery that few competitors had the skill to unravel.

"Hello, Martin, what's so important?" he asked.

"I'm here at Union Square and have a Japanese client who wants to buy your building."

"Of course, you know it isn't for sale."

"Of course. Can you give me a number?"

"Why would I give you a number if it's not for sale?"

"All right, what's the current net rent and when does the lease expire?" I asked. With those two figures, I could derive the cap rate and ballpark the IRR by escalating the rent to "market" when the lease expired and continuing it for the remainder of the ten-year projection period, thus ensuring a hefty residual value.

"Martin, you know every landlord in Union Square would like to have that information."

I pleaded for five minutes, occasionally waving and smiling to Mr. Mitsui. Finally, the owner relented and whispered the rent, which I scratched out on the notepad. I played with the calculator for a minute and then offered a price of $15 million, which represented "market value." I knew I could get to a higher number and still meet the buyer's IRR hurdle rate.

"Martin, I don't need you to sell it for that," he politely responded. "I can call three different people and get that price."

"What if...I could get them to $18.5 million?"

I heard the slightest pause before he claimed he had to leave. We haggled on and on and finally settled at $20 million. I told him I intended to draw up an offer over the weekend and personally deliver it to him Monday morning.

Hanging up, I exhaled and wiped my brow.

I tousled my hair in front of the mirror. Perfect. Two hours earlier, Mr. Mitsui and I had hammered out a verbal term sheet for an offer on the jewel box over dinner as his colleagues plied me with delicacies. They asked if I liked sushi and I said sure, as long as it was cooked well, and we laughed and raised our sake cups. I returned home exuberant.

Given that it was still early and a Friday night, I decided to pay a visit to my favorite Oakland club. I hung Gekko in the closet and donned a cream silk shirt, black wool trousers, and a soft black leather coat. I combed out the hair gel and took my measure.

Thirty minutes later, I pulled off the freeway and cruised for several minutes before landing a parking spot directly in front of the 5th Amendment. The establishment enjoyed traditional juke joint architecture: a nondescript storefront, maybe twenty feet wide, with a narrow door and a single small window, blacked out to conceal the goings-on inside.

A man-mountain filled the door, and, after patting me down, stepped aside and allowed me to squeeze past. At which point my forward progress immediately ground to a dead halt. The place was packed, shoulder-to-shoulder and wall-to-wall; any interstitial space was filled by a dense cloud of cigarette smoke augmented by discount perfume. From somewhere in the back, a band warmed up.

I slithered and sidled to the long bar and forced my way between two stools, creating a space out of thin air. Dennis, the stoic, pony-tailed hippie bartender, nodded at me in passing and soon produced a Budweiser.

"Here you go, guy," he said.

At either end of the bar, like bookends, hovered the cocktail waitresses. Extremely fine in appearance, they dished out more than they took. Holding fully loaded drink trays high overhead, they miraculously weaved through the crowd, fulfilling orders and making change without spilling a drop.

Suddenly, the band hit their lead-in and the joint started jumping. I relied on the mirror that ran the length of the bar to see what was going on in back. Freddie Hughes, a local soul legend, had hopped on the compact stage and opened the set:

"Oh baby, don't let the green grass fool ya . . .

Don't let it . . . change your mind."

How I don't know, but the agglomeration reorganized itself so that now a cluster danced in front of the stage. I pushed my empty forward and soon a fresh bottle appeared in its place. Freddie belted out three more standards and then paused, allowing the anticipation to build. Scanning the crowd, he clutched the mic:

"Ladies and gentlemen, if you will, let me welcome to the stage . . . NAPATA!"

Napata stood no less than six feet tall barefoot and towered over the band. A savvy diva, she marketed herself to a variety of audiences: a Motown revue for lucrative corporate events in San Francisco; a cabaret show for the fawning French in Neuilly-sur-Seine; a surprise appearance at an Oakland juke joint. I had met Napata a year earlier at a party and we quickly bonded, perhaps appreciating in each other the capacity for self-invention.

With a fierce demeanor, she tapped her foot one, two, three, and launched into the down-home classic "Hey Bartender" while the band shouted back the same in a call and response. Stepping down from the stage, Napata carried the song into the audience, whipping the crowd into a fever while snapping the mic cord behind her. The throng parted like the Red Sea as she sashayed past me. Reaching a crescendo on the chorus, she screamed "Hey Bartender!" and then suddenly spun around and shoved the mic in my face. I yelled "Hey Bartender!" in response, on key and on the beat. She snatched the mic away and the crowd went nuts.

I nursed another Bud through the remainder of the set and relaxed as people spilled outside during the break. I flirted briefly with an exceptionally sultry woman, with eyes like the vamps of old movies, as her boyfriend (probably played linebacker in school) ambled past me to the head. I wavered and then concluded that I had a busy day tomorrow and didn't need to get the crap kicked out of me anyway. I shot her one last smile and pushed away from the bar and bumped into one of the cocktail waitresses, who patted my cheek, "Later," and plunged out the door.

The next morning, I splashed water on my face over the bathroom sink and hurriedly brushed my hair.

I had never been late, not once, in picking Natalie up on Saturday mornings, but today I was running dangerously close. Rather than the customary 10:00 a.m. pickup, today's ETA was 7:00 a.m., and I had a forty-minute drive to

Alameda. I threw on my sweats and grabbed a hoodie and flew out the door.

Natalie had blossomed into a three-sport athlete, and now, at age 10, qualified for the Bay Oaks Soccer Club, the select team for players from Oakland and Alameda who in turn played other select teams throughout Northern California. We had an 8:00 a.m. game against the Pleasanton Rage and were about to enter the lion's den. The Bay Oaks girls were naturally diverse, a racial rainbow, who played for fun and struggled for funding. In contrast, Pleasanton epitomized the suburban juggernaut, with an organizational structure comparable to Real Madrid.

She was out the door before I even pulled up, dragging her duffel bag and clad in the yellow-and-blue uniform that I much admired, since those happened to be the colors of the Ukrainian flag.

"Hi, Dad," she said, hugging me and buckling her seatbelt.

We hopped on the Nimitz and sped off to suburbia. Since the passage of Title IX in 1972, women's sports had exploded in the US, and now the number of leagues and opportunities rivaled those for men. I believed that competition—a crucial component of success in adult life—could not be taught as part of a school curriculum. Sports filled the void, particularly for girls. Natalie demonstrated natural athletic prowess, but more important, the will to win. As a striker, her job was to get the ball in the goal, and she took no prisoners.

"How's Mom?" I asked.

Silence.

Wanda had enough trouble attending to her own issues. Even before the separation, I had assumed the role of providing discipline and structure in Natalie's life: homework, sports, extra-curriculars, anything involving dedication and outcomes.

Years ago, I had presented Natalie with a small plaque to hang on her bedroom wall, which read: "Because I'm your father, that's why." I advised her that our relationship was not a democracy but a dictatorship, which *might* ripen into an enlightened monarchy. Among her peers, this earned me the title of Strictest Dad, a sobriquet I secretly relished.

We pulled into an already crowded parking lot flanking a complex of soccer fields. I grabbed a folding aluminum chair from the trunk, and we scrambled to locate Natalie's teammates.

Trudging through the drizzle, Natalie stopped and eyed me solemnly.

"Dad, don't embarrass me."

"I promise, I'll be good," I said. My exuberance in cheering from the sidelines and admonishing the refs had gotten me in trouble and was a source of deep concern to Nat. I had unwittingly shamed her in the regular leagues, even once being issued a red card. Such behavior would not be tolerated in the select league.

With admirable restraint, I remained affixed to my chair through the whole game, cheered politely, and did not question a single call, although the refs were clearly in the pocket of the home team. The Bay Oaks played their hearts out and lost 4–1. Natalie assisted on the lone goal with a perfect pass after dribbling through half of the opposition.

We drove back to Alameda and gorged on breakfast at Ole's Waffle Shop, sitting at the counter in deference to the long line out the door waiting to be seated at a table. Later I dropped Nat off at a birthday party and made use of the free time to inspect a shopping center I had targeted for a listing, noting the customer foot traffic, the configuration of the stores, the ingress and egress, the maintenance of the common areas, the leaseability of the vacant shops, and all the other factors that Gary had inculcated.

That evening, back at my apartment in San Francisco, we did homework and watched 227 and the news, and then I tucked Natalie into her bed, kissed her on the forehead, and said, "Love you," to her "I love you too." I shut the door and sat in the easy chair, reflecting on how wonderful life was and how lucky Nat and I were to anchor each other's lives.

CHAPTER 6

Fault Lines

At precisely 5:04 p.m. on October 17, 1989, the earth moved.

A concessionaire had just handed me two plastic cups filled with tap beer, which proceeded to slosh around and spill on the dirty concrete floor. I peered out over the ball field, where the monstrous light standards swayed like tropical palms. The shaking persisted for ten seconds, maybe more, followed by the astonished silence of 60,000 fans. I collected my wits and moved quickly to find Ruby.

The earthquake had rudely interrupted the start of Game 3 of the World Series between the Oakland Athletics and the San Francisco Giants, an event billed as the Bay Bridge Series to commemorate the historic meeting of the two rivals in a championship game. A client had comped me two tickets for the contest at Candlestick Park.[11] The A's handily won the first two games in Oakland, and I expected them to sweep.

Ruby and I had started dating a few months earlier. She was a mature, decent woman who worked in sales and owned her own home. Honest and giving to a fault, she had inspired me to reconsider long-term relationships. That day, she'd driven in from Fremont, forty miles away, and had met me minutes earlier in the parking lot. I'd handed her an A's cap, grabbed her hand, and pulled her to the entrance.

"Pretty cool," I gushed.

"Really!" she said. "But this weather is kinda weird."

"Yeah, even for Indian summer," I said. Inland winds typically descend on the Bay Area in October and boot out the Pacific fog at Candlestick Park, cursed over the decades for its mist, cold, and overall miserable conditions, with out-fielders struggling to catch wind-whipped fly balls. But today was different: hot, dry, and totally still.

Now I navigated through the hushed crowd and found Ruby, who was . . . well, shaken. The ballplayers ceased their warm-ups and wandered dazed in the outfield. The stadium evidenced no apparent damage and the crowd no injuries; several fans nearby murmured that perhaps the game would continue. However, the loudspeakers remained mute.

"Baby, I'm scared," Ruby said.

I pondered what to do and then agreed, "Yeah, time to go."

As we left the grandstand, I noticed a police cruiser driving out to right field. I prodded Ruby to walk faster. Leaving the stadium, I heard the cop announce through the car's loudspeaker that the game was canceled. A man to my right, radio to his ear, exclaimed that the Bay Bridge had collapsed.

Another fan yelled that the Nimitz had pancaked. A third shouted that all the exits were closed and there was no way out.

I calculated that a crowd in panic is usually wrong and pulled Ruby in the direction opposite to where most people were headed. We squeezed our way along the chain link fence and finally found a small opening, barely wide enough for one person. The press of people at our back popped us out.

"C'mon, let's find our cars and get the hell out of here," I said.

"Think the freeway is closed?" Ruby asked.

I shrugged. "Everyone will be piling in that direction. Let's drive back around through the hood."

She followed in her own car as I maneuvered through the streets of Bayview–Hunters Point, where bewildered residents huddled on corners. The 101 freeway finally loomed ahead, and I spied the traffic inching along. I pulled over and ran back to Ruby's car as she rolled down the car window.

"You good to get home from here?" I asked.

"I'll be fine, as long as I'm on the freeway," she said, grabbing my neck and kissing me hard. She pulled away and disappeared in the dusk. As I headed back toward my apartment in downtown San Francisco, I spotted a pay phone at a gas station. I leapt out and snatched the receiver, which miraculously produced a dial tone. Fumbling a couple of quarters into the slot, I dialed Natalie.

"We're safe, Dad!" she confirmed. I warned her of aftershocks and told her I loved her.

Later that night I checked in on Ruby, who had made it
home safely after a four-hour crawl that should have been a
45-minute drive. The national and international news media
descended on San Francisco, generating wildly varying esti-
mates of death and destruction. A double-decker portion of
the Nimitz Freeway in Oakland had indeed buckled, flatten-
ing trapped vehicles like a scrapyard car crusher. A fifty-foot
section of the upper deck of the Bay Bridge also failed, but
the span otherwise remained intact. I concluded that this
earthquake was a big one but not The Big One.[12] Many businesses would reopen the next day, likely with skeletal staffs,
and life would go on.

In the morning, I called Tom, the buyer in a transaction I had in escrow: a recently constructed skyscraper in
the Financial District valued at well over $100 million and
the largest deal of my career to date. A leasing colleague
and I had arranged an increasingly rare "off-market" sale
whose closing was threatened by potential earthquake damage to the building. Tom ran a European investment fund
from Dallas that had been on the prowl for a signature San
Francisco asset and had stretched to make the price work.

Coincidentally, he grew up in the Midwest and attended
my alma mater, Campion Jesuit High School, a boys-only
boarding school named for the martyr Edmund Campion,
oddly plunked down in Prairie du Chien and drawing students from other states and even other countries.[13] The school
admitted a handful of local residents, dubbed "Townies," who
could pass the stringent admission test and afford the exorbitant tuition, which the Sawas, unlike Tom's parents, could
not. So I joined the labor force at age 13, sweating out sum-
mers at Campion pulling sandburs from the football field on

my hands and knees, and during the school year, washing dishes at a restaurant and performing the least enviable of other tasks.

By chance, Tom had also attended the University of Detroit and later started in commercial real estate in Chicago. He was now regarded as a heavy hitter who could commit ample sums of institutional investor capital on his word. I believed Fate had dictated the transaction and now, just as indiscriminately, could kill it.

"You worry too much," Tom admonished.

He calmly directed me to set up an inspection with their consulting engineer and then use all means necessary with the seller to prompt a city building inspector to pay a visit and sign off. He correctly predicted that the city would soon be swamped with calls and overwhelmed by problems at older masonry structures that threatened collapse. I followed his instructions and crossed my fingers.

During the pendency of the escrow and about three weeks later, another earth-shattering event shocked the world: On November 9, the Berlin Wall fell. The ideological symbol of the Cold War between the United States and the Soviet Union, the wall had been erected in 1961 by Stalin's successor, Nikita Khrushchev, and divided the city of Berlin, the country of Germany, and the world into the Eastern Bloc of communism and the Western Bloc of democracy.

"Marty, isn't this something?" my brother, Greg, phoned, breathless. The weakening and now potential dissolution of the Soviet Union after eighty years of hegemony was unprecedented.

"I didn't think I'd live to see the day," I said. "When Reagan called the Soviet Union the 'evil empire,' people laughed, but he was right."

"You think Ukraine will be independent?"

Rallies and peaceful demonstrations for freedom were occurring in a number of Soviet republics, including Ukraine, the largest Soviet state after Russia and of strategic economic and military significance. As a practical matter, no Ukrainian in the diaspora ever imagined that the Soviets might loosen their grip on our homeland.

"I read that Ukrainians are demanding the legalization of the Ukrainian Greek Catholic Church," I said. The suppression of religion—Karl Marx's "opiate of the masses"—and the promotion of state-sponsored atheism was a cornerstone of Marxist–Leninist ideology.

"Yeah, you found that church where Natalie was baptized," Greg said.

"If that happens, then that's proof the Soviets have lost the hearts and minds of the people," I said. "Stay tuned."

Several weeks later, I closed the sale with Tom. I tilted back in my office chair and gazed out the window at the cityscape and considered how much the world had changed and how much I'd changed in the past ten years. Now almost 40, I had inched toward the top of the broker food chain while juggling the demands of family and personal life. More than the money, I had developed a taste for the juice: the thrill of getting my way with sophisticated clients, of feeling in control, of closing the deal. I had not yet ascertained that the world has a way of smacking one upside the head.

She stood by the wall, idly chatting with another woman. I had noticed her upon entering the 5th Amendment. I had finished a late meeting in Oakland and stopped by to relax on my way home. On a rainy weeknight, the place was nearly deserted. I ordered the usual and mentally prepared for a listing presentation the next morning, challenging myself with the tough questions the client was sure to ask. I happened to glance in her direction, and she enticed me with a smile. I continued processing my thoughts and then, with nascent misgiving, turned around and slipped off the stool.

Young and built like a video vixen, Tina wore tight jeans and a red-checkered shirt. She did not flirt overtly but rather engaged me in polite chitchat. We talked into the night until the other patrons had filtered out. I offered Tina a ride home and walked her to the door of a house in the Oakland Hills, whereupon she languidly eyed me. I embraced then kissed her; she neither resisted nor reciprocated.

Having lived in Oakland for over fifteen years, I thought I knew the ways of city girls, at times a bit rough around the edges but usually up-front and clear in their motives. With Tina, her intentions remained a mystery, yet she penetrated the taproot of my psyche. Perhaps it was feeling the excitement as I had in business, or a garden-variety bad-girl fantasy, or merely acceding to vanity as men have done since the dawn of time. Or perhaps it was something more. Walking back to my car, I was hooked and knew not why.

The next week I broke up with Ruby. We had dated for over a year, and she cried softly at our last meeting. I felt like a heel and knew I had done wrong and incurred serious karmic debt.

After deliberating for a few more days, I phoned Tina, who intimated she was glad I called. I picked her up that night at the house she shared with her mother. Her brother, a prominent celebrity who happened to be visiting when I arrived, played dominoes with his posse. He nodded for me to join in—which I declined with a smile—then returned to the game without a word.

Tina and I went out for dinner and dancing, and as I drove her home, she flipped through my cassette tapes and loaded Smokey Robinson's *Greatest Hits*. "The Tracks of My Tears" piped through the car speakers, and we sang the lyrics in harmony, alternately tapping out the beat on the dash as electricity coursed through the car. She flashed a grin and suggested we hit an after-hours club and directed me to the House of Grapes in West Oakland.

I had never visited an after-hours and discovered an unadorned, if not dilapidated, building deep in the hood. We entered a large room furnished with cheap tables and chairs, with a makeshift bar in the front and a kitchen in the back where I spotted several women laboring over fryers spewing the scent of catfish.

Tina moved through the room and seemed to know everyone, including a habitué just getting started with his business day. After an hour, as I nodded off, I noticed her conferring privately with an extremely rough character. I don't recall her spending any time with me, only waking up the next morning with a historic hangover.

This outing set the pattern. Tina lived life in the moment, spontaneously reacting to her instincts; she promised nothing and asked for nothing. When the mood suited her, she lavished attention on me, which provoked me to please her, and if I failed, to blame myself.

The relationship (or whatever it was) continued for a few more months, not lacking in adventure. We celebrated one of my deal closings at the Beverly Hills Hotel, the famed landmark that harbored more secrets than any other Hollywood venue.[14] We partied at the Polo Lounge, where soon Tina was surrounded by moneyed men at the compact bar; an old-timer ribbed me: "You got your hands full there." The next day, Tina and I lolled poolside in one of the notorious cabanas and later watched the recently released *Silence of the Lambs* on the in-room television. She really dug Hannibal Lecter and laughed throughout.

At times, she would disappear for days. I resisted calling her more than once, since showing that I cared for her welfare would be perceived as weakness. I guess she boasted a fairly high IQ, and her mental agility added to the charm and enhanced my frustration. The intimacy deteriorated from her passive acceptance to indifference to avoidance. Tina's own kin warned me: Her sister would catch my attention and urge me with her eyes to come to my senses.

It got so bad that I sought counsel from a real estate colleague. Until then, I had never discussed my personal relationships, even my marriage to Wanda, with anyone. I had no close friends by choice. As a teenager, I preferred shooting pool, which I could both master and viscerally enjoy; you win or you lose, no gray area. I rotated among different peer groups—the athletes and the nerds and the average kids— and dodged the obligation to conform or to waste time doing nothing.

Since my interests were eclectic and varied and subject to change without notice, I avoided commitment. I believed, then and now, that it is extremely difficult to find someone who truly has your best interests at heart and who can handle an equal and reciprocal friendship. Besides, my life was hectic, with not enough hours in the day, and a true friendship required the investment of time and energy like anything else worthwhile.

In a pinch, George would have to do. A competent broker, he was much more accomplished than I in the pursuit of women. George dated across the ethnic spectrum and preferred runway models and edgy, manic types. I opened up about Tina as we strolled through the Financial District evaluating real estate.

"My head is truly messed up," I confessed. "I feel like shit when I'm with her and when I'm without her."

"So tell me something about this Tina," George said.

"Well, she's got spunk," I said. "She told me she drove to LA with a girlfriend in the middle of the night at 100 mph with the top down and wearing shades. Somewhere on the 405, a guy pulls up alongside and harasses them obscenely and finally speeds away."

"And?"

"She ran him down. Tailed him at high speed about a foot behind his bumper until he lost his nerve. She forced him off the freeway and then pulled up alongside, stopped in traffic in the fast lane, and asked the guy if he'd like to play some more."

George remained silent for a moment, drawing on his well of experience.

"How's the sex?"

"Awful," I admitted.

He snickered knowingly.

"Buddy, you're way out of your league."

I blurted, "I know it's not love or even lust—"

"You don't get it," George said with a hint of annoyance. "You don't have a clue what you're dealing with."

He pointed to an older commercial building and asked what I thought it would cost to renovate, implying that my dogged continuance of the Tina conversation merely reinforced my idiocy.

After several more months, I put myself out of my misery. In the summer of 1991, I announced to Tina the end of our relationship, at which declaration she displayed no emotion whatsoever and grew bored when I tried to explain my innermost feelings.

I felt compelled to analyze the matter forensically, to identify antecedents and latent evidence, and ascertain why I had temporarily lost my mind. Certainly, alcohol was a contributing factor. Most of the women I dated I had met in bars. From drinking as a teenager to partying in college, I regarded the cold beer in hand as a wingman who loosened me up, punched my shoulder, and enhanced my confidence. Clearly, my habituated behavior was to initially act under the influence.

But the morning after, I would squint and adjust to reality. In Tina's case, I never "sobered up," metaphorically speaking. I took pride in self-reliance, in not needing anyone to validate me. Yet I seemed to crave Tina's validation desperately, stimulated by the prospects of hanging with her. To George, I was obviously being gamed; to me, I knew it and didn't care.

I calculated there was something deeper to Tina's spell that I might never figure out. I closed the case file, feeling fortunate to have escaped relatively unscathed.

Or so I thought.

CHAPTER 7

Signs and Wonders

Attractive Black Female 30s, spiritual, seeks professional man. Serious only. 23709 ☎

After the Tina debacle, I didn't date for months. I moved back to the East Bay from San Francisco, a fine place to make money but not an inviting family atmosphere. The city was becoming an adult amusement park with fewer and fewer children. Natalie would be starting high school the following year, and her well-being ruled.

To the immigrant parent, no value is placed above the son or daughter obtaining the best possible education and thereby heightening the odds that the children will do better and be better than their forbears. My acceptance at Campion had thrilled the family; Grandpa had been a teacher in the Old Country, and his tutorial sessions in Ukrainian bore serious fruit. But no one matched Zenon's elation; my proud father bragged shamelessly to his cronies. I smiled at the memory as I helped Nat complete the early bird application process at Saint Joseph Notre Dame High School in Alameda.

On a Sunday morning in October of 1991, two years almost to the day after the earthquake, I noticed smoke billowing from the Oakland hills. I raced to the scene and snuck through the police line to watch the conflagration and discovered that the fire: a) moved faster than people ran; b) leapt over a freeway; and c) obliterated entire blocks in minutes but mysteriously left an occasional house untouched and pristine. What started as a small grass fire exploded into an epic firestorm that would kill twenty-five people and destroy over 3,000 homes. I deemed this particular fire a conspiracy of nature and Fate and became wary of Octobers.

As the holidays approached, I yearned for companionship and succumbed to sentimentality. I sensed that meeting women in clubs did not ensure the most advantageous prospects for a lasting relationship and decided to test the classifieds. I snatched a fresh copy of the East Bay Express[15] from a street corner news rack on a Thursday evening, quickly flipped to the personals, perused the section "Matches—Women Seeking Men," identified one that piqued my interest (see above), carefully composed my pitch, and after a number of hoarse and faltering starts, left a voice message in the numbered mailbox. To my wonderment, she called me back; we exchanged pleasantries and agreed to meet in person at a local restaurant.

Anita appeared as a goddess, framed in sunshine, hovering in the doorway of Skates on the Bay in the Berkeley Marina. I gawked at her from across the foyer.

"Anita?" I asked, still not believing my good fortune.

"Hello, Martin," she replied calmly.

"Uh, I got us a table by the window, near the water."

Over oysters on the half shell, Anita revealed that she lived with her daughter, Sonja, and two sisters in nearby Richmond, where she was also active in local politics. She worked in the San Francisco Financial District as the right hand to the regional manager for Digital Equipment Corporation (DEC), the iconic computer company that rivaled IBM in the 1970s and '80s. She was beautiful, intelligent, practical (a Capricorn), and very confident.

"I'll be 42 next month," I offered. "Way older than you."

"Oh, I turn 40 next month."

I regarded her with suspicion. "Your ad—didn't it say thirties?"

"Well, I *am* still in my thirties," she said with a twinkle.

I laughed and we toasted her marketing skills. I impressed Anita enough that she suggested another meeting at Skates, on the condition that she pay, and would I mind if she brought her BFF?

A week later, I shared cocktails and appetizers at the bar with Anita and Prudie, who impressed me as intense and earnest and dedicated to having Anita's back. When Anita conveniently repaired to the restroom, Prudie's demeanor transformed into the Grand Inquisitor: She was here to interrogate me and issue a ruling. And she quickly cut to the chase:

"Martin, how much experience have you had with black women?"

The question, however well intentioned, put me on the defensive, and I saw it as a trap. I can't recall my exact words, but I tried to make the case that, like Goldilocks, my experience was "just right." Sizing me up as a smart-ass, Prudie continued to grill me relentlessly as her brow progressively furrowed. By the time Anita returned, I needed air.

Anita never shared Prudie's assessment of me, which I suspect was a thumbs-down. I later observed that Anita considered all the trustworthy input she could gather on matters of significance but then made her own decision and stood by it. After several months of dating, Anita offered me the choice: "You can pass or play." She had no interest in a "meaningful relationship" of indeterminate term and vague objectives. We negotiated a timeline wherein I would make her an honest woman, and to evidence good faith, I bought us a house in the East Bay hills.

The day we moved in, a dove created a nest in the mailbox attached near the entry door on the front porch. I thought it odd that a mother-to-be would select such a heavily trafficked and vulnerable location, but Anita beamed and confessed that she had prayed the night before for peace and security at our new residence, and the dove would be just fine. Soon, Mr. Dove appeared, and then eggs, and then a brood. The family remained unperturbed at my gawking every morning as I snatched the mail from a flimsy cardboard box I had placed below.

I soon began to notice a pattern of what I would call anomalous occurrences around Anita, events that if considered singularly could be written off as coincidental or surprising or perhaps uncanny, but when regarded in total suggested something more. For example, Anita picking up the phone before it rang and launching into a conversation with her older sister Betty, her closest confidante on matters spiritual.

Routine events assumed significance. As I waited in the Safeway parking lot, I spotted Anita exiting with bags in hand and immediately being intercepted by an old woman, wizened and tattered. They talked for at least ten minutes.

"Who was that?" I asked, loading the groceries in the car.

"A very nice lady," Anita said. "She wanted to share some advice."

"You *know* her?"

"No, she's probably an angel."

After such repeated occurrences, I felt compelled to investigate.

"When you were a kid, were you . . . like . . . different?" I inquired as we relaxed on the patio. By now, I had internalized Anita's biography. One of eighteen (!) children born to a religious mother and an ethically upright father. Raised in rural Alabama on the outskirts of Mobile. As a child, spoke the King's English ("Hold my hond, Daddy!"), which she appropriated from an effete uncle. Educated in a segregated school system, which finally integrated in her senior year. Nineteen and pregnant, boarded a bus for California and never looked back.

Anita knew what I meant.

"There was this girl," she said. "A bully, in my sophomore year. She was jealous and wouldn't stop tormenting me. I couldn't take it anymore. One day I just blurted out that she had TB (tuberculosis)."

"Damn."

"It turned out she had no idea, but I already knew. She was positively diagnosed a couple of weeks later. After that, she was scared as hell of me. Word spread that I was not to be trifled with."

"How did you—?"

"I felt awful. I learned to hold my tongue. Whatever gift I had, it was a gift from God."

Anita often remarked that she had the best parents possible. Her father labored at a lumber mill until his untimely death at age 46. Tough but fair, he brooked no bullshit. Once, a shopkeeper laid a hand on one of Anita's brothers. Arriving spent from the mill, her father mustered the energy to walk to the store and beat the hell out of the man, who happened to be white, but which fact, I was told, scarcely mattered. There was right and there was wrong, and he would have whupped his own kin. Ultimately, the man declined to press charges, but I suspect Anita's dad was ready to accept the consequences without a flinch.

Her mother was no slouch either, birthing a baby every year or two throughout her adult life. Anita's mother established a Pentecostal parish and literally built a one-room church. She tried to instill the fear of the Lord in her offspring, which resulted in varying degrees of success.

"You must understand, the service would last ALL DAY," Anita said, "lots of yelling and testifying." Anita eventually shunned the ritual. Instead, she took to reading the Bible every night, performing her own exegesis, illuminating the margins with notes as well as penning lengthy, explanatory tracts in an extroverted, almost calligraphic cursive script on legal-sized canary-yellow lined tablets.

I had pretty much fallen away from Catholicism, maintaining but occasional contact with the Almighty. Nonetheless, I nurtured a regret that I should have done more to expose Natalie to religious instruction and hoped that Catholic high school would countervail my error. I admired Anita's individualized Christianity, which she applied to everyday living—she truly walked the walk—and perhaps unconsciously hoped she would straighten me out. But that was not her style.

Anita neither proselytized nor acted sanctimonious. She drank, smoked tobacco, and liked to party but always knew where and when to draw the line. And she framed the whole enterprise of life in a deeper context. When Prudie urged her to try ecstasy (MDMA), she insisted we do it together to enhance intimacy and open the doors of our perception.

As Christmas approached in the winter of 1992, Anita and I decided to throw a holiday party and toy drive. She invited her coterie of friends, which included salespeople at DEC who worked hard and played harder, and of course Prudie, who had warmed to me a bit. I tagged Napata and her fellow musicians, and George and his date, whoever that happened to be. Word filtered through the grapevine, and by 10:00 p.m., over one hundred people packed our house.

I maneuvered through little black dresses and stilettos and tight-fitting turtlenecks and even a dashiki amid the tinkle of glasses and the trace of reefer. Reaching the CD stereo player, I turned down the volume and called for quiet. "Thank you all for coming and bringing a gift," I said. "Now Anita has something to say."

Hoisting an apple martini skyward, she proclaimed, "Let the games begin!"

The crowd hooted and cheered. I quickly pushed the furniture against the walls and located a compact disc featuring Oakland's own En Vogue and punched up "Hold On." Sonja and her girlfriends sprang to the dance floor and set the energy level for the night. I drifted into the kitchen in search of the hors d'oeuvres and spotted Glen.

"Sup, my brother," he said while giving dap.

"Same ol'—trying to keep things moving," I said, finishing the handshake.

Glen was a bald, menacing, 6'5" black man whose handle was "The Big Nasty" and whom Anita had known for years. He admired her because she was so much fun to be with despite the fact that there was no hope of seduction. Early in our relationship, she brought us together and simply stated, "You two *will* be friends." At first, Glen and I had regarded each other warily and wondered alike what she saw in this other guy. But then we became running buddies, and our unlikely pairing developed into friendship, probably for the precise reason that neither of us gave a shit.

A very attractive woman who I did not know peeked into the kitchen and smiled cordially at Glen, and he was gone. I nibbled on the crudités and felt a tug on my sleeve.

"Martin, how are you?"

Anita's boss materialized by my side. Short in stature but very intense, he had emigrated from India and now reigned as regional sales manager for DEC.

"Great," I replied, shaking his hand. "How's business?"

He shrugged. "We just reported our first annual loss—everyone has to try harder."

"Including Anita?" I laughed.

"No, she's the only one I don't worry about."

"I know, she loves her job," I said.

"I'm sure she told you I've tried to promote her several times, but she has no interest in moving up," he said. "Money and success don't mean as much to her as the others."

Another of Anita's colleagues interposed himself and cornered the manager about a pending mainframe sale. I moved back to the living room and surveyed the crowd: a mix of people, all races, young and old, some well off, others struggling but always striving. Didn't spot any thugs or polemicists or generic bad eggs. I noticed Anita and Napata engaged in deep discourse. A pile of toys loomed in the corner; I would schlep them to the firehouse in the morning. All good.

Let me tell you about the day Anita and I visited an insurance broker in a small, faded, single-story professional office building on a Saturday morning. As I got out, I noticed a child sitting alone in a car with the windows opened. She appeared to be about 6 years old but with a peculiar appearance: an androgynous, adult mien with carrot hair and jagged teeth.

Since there were no other cars in the lot other than the broker's, and all the other businesses were closed, I approached and asked, "Where are your parents?" Anita had by now stepped up alongside. The child ignored me and focused on my wife. "Having issues with your family, huh?"

I rarely saw Anita flustered. She grabbed my arm and said, "Let's go."

"What's the matter, cat got your tongue?" The hoarse, grown-up voice trailed behind us.

As we approached the door, I whispered to Anita, "What's that all about?" Before she could reply, the voice squawked, "It's about you."

I yanked Anita into the office. "There's a kid by herself in a car outside." I motioned to the broker. "Do you know who it is?"

He rose from his desk and ambled out. "I don't see anyone."

I ran to the car and then looked around the parking lot and even around the corner: The child had vanished.

On the drive home, Anita hypothesized that the old soul was likely an imp, more mischievous than threatening. "What did she want?" I asked. "Just to instigate," Anita replied. "Believe me, if it was a real attack from the dark side, you'd know it."

A few months later, Anita trudged in disconsolate. She had been issued a speeding ticket—unjustly, in her opinion. I urged her to fight it and volunteered to help organize a defense. However, as the court date approached, she exhibited an increasing reluctance, due not to the merits of her case but rather nervousness about appearing before a judge. Notwithstanding her assertive personality, she panicked around authority figures, especially in formal settings. But I goaded her—"Look, the cop probably won't even show and you'll be home free"—and almost forced her into the car the day of the hearing. Anita sat stolidly as I drove down the hill, a route I had duplicated hundreds of times, when a flash streaked from my left. BANG! A car had run the stop sign and sideswiped our front fender. The teenage driver confessed he was lost and disoriented. Fortunately, there were no injuries and only minor damage. We waited for the cop to arrive and write the kid up, and by now, we had missed Anita's day in court. As we returned home, Anita would not meet my gaze. I was glad she felt guilty.

By now, I had accepted the fact that I had become an unwitting participant in Anita's excursions into the world of the unseen. I loved this woman, and the parallel universe added to the excitement, like playing three-dimensional chess.

One Saturday night, the women gathered for a girls' party at Napata's house near Lake Merritt. Glen had recently reunited with his high school sweetheart, Cynthia, who now joined our crew, accompanied by her sister. He didn't like the odds and suggested we visit the 5th Amendment.

The joint was packed, and we were fortunate to secure two barstools near the entry. Glen soon spotted an associate and wandered off. (Glen and I would sit and ignore each other, speak or not speak, and otherwise act as we felt.) He returned perhaps a half hour later and, bored, noticed a covey of sisters who had recently congregated to our side. Taking a pull on a vodka tonic, Glen grunted to gain my attention and then turned around and casually leaned toward the nearest woman.

"I'd like you to meet my friend here," Glen rasped.

The woman slowly looked Glen up and down, and then me. She sniffed, "And who might *that* be?"

"Count Yuri," Glen announced.

I hesitated for a nanosecond, and then caught on and adjusted my black hooligan cap and the collar on my leather coat and glanced away, taciturn . . . KGB-ish.

Another woman rolled her eyes. "Don't look like no count."

"Naw, baby," Glen said, "he's a . . . black Russian."

The third took interest. "For real?" she said, peering down her nose. "Then say something in Russian."

Russian I did not know, but perhaps I could captivate her with my Ukrainian (however meager), which I deemed close enough.

"*Dobry den* (good day)," I said.

"Oooooh, Yuri," she chirped, "you *are* a count!"

I winked at Glen and motioned to Dennis behind the bar for a round, and we told tall tales and the fun and the time progressed. Much later, convivial and bleary-eyed, I glanced at Glen, who directed my attention to the door. There stood Anita and Napata.

Napata reared up to her full height, spotted me, and cried to Anita with mock apprehension, "There's your baby!"

The two women bum-rushed the startled patrons and seized me, each grabbing an armpit. Smiling mischievously, they yanked me off the stool and dragged me out the door, my heels undoubtedly leaving impressions in the floor.

Tasting the night air, I heard Glen convulse with laughter and the sisters plead, "Yuri, come back and talk some more Russian to us!"

The pages flew off the calendar of our magical life, and it was soon time to legitimize the relationship. When Anita and I had first talked of marriage, I was apprehensive about finally divorcing Wanda, unable to predict how this wild card would play out.

Remarkably, Anita and Wanda achieved cordiality. I believe the fact that Anita smoked cigarettes endeared her to Wanda, and they would puff together off to the side at family picnics, where I'm sure Anita got an earful. I secured the services of Divorce Helpline, a group of family law attorneys in Santa Cruz, who handled the matter by phone, charged $2/minute, and had no ax to grind. Wanda and I divorced amicably and under budget.

"Hah, you're a spinster," I chortled.

Anita rolled her eyes. We sat in a private office in the Sandals All-Inclusive Resort in Montego Bay, Jamaica. The Reverend Terrence Gordon had just counseled us on the sanctity of marriage and the import of the vows. With our wedding but moments away, he entered the requisite information on the marriage register, whose solemnity demanded archaic description wherever possible, a remnant of British colonialism. My "Condition" was "divorced" and Anita's "spinster." Similarly, my "Calling" was "real estate broker," which I couldn't fundamentally disagree with.

The Sandals concierge and the director of fitness sported broad smiles while proudly signing the document as witnesses. Reverend Gordon entered the date, September 7, 1994, perused the certificate and, satisfied, led us out in a mini-processional to the beach amid the scent of hibiscus and bougainvillea.

We gathered just outside the reach of the pounding surf. Anita's dark skin contrasted starkly with her white gown, in turn silhouetted against the azure sky and the cyan sea. We all squinted into the refulgent sun reflected off the white sand. A welcome breeze prompted the concierge to adjust the orchid nestled in Anita's hair. The minister read from Scripture, and Anita and I exchanged vows and rings and kissed. Then all five of us hugged, accompanied by the clapping of couples lounging under thatched gazebos.

"Reverend, can you stay and have a toast with us?" I asked as we trudged back through the sand.

"Thank you, but I have one more wedding to attend to," he replied, glancing at his watch and politely excusing himself.[16]

We drank expensive champagne on the balcony of our oceanfront room. Anita and the concierge teared up and the fitness director admitted we were an unusual couple and he would miss us and hoped we would "soon come."

CHAPTER 8

An Unpleasant Surprise

I continued to prosper at Cushman & Wakefield as the new decade of the 1990s unfolded. The company had recently hired a manager to oversee all of the investment brokers on the West Coast. A proud Texan, he figured me out and nurtured my career despite my disinterest in socializing with my colleagues or with management. He became a crucial link in the assigning of "throws," the leads and often assured listings that came directly to the company and were then meted out to individual brokers.

The company was constantly looking for new talent and would funnel in young people for me to interview for an apprentice position. Trainees were now offered a draw on commission and substantial training, incentives unfathomable to me when I'd entered the business. Yet few rookies understood the requirements for this particular niche within the commercial real estate field: high-stakes investment sales remunerated by contingent commissions.

One day, the company produced a graduate from a prestigious business school that they were particularly high on. The young man sat in my office, extolling his accomplishments and iterating his demands for a guaranteed draw and generous bonus, a compensation package he claimed had just been offered to him by a competitor. I listened politely and asked, "What's that company's name again?" I pulled the yellow pages from my bookshelf, located the business, and shoved both the phone book and the phone toward the MBA. "Here, call them and say you'll take their offer. Then get out of here." He slunk out.

I undertook to observe rookies both within and outside the company, and noted those who did *not* last: graduates from elite schools with a high regard for themselves; professionals who transitioned from other fields, such as law, and who thought that technical prowess mattered; and particularly, individuals with a low tolerance for rejection and humiliation. Rather, the person most likely to succeed was typically the "C" student with an appetite for risk, an ability to independently problem-solve, and sufficient self-confidence that he would not be cowed by wealthier and more knowledgeable clients and colleagues. And I say "he" because very few women chose to pursue this specific career path, then and now.[17]

My most successful protégé was Steve, the son of a real estate syndicator, newly minted from a college known for its party atmosphere. During the interview, I asked, "So what's your dad like?" Steve replied without hesitation, "Oh, he works all the time and is kind of crazy, doesn't trust anyone." I struggled to contain my excitement.

"Since you don't know anything," I said, "you should pay *me* for the experience." Steve shrugged. "I would, but I don't have a lot of money right now." I endeavored to break him, explaining the long, hard hours, and, at times, the months between paychecks. He refused to capitulate, and I finally offered him the position.

"Any questions?"

"Yes . . . uh . . . when will the apprenticeship end?" Steve asked.

I frankly hadn't thought about that, given that I didn't expect anyone to last. I fashioned a steeple with my fingers and reflected quietly for almost a minute. Finally, I said, "Grasshopper, when you are ready to screw me on a deal, my work is finished."

The Japanese asset price bubble burst in 1991, to the surprise of everyone and no one.[18] I instructed Steve that it was time to find the next hot buyers. Given the impact of globalization, the money could come from anywhere, and so I demanded he study the psychology and negotiating styles of the Chinese and the Brits and the Germans and the Arabs and the Israelis. Friends and foes alike since World War II, all sought a safe haven for capital in a reasonably democratic society with a rule of law and liquid markets.

Nor could we ignore the burgeoning investment from domestic pension funds, sovereign wealth funds, and a previously quiescent vehicle known as a real estate investment trust. A REIT was principally a creature of tax law, and so skill was required in correct deal structuring. I took professional pride in negotiating one of the first UPREIT transactions in the Bay Area, a particularly complex variant of the typical REIT, for a research and development park in Silicon Valley.

In 1993, Cushman & Wakefield fired the investment manager for no apparent reason and hired Pete as his replacement. A company man who had opened the San Francisco office years ago, Pete strayed from the fold to try his hand at an investment firm, and now returned to the flock. I had never met him, although he was well known to the older brokers in the office. I scheduled a meeting to impress him with my past accomplishments and thereby ensure I would continue to receive my fair share of throws, as well as to sound him out on a better commission split with the house.

Pete's secretary detained me longer than necessary and then escorted me into the spacious corner office. He scarcely looked up as I eased myself onto the couch and watched the secretary close the door, and suddenly I felt as if I were encased in a tomb.

"So, Martin, what can I do you for?" Pete asked with naked disinterest.

"Well, Pete, we haven't really had a chance to talk since you came on board," I said. The vibe was off, but I stuck with my rehearsed script. "I look forward to working together."

"I'm glad you're a team player."

"There's a couple of high-rises I'd like to go after, and it would be helpful if you could give me a little support."

"No can do."

"Huh?" I gaped.

"I've decided to make Jeff my go-to guy for the institutional listings."

"What? That's crazy!" I said. "Have you looked at my production, the money I've made, the deals I did with the Japanese?"

"I know all that. Don't worry, you're not in any danger of being let go."

As I stood up, my knees wobbled, and the room whirled around me.

"How can you say this?"

"You know Jeff and I go way back—hell, we just spent a week at the Bohemian Grove."

"This is about business, about who's best for the job!" I fumed.

Pete stifled a yawn. "Nothing personal, but frankly, Jeff's a better fit for these types of assignments."

"That's *it?*"

By now, Pete had resumed shuffling his papers. I flung the door open and stomped out, glaring at the secretary as I gave Pete's office the finger.

I immediately left the premises and headed to Lake Merritt, where I parked and proceeded to power walk the three-mile circumference, vainly trying to discharge steam. Three loops later and sunburned, I still seethed with rage. Shocked and humiliated, I drove home and blurted to Anita the outrage that had been perpetrated on me and the assault

on my manhood. I vowed to quit as soon as I lined up a new
gig, and I privately cursed Pete for many years.

A few months later, I joined CB Commercial—Cushman
& Wakefield's chief rival—in their San Francisco office. CB
Commercial was spawned by the partnership of Colbert
Coldwell and Benjamin Banker and the founding of the
eponymous Coldwell Banker in 1914; the commercial group
was spun off from the residential brokerage in 1989. It was
already a national enterprise and was growing rapidly by
acquiring related businesses in the areas of investment
management, mortgage banking, and corporate facilities
management.

I found the atmosphere more collegial than at Cushman
& Wakefield. However, the investment brokers simply did not
operate on the institutional side of the business—the megadeals involving skyscrapers, shopping malls, and industrial
parks—and were content consummating smaller sales. For
the next two years I put up respectable numbers generating
my own deals while also socializing with my colleagues, concentrating on the care and feeding of managers, deciphering
the corporate structure, and hunting for an edge.

The company formed an Investment Properties Group to
link the investment brokers in all the offices so as to provide
a united front to national and international clients, rather
than the perception of independent mercenaries scaveng-
ing in individual cities, which we were. This necessitated my
attendance at periodic gatherings in Las Vegas and other
resorts meant to reward achievement and promote unity,

events that were typically accompanied by heaving drinking and outings to strip clubs.

I knew this behavior dismayed Anita, but she rarely verbalized her emotions. She knew that I knew how she felt, and it was up to me to take responsibility, which I rarely did, too caught up in the moment and oblivious to her well-being. One evening, I came home to find Anita sitting on the bed in tears.

"What happened, Pooh?"

She shook her head without looking up. "Some of my jewelry is missing."

"How is that possible?" I asked. "Did someone break in?"

She nodded softly.

"Who? How?"

Anita now stared at me, almost as if expecting me to explain the theft. I checked all the doors and windows for any evidence of tampering and then asked my wife if perhaps she had misplaced the items. She remained silent as I told her we could file an insurance claim and buy substitute pieces.

"Their value is personal," she said. "They can't be replaced."

With time, I forgot the incident, not fully trusting Anita's intuition that this was no haphazard burglary, if it was a burglary at all. A regrettable decision.

In the summer of 1996, I finally spotted an inefficiency, a situation that seemed odd to me but went unquestioned by anyone else. The corporate headquarters of CB Commercial was located in downtown Los Angeles, yet the investment brokers in the home office did even less institutional business than in San Francisco. I interviewed the company's subsidiary businesses and discovered that they were actually giving away their property listings to competitors! I quickly devised a plan and met with Rich, the amiable office manager in San Francisco.

"Rich, I'd like to move to LA," I said.

"What?" he said. "Why would you leave the Bay Area for all that smog?"

"I'm the only broker with major deal experience. I want to put together an institutional team and compete for the trophy listings."

"But why not do it from here?" he asked. I knew that his primary concern was my leaving his profit center.

"I need to be at the headquarters," I said, "and have top management twist the arm of the subsidiaries into giving us their business, to jump-start the process, to help us build a track record, to support us unconditionally."

He sat silent, unable to argue with my logic.

"Look," I continued. "We'll be active all over the West Coast. Heck, I'll probably wind up doing *even more* deals in San Francisco."

"Martin, you've done well here. The boys like you."

"It has to be LA and it has to be now, otherwise we'll have lost the institutional brokerage business for good," I said, exaggerating a bit.

"I can get you an assistant here—"

"Rich, will you talk to Jim?" I pleaded. James J. Didion (brother of acclaimed writer Joan Didion) was the CEO of CB Commercial, a hard charger who had worked his way through the ranks and who valued initiative. Rich had been his close friend for many years.

Rich and I locked eyes for the longest time, the classic sales moment when each side is loath to speak first. Finally, he offered, "I trust you when you say you can pull this off— I'll bring it up with Jim."

A week later, the transfer was approved. I had sold CB Commercial on the idea; I still needed to sell my wife. I hadn't seen the merit of broaching the subject until I had secured the company's concurrence, but now I felt uneasy.

By this time, Anita and I had become empty nesters. After living with me on weekends for eleven years, Natalie would be off to college in a month. A summer earlier, Natalie and I had created a short list of schools and planned a road trip to evaluate the most promising. This exercise carried particular weight for me since it evoked the time when I broke my father's heart.

While a senior at Campion, I had not only been admitted to college but to the University of Detroit, another Jesuit-run school, with a full, four-year scholarship. I had completely, wildly, fulfilled his dream. Yet when I arrived in Detroit in the fall of 1968, it was a "city on fire." The 1967 riots demarcated a turning point in the once great city's fortunes, which had already faced years of economic decline as the auto companies vanished.

My summer in Chicago had hardened me to urban life but not to life in Detroit. I could not deal with the one element that eluded the statistics: utter hopelessness. I phoned

home before Thanksgiving and let slip that I was withdraw-
ing from school. I can't imagine the hurt and humiliation
that Zenon felt, the loss of face with friends, the open wound
that my subsequent business success did not totally salve. He
kept the somber letter he received from the school 'til the
day he died.

"A great adventure!" I proclaimed as Nat and I hopped on
the Nimitz at dawn for our road trip; having vetted Bay Area
colleges, we headed for Southern California. I let her drive
occasionally—among her girlfriends, she alone could read a
map with authority, drive a stick, and change a tire.

"What's our first stop?" she asked.

"Santa Barbara," I said. Four hours later, we beheld the
shimmering Pacific at Morro Bay and then cut inland until
we reached the coastal community. The seaside location of
the University of Santa Barbara was compelling, but a drive
through the adjoining residential district proved fatal.

"There's no way you're going here," I declared upon witnessing rampant inebriation and debauchery at Isla Vista.
"It's only noon on a weekday!"

"Dad . . . ," Nat said, rolling her eyes.

We hugged the coast and cruised down the famed Pacific
Coast Highway to Pepperdine University, positioned on the
Malibu Bluffs with unobstructed ocean views. A private
school affiliated with the Churches of Christ, Pepperdine
offered more promise, and we hurried to catch the last campus tour of the day. "All I remember is that we saw Gary
Radnich (a Bay Area sportscaster)," Nat later laughed.

We followed PCH straight to Santa Monica Pier, where
we dined at the Pier Seafood, and I excitedly described my
(redacted) introduction to California twenty-five years

earlier. Nat had also embraced the Golden State and was not considering any out-of-state schools.

"I still don't know what I want to be when I grow up," I said in partial jest. "So you need to discover on your own which career path to follow."

The next day we would be visiting UCLA, with its notoriously low acceptance rate, and I didn't want my daughter to think that parental bragging rights were even a factor.

"It's important that you feel comfortable with the campus and the environment, and that you're challenged intellectually," I said, speaking to the sunset haze. "But the main thing is that you strive to be a good person."

Our journey continued through the vastness of the Southland, ending at UC San Diego, located atop a mesa near the sea. We returned home weary but satisfied. I commiserated with my daughter that the coming year would be a flurry of admissions tests, applications, personal essays, and nervous waiting, and that she shouldn't get too stressed and that Fate would prevail.

To our mutual surprise and delight, she was accepted to the University of California, Berkeley, one of the top universities in the world, a mere five miles away from home. She finished her senior year at Saint Joseph Notre Dame High School honored as chemist of the year and rewarded with a new element named in her honor: Sawanium. I cautioned her to take everything the radical professors at Berkeley declaimed with a grain of salt and almost exacted her promise to phone me from the dorm and go over homework.

That year, my father passed away after a series of strokes that debilitated him physically and compromised his mind. Mom cared for him to the end despite all their fights and his foibles; for example, when Lydia asked Dad to teach her how to drive, Zenon made her so nervous that she bumped into a garbage can, whereupon he ended the lesson and her desire to ever take the wheel.

He had also sworn her to secrecy about any mention of the War. Dad had been most adamant about not discussing "what happened" in Ukraine except in the most general and innocuous of terms, an Eastern European refugee variant of *omertà*, the code of silence.

At the funeral, his former employer humorously related the day when two men in suits and sunglasses strolled into the meatpacking plant and asked for Zenon. He recounted that my dad calmly removed his butcher's apron and accompanied them outside, where they conferred in a late model sedan for the better part of an hour.

"What was that all about?" his boss asked. Dad re-donned the apron and resumed cutting a hindquarter with nary a word. Only months later did he confide to his boss and to no one else that the FBI had solicited his assistance for Cold War counterintelligence, which he declined. I wondered what other stories accompanied him to the grave.

We mourned Dad's passing and pled with Lydia to come live with Anita and me, or with my brother, Greg, and his wife in New Orleans, whichever she preferred. But the thought of leaving home was unthinkable. She had hoarded possessions accumulated over the decades, evidencing her success since first touching American soil empty-handed. And which included Charlotte's belongings, for whose return she prayed daily.

Unlike Natalie, Sonja, now 24, had grown increasingly wary of the world. Quiet and introverted, she actually enjoyed living at home as an adult. I couldn't comprehend this growing trend; although I loved my parents, I found the thought of living with them a day beyond my high school graduation totally abhorrent. Yet, I couldn't force myself to take a strong position with Sonja—who was I to judge? The matter caused Anita considerable emotional pain. Finally, she expelled her daughter after a huge scene.[19]

I frequently saw David and Alice, who had moved back to the Bay Area. Now finding their own way as adults, they reconciled with Wanda to a degree. David had recently secured employment with BART as a train operator, and I would reflexively check the conductor's window whenever I waited on the platform. Alice had just returned from living in Hawaii for two years, which she found even more laid-back than California, but she missed the family. Both David and Alice remained very close to Natalie and eased the burden of dealing with their mother.

And so I reasoned that with the daughters out on their own, Anita would be more willing to relocate. Her company liked her so much they'd probably let her transfer. Yet I also appreciated how much she had settled in, valuing the home environment above all else. Here she read the Bible, cooked healthy meals, organized her perfumes, created floral arrangements, and hosted our parties. Guardedly optimistic, I waited until Saturday evening, when Anita would be relaxed.

She reclined serenely on the sofa with legs tucked underneath, like a lotus flower on a tranquil pond. Her cat wedged himself under her thigh and eyed me defiantly. As a fine mist from a rare California summer storm migrated through the patio screen, Anita sipped a chardonnay while I nervously gulped a Heineken.

"Hon, what's troubling you?" Anita asked.

"Oh, nothing's wrong, Pooh," I said. "In fact, I have some great news! I've been offered a tremendous opportunity at CB's Los Angeles headquarters."

Anita froze momentarily, and then gathered herself.

"LA?"

"Yeah, I'll be the go-to guy for the big deals—"

"LA?"

"Now, of course we don't have to live downtown; we'll find a nice place on the Westside."

She set the wineglass on the end table and eyed me suspiciously. I surmised she had deduced that I had a hand in this "offer" and hadn't consulted with her first. I took another swig and quavered, "I thought you'd be a little more . . . excited."

Anita rose and faced the screen, absorbing the mist.

"Nothing good will come from LA," she said. "A land of illusion and delusion."

"But the beaches, the sunshine, the—"

"Our families are here, our friends are here, *my* work is here."

"DEC has an office near LAX," I meekly offered.

"Martin, I have a bad feeling around this."

"What? How can you say that?"

"There are things you don't understand."

I rose and paced the floor, choking the neck of the beer bottle. "I'll make a lot more money," I stammered.

"Is that what's so important to you?" Anita whispered, her eyes moistening.

"And prove my worth," I blurted, addressing the wall.

Anita eyed me sadly.

After consultation with her sister Betty and deep prayer, Anita acquiesced to the move and never discussed it again. She was able to transfer to DEC's Los Angeles office, despite the fact that the company had laid off numerous employees and was hemorrhaging financially, a testament to her value. I wrapped up business in San Francisco and closed my last pending sale, a vacant, renovated brick-and-timber warehouse in the South of Market area, a neighborhood of old warehouses and rave parties. The prior developer had spent too much on the rehab and couldn't induce any tenants to leave the Financial District. The bank foreclosed and hired me to quickly unload it.

Two young men, scrounging money from family and friends, stepped up with the best offer and the intention of leasing the building not to established San Francisco businesses but to start-ups they hoped to lure from Silicon Valley. I thought it was a dumb bet and wished them well.[20]

The kids threw Anita and me a farewell dinner. They wondered why anyone would voluntarily move to LA and urged me to get an audition since people said I looked like Robert De Niro. I gamely tried to enumerate SoCal's redeeming qualities but then surrendered and vowed that we were only an hour away by plane and would be back all the time.

Basking in the glow, I paid no heed to my own counsel. I had often advised clients that when you have a deal in escrow, and everybody is relaxed and smiley-faced, it doesn't mean that things are going smoothly. It only means that as captain of the Titanic, you haven't spotted the iceberg yet.

CHAPTER 9

Powers and Principalities

Anita and I settled into the heart of La La Land among the boat slips of Marina del Rey. Over a decade earlier, Gary and I had sold a shopping center in the Marina, and I thought the location embodied the best of LA living.

My wife found the phony air kisses particularly annoying. Of course, we could not visit a restaurant, dry cleaner, or hair salon without being attacked by a wall full of 8 x 10 glossies of people we didn't know. And when we did accidentally encounter a movie star, we registered mild dismay that their appearance did not match the screen persona. Yet Anita conceded that the Marina views were nice and the healthy negative ions from the ocean breeze made for perfect sleep.

We lived just minutes from the beach, and I sought to take full advantage. I joined the legendary Gold's Gym in neighboring Venice where Schwarzenegger and Ferrigno had trained and where I balanced on BOSU balls amid steroid-infused giants. I bought a pair of rollerblades and discovered my second calling, skating along the Strand, the famed oceanfront path that runs from the Marina to the end of Will Rogers State Beach, a seventeen-mile round trip.[21]

Particularly on crowded weekends, the Strand represented a microcosm of LA, with pedestrians, joggers, bicyclists, skaters, and other beach denizens competing ferociously for a five-foot-wide piece of real estate. A typical excursion:

I hop on at Washington Boulevard and proceed north, moving in and out of traffic.

I skate through multi-racial and multi-everything Venice Beach, noting snippets of conversation from the crowd:

"Had to change therapists last month."

"José . . . ¡ven aquí!"

"The waves are bitchin' at Zuma."

And so forth.

Suddenly, bicycle tires squeal as a perfectly tanned bikini blonde, going too fast, brakes for a tousle-haired, brown-skinned boy, darting toward the surf. Catastrophe averted by an inch; neither looks at the other.

I speed up and assume a skier's crouch as I disappear under Santa Monica Pier. Rough-hewn wooden beams and columns brace the boardwalk above me. The fenestration produced by the planks admits thousands of specks of sunlight; the smell of the creosote embedded in the wood overwhelms the bouquet of hot-dogs-on-a-stick, while the slap of waves against the piles muffles the thud of footsteps over-head. I exit the tunnel, smitten anew by the intense sunlight, sea air, and clamor emanating from the amusement park.

The crowd dissipates as I rollerblade through north Santa Monica and the rarified confines of the private beach clubs, with their brightly colored umbrellas and matching towels and vigilant attendants keeping the hoi polloi at bay. I strip off my tee. Now clad only in board shorts, I fall into a rhythm of long, smooth strides. By the time I glide by the Palisades, I am in the zone and going full throttle.

I eschew protective gear on the theory that most accidents are the result of people acting without thinking and the best way to avoid mishaps is by maintaining a heightened state of awareness. If I keep my focus, remain poised, and concentrate on anticipating errant human behavior, I will complete my journey intact.

On a Monday morning, I drove out of the Marina, past the procession of towering Mexican fan palms with their spindly, denuded trunks, and hopped on the 90 to the 405 to the 10 freeway. I powered down all the car windows and pounded the steering wheel to the beat of "California Love" by the recently deceased Tupac. With the Century City skyline looming ahead, I adjusted my Ray-Ban Wayfarers and mused that, on rare days, LA could still resemble the postcards (albeit with fake, airbrushed blue skies).

Three months into my new position, I had already made an impact, securing the listing on a Westside office building from a CB affiliate. I then obtained an audience to preview the deal with Jordan, the head of acquisitions for a privately held company that over the years had accumulated a number of trophy properties that commanded the highest rents and the most coveted tenants.

As I pulled into the garage, I felt out of place in my suit and tie, which remained the uniform of the day in Downtown Los Angeles but which seemed staid and even anal on the hip and trendy Westside. Downtown was a non-place where nothing happened and the workforce disappeared after 5:00 p.m. When someone said "New York" or "Chicago," images of the skyline sprang to mind. When someone said "Los Angeles," people reflexively thought of the Hollywood sign. A local real estate developer was currently negotiating with the city to build a new arena for the Lakers, the most recent in a litany of proposals to turn the barren landscape into a 24/7 venue.

The entertainment industry, with its myriad agents, accountants, attorneys, real estate people, and other ser-vice providers, powered the economy of West Los Angeles. Scarcely a dozen miles from my downtown office, the Westside could have been on Pluto. An attorney once remarked that he would more likely be called to a meeting in London than in Downtown. Apocryphal accounts allege that children grew to adulthood in Bel Air without ever setting foot in Downtown Los Angeles.

In the elevator, I reflected that perhaps Jordan would be interested in my building, perhaps not. But I was a stranger in a strange land, and what I really needed to know was how he thought.

I entered an office adorned with framed photographs of imposing office buildings. Jordan motioned for me to sit and then leaned back in his chair. Clad in movie producer attire, he dispatched with formalities.

"So, Marty, what do you have for me?"

"I'm going to market soon with a property around the corner from one of your buildings," I said as I handed him an attractive, four-color investment brochure that I had labored weeks in preparing.

He flipped through it nonchalantly, undoubtedly more familiar with the asset than I was.

"How come I don't know you?" he asked.

"I just moved down from San Francisco," I said. "I'll be handling CB's institutional business."

He studied me curiously and then motioned to the photos.

"Do you know how we buy so many Class A buildings?"

I simulated attentiveness and waited for the canned response of how they had a vast network of relationships, or were able to move quickly, or focused on off-market transactions, or could exploit inefficiencies, or were simply superior negotiators.

"We pay more."

Those three words produced a revelation. In nearly twenty years of brokerage, I had never heard a buyer admit to the obvious. I caught my breath, unable to mouth a response.

"Now, let me explain why."

Jordan proceeded to educate me on how the commercial real estate world was again changing. I knew the business as it had been for most of the twentieth century: a local market dominated by private entities, as typified by the real estate dynasties of New York City.[22] These men developed and bought wisely and rarely sold, preferring instead to refinance and reinvest the profits and, most important, to train their sons in the business.

But many of the dynasties fragmented as the succeeding generations often lacked the acumen and/or the desire to carry on the family business and as the deals became larger and larger, requiring partnerships with institutional investors. The acceptance of commercial real estate as a legitimate asset class, like stocks and bonds, allowed insurance companies and pension funds to pour money into megadeals in the major urban centers. And now there emerged a new option for liquidity: the public markets.

Whereas Jordan's portfolio was significant in comparison to other LA property owners, it was dwarfed by the market cap of many US companies. To go public, Jordan explained, they had to "bulk up," which meant implementing an aggressive buying campaign. He explained in detail which buildings fit and which didn't, then swore my allegiance in helping him achieve his ambitions.

"You know we're at the top of every broker's list," Jordan warned. "And you . . . you still need a map to find Wilshire Boulevard."

I reflected for a beat and then said, "Don't worry—I get it."

In the span of the next fifteen months, I sold Jordan five office buildings via separate transactions, which was some kind of record for me and probably for most. After one closing, he gifted me with a new pair of inline skates. These sales not only padded my track record but also provided a valuable client reference and instant credibility among the heavy hitters.

Concurrently, I assembled a team to compete against other brokerages in what came to be known as "beauty contests," pitch-fests held by the institutional sellers of major assets to interview and select a worthy marketeer. I hired an assistant (an Irish kid who gamely accepted my outbursts), along with the services of a marketing coordinator, rounded off by a leasing broker selected from whatever city the property happened to be located in so as to provide local market knowledge. And I would usually bring along a manager to truckle to the client and plead for the assignment.

Gradually, we started to win business in these head-on competitions, and within two years, we chalked up significant sales, such as a 500,000-square-foot office building in the Bay Area, a 7 million-square-foot industrial park in Utah, and a 400,000-square-foot shopping center in San Francisco, to name a few.

I traveled more frequently, both pitching new business and hunting for fresh capital on the West Coast and in New York, as well as internationally, for example, in Hong Kong, where wily entrepreneurs were spiriting money out of mainland China and where my chop came in handy, and in Tokyo, where the Japanese had now become sellers instead of buyers and were unloading their US properties at cents on the dollar.

Of course there were the conferences and award functions, not to mention languorous Friday afternoons at Spago, bonding with CB's Beverly Hills office manager, sitting next to a table permanently reserved for a Hollywood billionaire, whose enormous girth and even greater appetites demanded such accommodation.

The more I traveled, the more I drank, with alcohol serving as a relaxant and sleep aid. On an overnight trip to the Bay Area, I was arrested for a DUI[23] and spent the night in the Alameda County jail in downtown Oakland, a sobering experience. I was released early in the morning and kept it a secret from Anita, although I suspect she knew, given her powers. I deduced that the problem was in fact driving, not drinking, and vowed to be more cautious, and, as a safeguard, practiced the demonstrated field sobriety test in my spare time.

And then one day Tina phoned. The mere fact of the call, nearly seven years since our last contact, would have raised questions in a sober mind. She called with words to the effect that she "wanted to see how I was doing" and it would be "nice to catch up." I told her I was married and living in Los Angeles, and she congratulated me and said to call when I happened to be in the Bay Area. I responded that I was glad she was doing well. Late for a meeting, I wished her well and hung up.

Several months later, in Oakland on business, I contacted her. Why? I'm sure I had convinced myself that I intended only to satisfy my curiosity and not seek out baser inclinations, and that I had matured, and what better way to prove that I could exercise self-control. I suggested dinner at the Gingerbread House, a Cajun/Creole restaurant near the Waterfront Hotel in Jack London Square where I was staying. She had not aged much, and we hugged lightly and I noted that she was unusually heedful and pleasant. After hours of drinking and incidental eating, Tina dropped me off at the hotel.

In retrospect, the fact that she made no effort to seduce me likely provoked me further. I invited her for a drink at the hotel bar and then to the room, and the rest of the night disappeared into a haze. The next morning, I hurriedly packed and left Tina asleep and checked out. As I pulled away in a cab bound for Oakland Airport, I sensed an odd finality. She had enabled me to find the worst in myself, and I never saw her again.

I drove directly home from LAX and called in sick. Haggard, I awaited Anita's arrival from work. When she walked through the door, I struggled to act normal until my guilt created an immense tension.

I stood before my beautiful wife, tears in my eyes. "I need to tell you—"

"I know," Anita said softly.

"You know . . . what happened?"

She opened the patio door and stepped out on the balcony. The flotilla of boats in the marina bobbed gently at their moorings, bathed in the orange glow of twilight.

As I inched closer, she spoke with her back turned. "She called me months ago, anonymously, promising to 'get my man.' I didn't know who she was, but I knew *who* she was . . . I could discern her character . . . what she looked like."

"You *talked* to her?"

Anita slowly turned, trembling.

"You remember," she said, "before we left the Bay Area? I told you some of my jewelry was missing and you didn't believe me?"

I nodded.

"She took it—somehow broke into our house, our *home*."

Beyond astonishment, I staggered to the couch and collapsed while Anita put her hands to her face and wept.

In a haze of alcohol and hubris, I had been oblivious to what
was really happening. On reflection, I imagine Tina probably
regarded me as easy prey and an unworthy opponent from
the very first day we met. No, this wasn't about romance or
jealousy or blackmail. Tina had initiated spiritual warfare:
She was the instrument and Anita the target, not me.

At the time, I knew little about the concept of spiritual
warfare, assuming it was a metaphor for doing battle with
temptation, invoking militaristic language for effect. But for
Anita it represented a very real struggle with what the New
Testament calls principalities and powers, those negative
forces that we battle in the spiritual realm.[24]

The ultimate enemy was Satan, if you will—not the red
horny guy with a pitchfork but the external, oppositional
force of evil in the world of the unseen. And my affair was
not just a one-night stand with an old flame but the conspir-
atorial defilement of a marriage where "the two shall become
one flesh." All I knew was that Anita was under attack and
there was nothing worse.

Throughout this crisis, Anita had prayed hard and
through grace, obtained the aura of light and the mantle of
protection. But I had surrendered my self-respect and con-
taminated our marriage. I had let down and put in harm's
way the person I admired the most. Hearing all this, I could
barely function, as my self-image proved to be a fraud. My

ego shattered like a porcelain plate dropped on concrete. I begged her for a forgiveness I did not deserve.

For the next several days, Anita deliberated on our future together as I quietly stayed in the background. I believe she talked with her sister Betty, whose judgment on matters of consequence was beyond reproach. Betty was churchgoing but not Bible-thumping; she had enjoyed a long marriage maintained by occasional incidents of wielding a skillet to modify spousal bad behavior. Betty shared the gift of discernment and could tune in on Anita's spiritual wavelength.

To my knowledge, Anita talked to no one else. I had feared that word would spread and Natalie and Sonja would find out and I would be completely diminished in their eyes, a terrible thought. But Anita kept it to herself and followed her nightly ritual of reading the Bible and praying, which for her was a very real conversation, a back-and-forth with God.

And then, one morning she rose and pulled back the drapes and allowed the Pacific sun to bathe the room. I handed her the morning coffee, and she mumbled over the mug, "You don't junk a Cadillac over a few dents" (although I suspect she really felt that the car was almost totaled) and advised me we would keep on but I had to change. I hugged her fiercely and gave my word.

Forthwith, I found a counselor who specialized in both chemical dependency and marital counseling. Anita and I tracked him down not to a snug office in Beverly Hills but to a cottage behind a main house somewhere in Mar Vista.

I knocked and a voice declared, "Door's open." We entered what was essentially one room that served as office and living quarters, piled with journals, bottles of herbs, and the accouterments of a hippie commune. Daniel, bearded and weathered, resembled an Old Testament prophet.

He welcomed us in and cleared space on a threadbare sofa where we sank several inches. Wheeling over in a desk chair, he hovered above us, ordering me to describe what brought us there and then hearing Anita's version. Satisfied with a command of the facts, Daniel addressed my wife.

"I could start therapy for him or the two of you, but it would be a waste of my time and your money," he said.

She frowned.

"The reason is, until he quits drinking, no other intervention is effective."

As he pivoted and rolled up in my face, I finally connected the dots and fully comprehended my alcoholic inheritance. My most vivid memory of childhood was accompanying my dad to the Eagles Club, the local "aerie" for the Fraternal Order of Eagles, a national organization engaged in charitable activities, but for me a bastion of manhood.

Dad ushered his son, perhaps 7 years old, into the dim, oaky bar.

"Hey, Zen, I see you brought the boss," the barkeep chortled as my dad broke into a grin. He hoisted me onto a barstool amid a cloud of cigarette smoke and camaraderie. The men had come to escape their wives and drink to forget; certainly, my dad had more to forget than most.

He regaled his confederates with my accomplishments, that day averring that little Martin was devouring the epic novel *Ben-Hur*. "Do you understand what you're reading?" a gruff voice asked, inches from my face. I nodded solemnly and the conversation shifted to the Milwaukee Braves, the hottest team in baseball.

But the solace lasted for only a little while, and eventually, the men filtered out one by one to their families and the arguments that were certain to ensue. Dad packed me into our black Buick Special with its three chrome-ringed "VentiPorts" on the forward fenders and wove home unconcerned with his driving, as our next-door neighbor was a cop and himself an Eagle. I sat back and relished the day when I could fully participate and trade my Coca-Cola for a Budweiser.

"Martin, I could make this complicated, but it's not," Daniel said as I blinked to attention. "You first have to get out of the fog so you can think and act coherently—then we can deal with your issues."

"You mean like AA?" I said.

"Going cold turkey, that helps some but not others. I'll give you a few options to consider."

"You seem to know a lot about this," I said.

"Personal experience," Daniel grunted.

He proceeded to elucidate various methods for reducing dependency. Fifty minutes later, he saw us to the door.

"I've got my work cut out," I said.

"You know you have one shot," he said. "Otherwise, she's gone."

CHAPTER 10

Trial and Error

"Each of you lives this life to understand the worth of yourself."

Mary Jo spoke with eyes shut in a disembodied Irish brogue. An audience of perhaps thirty people, including Anita and me, listened attentively in a small conference room in the Hollywood Holiday Inn. Mary Jo had entered moments earlier and sat on a stool and introduced herself as a psychic medium as well as a suburban homemaker. "Dear ones, I'll soon go into trance," she cheerily stated. Cautioning that her voice would change, she explained that she would speak to us all as a group and then individually, identifying a personal issue of concern and means of alleviation.

I honestly cannot recollect how I found out about this event, her only appearance in LA (she later confessed she found the energy troublesome and had no desire to return), or why I felt drawn to attend. Perhaps my road to sobriety had opened tiny windows in my mind. Notwithstanding my exploits with Anita, I had no previous contact with, knowledge of, or interest in people who identified themselves as psychics. I embraced the crystal ball stereotype and dismissed the premise. But now, I only knew that I had to go.

Casually, I mentioned the event to Anita, who to my surprise proved less than enthusiastic. I had assumed that given her experience with the anomalous, Anita would naturally be curious about mediumship. Quite the opposite: She directed me to several passages in Scripture that dealt harshly with mediums, sorcerers, and spiritists. But I persisted in convincing her to attend—"It'll be fun, probably all a con"—and she eventually relented.

Seated near the back of the audience, I now chuckled to Anita that this would be a hoot, to which she rolled her eyes. I expected to hear generic descriptions of garden-variety emotional problems. Instead, Mary Jo bore into her first target, a man in the front row, and revealed a "secret" with such specificity that it devastated him and shocked the rest of us. As she continued down the line, I grew nervous. Anita elbowed me and whispered, "Careful what you wish for."

My wife barely maintained her composure as Mary Jo counseled her on coping with the death of a brother who had drowned years before, the details of which even I didn't know. I cringed now that it was my turn, certain that the intuitive would reveal what a horrible person I was in my actions toward Anita. Instead, she took it easy on me, telling me not to worry about an upcoming surgery that was on my mind, and quickly moved on.

After the session ended, Anita and I left, hand in hand. At the parking garage, we noticed the man who had received the first reading rush to his car. Visibly shaken and desperate to escape, he promptly backed his car into a concrete column—BAM!—and then sped away. I murmured to Anita, "How could this woman possibly know these things?" She answered me with her silence.

By the summer of 1998, I had made progress in my bout with the bottle.

I thought of my dad suffering a heart attack in his mid-40s. Years of walking in and out of a meat locker, pack-a-day smoking, and two-fisted drinking had weakened the ticker. The cardiologist admonished that surgery would give him a conditional reprieve, but unless Zenon altered his lifestyle, the odds favored that he wouldn't see 50. With incredible resolve, my dad swore off alcohol and tobacco, attended a community college sixty miles from home, graduated with a business degree, and obtained a desk job with 3M Corporation.

However, his personality changed. He would read or otherwise sit silent for hours in his easy chair, no longer the happy inebriate. He had uplifted himself and his family, but the abstinence had created a hole that he knew not how to fill.

Rather than grit my teeth and repress the temptation, I adopted a program of controlled moderation. I concentrated on retraining my mind to see life without being drunk as a benefit, not a deprivation. I frequently went days without;

on social occasions, I limited myself to two to three drinks at any one time and monitored my blood alcohol content. Eventually, I climbed out of the fog, and through sustained personal effort, reestablished an element of self-control, cutting back on the socializing and networking component of the business.

Nominally, I was at the top of my game, winning coveted sales assignments from the dominant institutional property owners. I had just closed the sale of the Ordway in Oakland, the tallest building in the Bay Area outside of San Francisco and located only three blocks from where I started in commercial real estate twenty years earlier, an apt reminder of the road traveled.

And I had recently completed the pricing of Treasure Island for the US Navy, a feather in my commercial real estate cap. Decommissioned as a military base, this man-made island halfway between Oakland and San Francisco would soon be sold to the City and County of San Francisco for a future, multi-billion-dollar redevelopment project. I deemed this the most complex valuation of my career, as the site suffered from poor soils, environmental contamination, aging infrastructure, and restricted vehicular access measured against the interests of two very competitive public agencies.

Yet despite such challenging assignments, I became increasingly disaffected. Perhaps 25 percent of my time was spent actually negotiating deals; the majority was dedicated to making listing presentations, preparing marketing brochures, supervising due diligence "war rooms," dealing with administrative matters, adjudicating commission disputes, and the like.

The sale of investment properties had been thoroughly commoditized and accompanied by the compression of brokerage fees. Market information—the linchpin of a broker's value proposition—was being aggregated by techies online and given away. The only way to remain competitive was to add more people and manage an assembly line operation; for me, the process had become rote repetition, lacking in creativity and imagination. But I soldiered on.

"Hon, what do you think I should do?" Anita asked one day. Compaq Computer had announced its acquisition of her employer, Digital Equipment Corporation, in a deal valued at $9.6 billion, the largest merger in the computer industry to date. Once-mighty DEC had fallen hard; the "restructuring" would result in 15,000 pink slips. Anita was offered the opportunity to accept early retirement or take her chances under the new leadership at Compaq.

"It's your choice, but why stay?" I said. "Times have changed; life at Compaq will not be the same." Her manager and a number of colleagues had already been let go. "You'd only be doing it for the money."

"I need to stay busy . . . "

"Look, I'll teach you how to rollerblade!"

Anita retired and found things to do, and we threw a holiday party at year's end. A dozen friends flew down from up north, and it was almost like old times. I closed out 1998 with impressive numbers and then followed my own advice.

Compared to my colleagues, I had always lived a relatively modest lifestyle. Nor was financial net worth a yardstick for measuring my self-worth. While I respected the kingpins of commercial real estate, I didn't desire to be like them, didn't covet what they had. Moolah was important in that it subsidized freedom of choice. But if the action wasn't there, if I didn't wake up with excitement at what each day might bring, it didn't matter.

I resigned abruptly, not only from CB Commercial but also from the business that had been my lifeblood for two decades, to the disbelief and dismay of everyone.

Except for one person. I had previously broached the subject with Anita, who remained remarkably detached. The brokerage business, with its workaholism and temptations, had nearly cost us our marriage. While I fully accepted personal responsibility rather than blame commerce, I knew Anita was not unhappy to see me leave.

"Do I need to go back to work?" she had asked.

"Naw, we're fine."

"Do you know what you're going to do?"

"Not exactly."

"How about Mexican for dinner?"

I had not forgotten the encounter with Mary Jo many months earlier, but with the press of business and self-rehabilitation, I didn't follow up. Now with time on my hands, I decided to investigate the matter further and reflexively turned to my former colleague, whom I could rely on to render an unvarnished opinion.

"Buddy, are you serious?" George said after hearing my story.

"I know it all sounds weird in my retelling, but she . . . *knew* things."

"Yeah, she knew how to play you for a fool."

"It was different," I said. "No 'tells' that I could detect. She wasn't cold reading. I don't believe she paid thirty other people to act as shills."

"You know what they say," George said with a snort.

Okay, what?

"If you've been playing poker for half an hour and you still don't know who the patsy is, you're the patsy."

But I remained unconvinced. What I knew for sure was that I couldn't really discuss this topic with my business associates or even with Anita, so I undertook independent research. I subscribed to Skeptic magazine and read books on stage magic and paranormal trickery and the methods psychics have used through the ages to bamboozle a gullible populace. I studied the lives of noted mediums and clairvoyants—the many that were debunked, to my satisfaction, and the few that weren't.

I reflected on my personal experience of negotiating with some of the most ingenious people in the real estate industry who elevated misdirection and sleight of hand to a high art, particularly where financial gain hung in the balance. I applied my bullshit detector not only to Mary Jo but to the most vocal skeptics as well, a preponderance of whom were atheists and who considered religion equally ridiculous.

I then induced Anita, still reluctant, to attend a retreat Mary Jo was hosting in a beach town on the Florida Panhandle. Mary Jo opened the program by stating that she was merely a transmitter for messages she received from her "Guides," discarnates with advanced wisdom and a long view. She then "read" each of the attendees, again revealing specific and detailed personal information no one else could possibly know. The sessions that followed were organized around different topics, such as past lives and connecting with the soul self, and accompanied by tips for better living that my common sense could not refute.

On a balmy evening, Anita and I shared a private moment with Mary Jo on the hotel veranda.

"I grew up in rural Tennessee," she revealed. "Of course, I couldn't talk about the experiences I was having with anyone."

"How did you . . . break out?" I asked.

"At some point, I heard about Edgar Cayce,"[25] she said. "He was raised on a farm in Kentucky, not far away. I felt this strong connection with him and decided that this is what God wanted me to do."

As our conversation continued, my wife discovered that Mary Jo was a decent Christian woman with a good heart who didn't operate from the dark side. Anita's resistance eroded, although she still struggled with how all this fit into a Biblical worldview.

Flying back from Florida, I concluded that the overwhelming majority of psychics possessed no special skills and/or operated a fraudulent enterprise and therefore were not to be trusted. But I also believed that, in an asymmetric distribution, a tiny percentage were adepts who recognized their unusual gift at an early age and accessed extremely valuable information through unexplainable means. They dedicated their practice to helping people deal with suffering and loss rather than making predictions or telling fortunes. And I intended to avail myself of this resource.

But first I had to pay the bills. I put my twenty years of commercial real estate experience to the side and considered all business options except one: getting involved with Hollywood. A former associate, perhaps the greatest prevaricator I had ever met, moved to LA and dabbled with investing in feature films. He soon returned to the Bay Area, thoroughly chastened and grumbling, "Those people lie."

I rollerbladed daily, turning ideas over in my mind on the long, quiet stretches of the Strand, imagining from whence might emerge the next generation of hunters: solitary, living on the edge, relying on his or her wits moment to moment. The epiphany occurred on a Tuesday afternoon halfway between Santa Monica and the Palisades.

Day trading!

In 1999, no endeavor resembled the Wild West more than online, intraday stock trading. The convergence of new technologies and regulatory accommodations now allowed an individual to directly buy and sell stocks over the internet, historically the province of large stock brokerage firms. The spectacular recent rise in stock prices, particularly of technology stocks and especially the dot-coms, along with unprecedented levels of volatility, poured fuel on the fire. The combustible material was the small investor glued to a personal computer, typically located in the bedroom or a secluded nook of a personal residence.

Having acquired some measure of savvy over the years in placing bets while controlling risk, I didn't consider myself a sucker out to get rich quick. I regarded day trading as an enterprise similar to brokerage, except that I would be making many small bets very quickly and I would be hazarding my personal capital. I bought a new computer, upgraded the connectivity with a digital subscriber line (DSL), and gave myself six months to break into profitability.

Training and encouragement were marginal or non-existent. I finally located a shop that claimed to teach the rudiments, and I eagerly anticipated the first class. When the alarm clock rang at 4:30 a.m., I bolted upright in bed, disoriented; Anita placed her hand on my forehead and tittered, "You okay, baby?" I had been instructed to arrive at 5:30 a.m., an hour before the opening bell on the West Coast, so as to absorb the breaking news, monitor activity in the futures markets, and plan out the day's trading strategy.

I sped across the Westside in the darkness and exited the 10 at Western Avenue, the second longest street in LA after Sepulveda and the most ethnically diverse, passing through a multiplicity of communities, its vertical length on a neighborhood map resembling the strata of a soil boring. I maneuvered through Koreatown, already abuzz at this abysmal hour, to Wilshire Boulevard, where I pulled into a dank garage.

I entered a dimly lit, windowless room, the fluorescent lights casting ghostly shadows on myself and six Korean newbies, young men in tees with chubby feet in laceless sneakers, staring at cheap monitors and jabbing at primitive keyboards. A youthful instructor directed me to an empty seat as the class commenced, and I concentrated on the mechanics of stock trading. The trainer paced the room, barking out commands and occasionally lapsing into English for my benefit.

In the ensuing days, I learned how to paper trade. Admittedly, I once let my concentration drift and thought about my big real estate deals and private offices and wondered aloud, "WTF?" Whereupon the instructor hovered over me and scowled until I refocused and correctly entered a buy order with a trailing stop-loss.

The time soon arrived to trade in real time from my home computer. I quickly deduced that the relationship between paper trading and the real thing was tenuous, much like studying military history and then going to war. I also realized that I was not alone in my bedroom. Behind the monitor sat Goldman Sachs and Morgan Stanley and others who boasted unlimited capital and unmitigated greed, salivating to take my money. I imagined their hands reaching toward me through the screen, zombie-like.

An intense battle raged daily between myself and whoever happened to be on the other side of the trade. By definition, a day trader closes out all positions by the closing bell, which necessitates constant vigilance and monitoring. I would be mesmerized by the flickering images on the screen, toggling between candlestick charts and elusive bid-ask spreads, frequently forgetting to eat until forcibly reminded by Anita. The volatility was insane.[26]

By the fall, I had not only failed to meet my goal but had seriously dipped into personal savings. When Anita asked how we were doing, I would reply, "Just fine, Pooh." Who was to say that the next month would not put us in the black? Yet the recognition had set in that perhaps I had not found my true calling, that success in one area of business does not ensure success in another. I studied all my trades and discovered a pattern of exiting prematurely and not sticking with the plan, emotional decisions based on the fear of losing money. I was the poster child for the market shaking out the weak hands.

Simply, I was loath to risk the hard-earned capital I had earned. As a commercial real estate broker, I didn't sell properties—I sold time. I might not make money, but I did not lose money since the company covered my overhead. The memory of being broke and Wanda pregnant played a role—I still kept all my credit cards (by now augmented with high borrowing limits) active as an emergency line of credit, just in case.

Undoubtedly, my family history also contributed to this mindset. My parents arrived with nothing; any material gain could be directly attributed to their hard work and personal sacrifice. Zenon built our house with his own hands, assisted by his neighbors. He and Lydia scrimped and saved to pay the mortgage and grow a retirement nest egg. And then Dad dabbled in the stock market and lost most of our savings and suffered terribly.

I concluded that the most successful traders, like other gamblers, tend to win only slightly more than half the time and that losing is inherently part of the enterprise. The skill comes from minimizing the size of the losses and letting the winners run, requiring extraordinary emotional discipline. With diminishing confidence, I implored Fate to smile more kindly upon me.

And she did.

CHAPTER 11

Anatomy of a Deal

The call interrupted me in the middle of a bad trade.

Barely 9:00 a.m., the merciless August sun somehow penetrated the drawn blinds as I sat at the computer. The lights were flashing red on the screen—not a good sign. I had decided to fade Yahoo despite my better judgment and now the stock was moving fast against me. At that moment, the phone rang. I made it a rule not to answer during trading hours, but for reasons unknown, picked up the handset.

"Hello?"

"Martin, it's Dave."

I was slightly surprised to hear the voice of a former associate. Dave was the foremost appraiser of commercial real estate in San Francisco and maintained a side hustle of helping clients acquire properties, a rare melding of right- and left-brain functions. We had made money together years ago; he had referred a client to me, and I had brokered the sale of a property he was involved in. However, after I moved to LA, we had only intermittent contact.

"Listen, can I, uh, call you back?" I said, watching the losses mount.

"It's really important—I have a deal."

In business, until you go down the road with someone with money at stake, you really do not know that person. I had with Dave and trusted him implicitly. And to any real estate pro, the mention of that four-letter word is all it takes.

"Hang on a sec," I said. My finger hovered over the key and then pressed reluctantly, closing out my position. *Shit, another loser.* "What's the building?"

"799 Market—Bank of America's going to quietly sell it off-market."

I knew the property, as I did all the buildings in downtown San Francisco: an eight-story office-and-retail building at the corner of Market, Powell, and 4th Streets, the busiest intersection in the city and an absolutely golden location. Dave confided that the property would not be auctioned off in a buyer feeding frenzy. Rather, the bank intended to move it off their books without fanfare. This was the perfect storm.

"What do they want?" I asked.

"Thirty-five," Dave said.

"Who else knows about it?"

"Only the bank's broker—he owed me one and gave me a day's head start before contacting the usual suspects."

"Let's go through the numbers."

Having appraised many of the signature assets in San Francisco for serious clients, Dave ran conservative financial projections I could rely on, unlike a broker's projections in a marketing brochure, which were pure fantasy. Nonetheless, after he emailed me his figures, I relentlessly questioned each and every assumption; trust and verify, as they say. We went back and forth for over an hour.

"At thirty-five, this is a *very* good deal," I finally concluded. "So let me get this straight. You think you and I should buy it . . . "

"Yes!"

"And all we need is 35 million dollars."

"Uh-huh."

I had never acted as a principal in real estate except as a home buyer. In the arena of signature commercial real estate assets, the difference between acting as a broker and a principal is, to paraphrase Mark Twain, "the difference between the lightning bug and the lightning." To have skin in the game, to put personal capital and reputation at risk, not to mention to incur outsized liability on potential borrowings . . . well, over the years I saw what could happen. And to entertain this proposition at the precise moment I was losing my ass day trading?

I have held to the belief that, in whatever endeavor of life, if an individual lives to a reasonably ripe age, he or she may be presented with one or two, or at most three, opportunities that can truly alter one's personal trajectory in a radically new way. The vast majority of people do not recognize the opportunity for what it may be; a small fraction recognize it but don't act on it; and the tiny remainder both recognize and act on it.

Wavering, I suddenly felt my neck hairs bristle. It was the juice, dormant for so long.

"Let's do it."

I instinctively sprang into action, like a cheetah upon spotting the wounded gazelle. Dave and I had twenty-four hours, our only advantage; one quick shot at the prey and that was it. I had to find a financial partner with both the capacity and the immediate desire to invest in this type of property in this specific submarket. In other words, an investor who hankered for the asset and was willing to stretch rather than foolishly attempt to steal it.

I mentally filtered through all of my clients and relationships faster than IBM's Deep Blue and settled on a private equity source who advised a number of institutional investors and whom I knew could perform. I hesitated—months of solitude may have diminished my phone skills—and then dialed the acquisition officer.

"Hey, Phil, it's Martin!"

"I heard sightings of you at Venice Beach," he snickered.

"I've got a deal for you."

"On my way to LAX," Phil said. "I'll be back next week—call me then."

Nuts. Think . . . think.

"Let me meet you at the gate—I'm in the Marina, only minutes away."

"Can't promise you much time. I'm running late as it is."

"If you look up, you'll see me coming."

Armed with Phil's flight information, I snatched up Dave's proforma and bolted out the door, nearly running over Anita, who was returning from Gelson's Market. "Gotta go, Pooh," I said, and added, "It's all good," over my shoulder. Fortuitously, I breezed through security,[27] and less than a half hour later, I pitched the deal to Phil between gasps. We had made money together, and I knew he trusted my opinion.

I finished my spiel tagging alongside Phil as he strode toward the gate, weekender bag in one hand, boarding pass in the other.

"Can you give me an indication, kinda like right now?" I asked.

As the flight attendant snatched the pass, he calmly turned toward me.

"I have an investor in mind. You know what the drill is, due diligence and all that, but yeah, we can place it."

I fist-bumped the sky as he disappeared into the gangway.

I drove home, pondering the next challenge. I had identified the end investor, but they would not put up any money until completing the vetting process: studying and underwriting the transaction; poring over banker boxes of documents; and physically inspecting the building with teams of specialists. I needed someone to immediately pledge the earnest money— the good faith deposit—to tie up the property and convince the bank we were serious players and not just a couple of guys way in over their heads.

Such high-risk money does not come cheaply and usually provides the plot line for a gangster movie. I required a very savvy guy who could grasp the deal instantly and evaluate the risk and say yea or nay. I immediately thought of Jack, another former brokerage client. His Manhattan-based company operated in the netherworld of foreign capital, investing on behalf of offshore clients, primarily from the Middle East. In this case, the fast cash fit the profile for his personal account, which sought high-risk/high-return investments.

Rushing inside, I thanked Anita for the gourmet sandwich she had placed on my desk and dialed between bites.

"Hi, Jack," I said. "Whoops, better not say that on an airplane."

He groaned. "You still alive, Martin?"

"I need some money, half mil at least—the deal's in San Francisco, one hundred percent location."

"Tell me more."

Thirty minutes later, I had my earnest money. Jack negotiated hard for a cut of the action and a seat at the table and honorably refrained from end-running us and doing the deal himself. I called Dave and assured him we were ready to rock and roll and I would meet him at 8:00 a.m. in his office.

That evening, Anita and I feasted on soul food at Aunt Kizzy's Back Porch in the Marina, the walls festooned with signed photos of black celebrities. She admitted her concern: Here I was again with that look of excitement in my eyes and crazy shit happening a mile a minute, and now, an overnight trip, and what next? I asked her to believe me that I had put the past behind and that this deal was different and might open new doors, and without her support, I wouldn't go.

We kissed as she dropped me off at LAX. On the last Southwest flight for the night, I finally had the chance to relax and reflect on the opportunity at hand. The top commercial

real estate brokers can earn an outsized living from commissions, ordinary income. But fortunes in real estate result
from owning assets, from having equity, from realizing
capital gains. The size of significant commercial real estate
transactions puts them out of reach of any but the wealthiest
individuals if acting alone. However, a shrewd player able to
control other people's money and garner a piece of the action
for the effort while minimizing personal investment and liability . . . well, he or she can, in the words of Gordon Gekko,
"piss in the tall weeds with the big dogs."

I sipped on a Starbucks Venti, half decaf and half regular,
part of my regimen to reduce the intake of excitable chem-
icals and, like the Buddha, take the middle way. The coffee chain had proliferated throughout the San Francisco
Financial District, such that there was now a store directly
across the street from Dave's office, where I paced.

"So they said they would do a deal at $35 million, not a
penny less?" I asked.

"That's what the broker told me, and I believe him," Dave
said. "If we start negotiating, we'll get blown out."

"Think we can get thirty days?" I said, referring to the
duration of the due diligence period before the deposit went
hard.

"Maybe, if none of the other terms are squirrelly."

I drafted a letter of intent outlining the salient features
of our proposal, which Dave's secretary quickly typed up
on his business letterhead. Unlike residential transactions
where a buyer signs a canned purchase and sale agreement,

commercial sales start with a term sheet, thus opening the door for handsomely paid attorneys to run up staggering bills while arguing obscure points in protracted contract negotiations. We signed the letter and faxed it to the broker, who confirmed receipt and said he would promptly walk it over to the bank.

Dave and I labored the rest of the day putting together an investment package for Phil's client, replete with a property description, financial analysis, rent and sale comparables, and a forecast of the enormous value we would create in the future by raising rents. Also, the building had been run by the bank's corporate facilities department, which intrinsically meant that two hungry guys could trim the expenses and further increase the bottom line.

Slightly before 5:00 p.m., the broker called, and Dave switched to speakerphone.

"I've got Martin here," Dave said. "How did it go?"

"Kirsten wants to talk to you both in ten minutes," the broker said.

Kirsten was the asset manager charged with running the sale for the bank. While it was ultimately subject to committee approval, her recommendation carried significant weight. Her request was unusual since the opposing parties rarely communicated at this early stage, preferring to negotiate through the broker.

"Why?" I asked.

He continued, "She doesn't know either of you. You've met their price and the upfront money is fine. But she needs to hear you say that you are going to close and close on time."

"Is there some deadline?"

"Yeah, they have to book the sale by the end of the third quarter, otherwise it's a no-go."

Dave and I grimaced at this fresh piece of information; we now had zero wiggle room.

"And there's one other thing. Kirsten's already booked her vacation for the week after closing. She's going to Siberia to hunt brown bear—complicated logistics—and wants you to know she'll be very unhappy if she has to cancel the trip."

A huntress!

"Let me put you on hold for a minute," Dave said to the broker, muting the call. In every deal, there is a moment of truth, and this one arrived early.

"Is your investor going to perform?" Dave asked nervously.

"You know how it goes," I said. "Nothing's certain."

"If we don't close—"

"Yep, we'll wish we were that Russian bear, and we won't do business in this town again."

A pigeon alit on the windowsill and eyed us curiously. Finally, I offered Dave a thumbs-up. He hesitated, then reciprocated and turned the speaker back on.

"Tell Kirsten no problem."

I tossed and turned in bed that night despite Anita's best efforts to soothe me. Kirsten had grilled us mercilessly and we had scrambled to offer evidence of our accomplishments as well as the names of prominent locals who would vouch that we were men of our word. I couldn't read her and had no clue as to which way she'd lean; she only committed to letting us know the next day.

I woke at dawn, and, too nervous to trade, threw on my shorts and grabbed my blades. I skated on the virtually deserted path in the breaking light and thought how limitless the ocean was and how insignificant I was and to hell with worrying about a mere deal. There was always another train pulling into the station—that's what I told buyers—but I scarcely believed it that day.

Later, I nursed a half-caf on the Venice Beach Boardwalk, my new Nokia cell phone poised upright on the table. A reed-thin man, wearing nothing but a Speedo, flashed past me on the Strand, deploying five-wheel rollerblades at a tremendous velocity while skating *backward*, his shaven head glistening in the morning sun. Suddenly, the phone vibrated frantically and then displayed Dave's number.

"Howdy, partner," I said.

"We got it."

Reaching agreement in principle is not the end but only the beginning of what I would describe as deal frenzy, a month of constant negotiation and on-the-spot decision-making. As if we lacked sufficient pressure, our broker confided that offers from the name buyers had started to roll in; Kirsten would remain true to her word, but we'd better not screw up. Dave and I immediately engaged the only honest attorney we knew to handle the contracts for both the purchase of the real estate and the formation of a joint venture with the investor, effectively two parallel transactions.

Phil had just identified our prospective partner: Commonfund Realty Investors, the real estate investment arm of Commonfund, a Connecticut-based money manager representing college endowments and other nonprofits. They were growing their portfolio, and this would be their first acquisition in San Francisco. He confided that the deal fit perfectly and they were very motivated; a contingent would arrive next week to meet us and tour the property.

We slogged through the leases and boxes of documents furnished by the bank, searching the fine print for language that could come back and bite us in the butt, since we were buying the property "as is." Caveat emptor. We lined up all the physical inspections—architectural, structural, environmental, survey, to name a few—and paid extra for the rush job and sweated out the results. We opened escrow and instructed Jack to wire funds, which he did, but then made it a habit to call daily and ask what was going on and had we done anything stupid.

The day of the Commonfund tour soon arrived. Dave and I walked briskly to the building a few minutes early to evaluate the scene: a fabulous sunny day at the end of summer. A long line of tourists queued at the cable car terminus across Market Street, waiting to board, as the fabled vehicle, bursting with bodies, pulled in with bell clanging.

The major tenant in our building was Ross Dress for Less, the behemoth off-priced retailer that occupied four floors for its flagship store. The crush of foot traffic today boded well for their sales and therefore the payment of percentage rent.[28]

However, we were immediately accosted by several aggressive panhandlers who had also staked out this prime corner. Ever resourceful, Dave offered each one cash to move down the block for a bit. As is often the case, the last of the group, recognizing his advantage as holdout, demanded an outrageous premium. As Dave resisted, I spotted Phil and the Commonfund people in the distance. I motioned to Dave, who scowled and then forked over the remaining cash in his wallet.

We greeted the investors and shook hands. Riding the escalator up through Ross, I lingered with Phil at the rear. "Are they . . . on board?" I whispered. "Don't worry," he said. "I've hyped you guys. But you have to walk them around Union Square and show them you know the market cold." Fortuitously, one of the few people who knew this market as well as I was Dave, who over the years had assembled a cache of those secretive retail leases and their landlord-friendly clauses crafted by wily operators—where the addition or omission of a single word could materially alter the consequences—and could authoritatively expound on multi-level retailing.

Three hours later, the contingent returned to their hotel with Phil, tired but satisfied. Dave and I had impressed them with our acumen, answered their questions truthfully without hesitation, and made them forget that they were dealing with a broker and an appraiser who had conjured up a deal on the fly. They avowed their attorney would call our attorney the following day.

The negotiation of a real estate partnership is akin to a prenuptial agreement. The parties will soon be married and lovey-dovey; however, until that time, they seek to protect their respective interests. With the added involvement of attorneys schooled in adversary theorem, a weird emotional ambiguity results. The Golden Rule—"he who has the gold makes the rules"—favored Commonfund in the ensuing negotiations, but when things got a bit one-sided, we threatened to pull the deal and walk.

As the closing date loomed, all hell broke loose: "Ross Stores won't sign their estoppel"; "Commonfund is squeezing you on the buy-sell"; "The bank will make no reps or warranties, other than they might own the property"; "The property management company says you have to go union unless you prefer to bring pizzas for a bunch of hardworking people with signs."

I felt my head compressed in a vise, each day equating to a quarter turn. I had repeated this exercise numerous times while assisting buyers but now felt suffocated by the stress. My repeated trips to San Francisco had started to wear on Anita, although she continued to exhibit stoic resolve. The only positive sign was that while Dave and I squabbled on this matter or that, we quickly reached consensus and didn't personalize our differences. We had structured our relationship on a straight-up, fifty-fifty basis; our work ethic matched, and we were never plagued by doubts of who was contributing more.

On the last day of September, we closed on time and on the money.

CHAPTER 12

Urban Realty

I turned 50 shortly after the onset of the third millennium AD, with both events transpiring without calamity.

Y2K[29] had proven to be a dud, and the only remaining debate was whether the millennium technically started in 2000 or 2001. The financial mood was euphoric: The NASDAQ Composite was hitting all-time highs almost daily; Bill Gates was the world's richest man, the first tech geek to achieve this distinction; and the internet was linking all the world's inhabitants.

Commonfund had immediately bought us out of 799 Market, determined to manage the asset themselves. While Dave and I would obviously have preferred to stay in, we nonetheless had created significant value by conceptualizing, structuring, and closing the deal and thus were properly rewarded. We divvied up the pot—a tidy sum—and concurred this was an excellent way to make a living.

I had given up day trading and temporarily reunited with my colleague Adrian from Cushman & Wakefield days. He had joined a boutique investment bank, only to watch his business partner, accompanied by the entire staff, defect to a competitor, leaving him empty-handed in the midst of several significant marketing assignments. He pleaded with me to help him out for a bit, which I did.

On March 10, the NASDAQ hit 5,132; on April 17 . . . 3,227. A drop of nearly 40 percent in five weeks was deemed consequential by most observers. The dot-com bubble burst with a fury, resulting in the disappearance of a plethora of fake companies and wreaking havoc on the commercial real estate industry, particularly in Silicon Valley and the Bay Area. Vacancies soared, rents plummeted, and confidence evaporated.

Yet I couldn't get my mind off 799 Market and the ability to leverage time and money and creativity. Dave and I held theoretical discussions about putting more deals together, notwithstanding the market collapse. We had both lived through the cyclical troughs endemic to commercial real estate and noted that, if the objective was to buy low and sell high, what better time to buy low? It was merely a matter of aligning with the proper capital; we had a track record (one deal!), and, equally important, no baggage from having screwed investors.

But this time I would do it right and consult with Anita, conditioning any plan on her approval. I would not risk my marriage for money. As we relaxed one evening on the balcony and watched the planes obediently queue up to land at LAX, the time felt right.

"Pooh, how would you like to move back up north?"

Anita eyed me warily as she drew on her smoke.

"No kidding," I said. "Dave and I have bounced around the idea of putting more deals together, of maybe starting a company in San Francisco. It would be a major commitment."

She shook her head. "You asking me or telling me?"

"We're in this together."

"So what exactly does this 'idea' look like—for us?"

"Well, I know we can't turn back the clock, but we can probably do a pretty good imitation," I said. "We'll move back to the East Bay hills, get a nice little house; I'll put in a normal day, won't travel much, come home at night . . . sober."

"And me?"

"You do all the things you truly enjoy."

She focused on the planes, perfectly spaced, like giant geese suspended in flight. A minute passed, then another. Finally, she slowly nodded. "One thing we must do."

"And that's?"

"Consecrate our new home."

I leaned over and laid my head on her breast.

Dave and I named our company Urban Realty.

We set up shop in the San Francisco Financial District at 364 Bush Street, a diminutive two-story historic building oppressed by the adjacent high rises. Our headquarters was a second-floor walk-up above two ground-floor tenants: Sam's Grill, a landmark seafood restaurant established in 1867, and a postage stamp shop. The ancient offices sported half-lite doors with transoms; our HVAC consisted of sash windows when they didn't stick. Admittedly, the Sam Spade décor was not cutting-edge, but the rent was cheap.

Setting up an operating company took the entrepreneurial spirit a step further by introducing me to overhead. In addition to committing time and capital to tie up deals, I now had payroll, rent, and other expenses to more quickly siphon off savings. Having a partner to share costs was beneficial but not the primary reason for forming a partnership. Nor were mutual honesty and a common work ethic—these were givens, *a priori.* A partnership only made sense if the parties brought divergent, complementary skill sets to the table at an equally high level, such that one plus one equaled three.

We divided responsibilities according to our expertise and personalities: I would hunt for deals and capital and develop strategy while Dave would handle investor relations, diligence, and ongoing management and administration, pretty much the way the cards fell on 799 Market. We rarely socialized; Dave had a wife and three children, and with his appraisal practice, little time for extracurriculars. Urban Realty was all business, ready to crouch motionless and then pounce on short notice.

Anita and I found a home in the fire zone above the Caldecott Tunnel. Newly constructed residences now dotted the landscape that had been ravaged ten years earlier by the firestorm. And the human fabric of Oakland was also changing. The expansion of tech firms into San Francisco had driven up residential property values, and the ensuing gentrification rippled throughout the Bay Area.

Early data from the 2000 Census revealed that the black population in Oakland had declined significantly over the past decade, as it had in most California cities. For many African Americans, the California dream was simply not panning out. The high cost of living, coupled with crime and poor schools, had triggered a reverse migration back to Texas and the South. The 5th Amendment still offered live music more often than not, but other watering holes had disappeared.

With the fall of the Digital Equipment Corporation, many of Anita's colleagues had dispersed, and Glen and Cynthia moved to Las Vegas. However, Napata and enough others remained such that we quickly found an excuse to throw more parties.

Natalie graduated from Cal and was now employed by a law firm. I promised to help her out financially for exactly one year after graduation with the understanding that she would prepare a personal budget and achieve economic self-sufficiency and thereby never have to marry a jerk for the wrong reasons. I hadn't anticipated that she might drift into law but held my tongue as best I could.

My millennial resolution was to improve my life in the spiritual area. I had tried to "first do no harm" and eliminate bad behavior, but one can be an ex-whatever and still be lacking. Now was the time to effect positive, proactive change.

I started with several private phone sessions with Mary Jo to give me context for my actions. In a sense, it was like talking to a therapist, in terms of resolving personal issues.

However, unlike a therapist, a skilled intuitive does most of the talking, based on receiving a flow of mental images—letters of the alphabet, pictures, numbers, and other symbols—which he or she then translates into concrete expression.

The messages may involve communication with a loved one who has passed, or the status of a relationship with the living, or advice on health issues. The intuitive is akin to a radio, not the source of the information but a receiver. At times, the reception may be spotty and the message inconclusive; no accomplished intuitive claims complete accuracy. At other times, the message may be astounding in its clarity.

"Martin, I don't want you to volunteer any information or say anything once I'm in trance," Mary Jo directed on our first call. "If I ask you a question, just answer with a simple yes or no."

I admired her confidence and honesty: Mary Jo recommended only a couple of these intense private sessions per year and cautioned against overuse. "Sweetie, you don't want to use this as a crutch," she said. "We're here to help, but only you can live your life."

And so I gained a glimpse into the other side, an aspect of reality unbounded by the perceived constraints of time and space, where life does not merely start at zero and end at zero but is defined by the survival and evolution of the personality along a dharmic journey—a process of soul-building—in a parallel world, a world without kings and paupers, where financial success and material accumulation don't matter and we all stand naked under the same spotlight.

I now determined that what I lacked was a spiritual mentor—someone whom I both trusted and admired—to emulate and thus accelerate the process by imitation and quickly realized that the answer was right under my nose. Why couldn't a wife and lover also serve as a spiritual guide and moral compass? Anita had all the right qualities: rock solid in her faith; dedicated to an individualized practice; didn't proselytize; led by example; and exhibited humility. Coupled with her discernment and charisma, Anita was the complete package.

It was not as if these qualities had gone unnoticed. Friends continued to pop in—as they had in the old days— for help with personal problems or merely to engage with Anita on a deeper level. Napata would drop by after a gig, and she and Anita would sit out on the deck, and I would go to bed and then waken to find them glued to the same spot with the sun well up in the sky.

"How can you talk all night?" I asked.

"During these marathons," Napata said, "we oftentimes find ourselves silent for long periods of time. The stillness is usually broken with the two of us saying the same words at the same time."

She reflected, "We realized that sometimes we simply do not need to talk to have a conversation."

One evening, as my wife and I relaxed on the sofa, I put down the *Wall Street Journal* and observed Anita as she read the Bible, reading glasses perched on the bridge of her nose. I asked Anita what chapter and verse she happened to be on, and maybe I could read along. She gave me a "Sure, why not?" look. I found I could cite many passages from my childhood catechism classes, but those were the result of rote memorization. I had never tried to penetrate the layers of meaning, probably sufficiently awed by the literary beauty of the King James Version[30] to accept it without question.

With patience, Anita instructed me on how to make the Bible my own, as she and countless others had achieved over the millennia. I discovered that the essence of the Torah was communicated to Moses at Mount Sinai and then passed down orally from generation to generation until written on scrolls over more centuries, eventually resulting in the canonical scriptures of the Christians and Jews.

Her exegesis revealed that the words were not archaic and irrelevant fabrications from antiquity but a guide to living in the present age, a framework to determine right from wrong and a roadmap to moral maturity. Anita stressed that all the religious instruction in the world was insufficient if not accompanied by prayer. Not just petitionary prayer in those rough moments but an ongoing dialogue with God, and thus a link to the Divine.

This made sense to me, and into the Anita basket I put my eggs.

Dave and I had come out of nowhere to buy 799 Market, but in the cynical eyes of the brokerage community, it could have been a fluke. We had to close another significant acquisition and make Urban Realty a household name in order to secure the brokers' attention and see every major deal. I began trolling Silicon Valley for distressed opportunities, but it was very early in the cycle. Credit shriveled as banks refused to lend on properties with weak tenants obligated to pay over-market rents. No one knew where the bottom was, including us.

And then, in early 2001, as I was wrapping up my business with Adrian, he came to market with a trophy property. One Montgomery Street was a historic banking temple at the corner of Post and Montgomery Streets and leased entirely to Wells Fargo Bank. The splendid architecture led most customers to believe that this was in fact the bank's headquarters. The stars had aligned: superb location, building, and tenant credit. (And, conveniently, right around the corner from our office.) Dave and I conferred with acute urgency.

"I think we should take it to Jack," Dave said. "This is perfect for his foreign investors."

I hesitated. "Look, Jack's a player, but we'll have just one bite at the apple. Offshore money . . . hell, you never know where it's really coming from and if it's even going to show up at all."

"What other capital do we have that will be aggressive in this market?" Dave asked. "And that will need us?" He was right—the deal was a passive investment until the bank's lease expired in five years. Not much to do for Urban Realty to justify an exalted equity position—but I had a notion.

"Let's call Jack," I said.

Of course, Jack was thrilled at the deal. He claimed to have the perfect investor match. Q: "Who is it, Jack?" A: "Oh, you know I can't say." I told Jack he would have to deliver the goodies at closing or Urban would be toast. While Dave and Jack prepared the offer, I paid a visit to City Hall. One Montgomery Street, while only two stories, occupied a substantial 28,000-square-foot corner lot. I knew the long-term value of the property lay in the land; I just had to prove it.

It had been assumed by the seller and everyone else that the air rights over the property had been sold off twenty years earlier when a controversial office and retail project was developed on the remainder of the block. In one of the few instances during my real estate career, I actually drew on my city planning background. I knew there were always last-minute changes and compromises on politically contested projects: The only way to know what really happened was to personally review all the documents for the entire block.

I ingratiated myself with the Planning Department and for several days pored over the archival material. Voilà! The air rights were still intact and sufficient to support a high-rise building. I regarded the discovery as the best single business idea of my life. Not only would this intelligence enable the investor to pay more than anyone else, but it would also justify Urban's skin in the game. As the knowledgeable local partner, we would pursue entitlements for a tower integrated with the existing architectural landmark, creating value out of . . . thin air.

We won the bidding and began the thirty-day cycle of deal frenzy. Jack put up the deposit for his client and assured us this was a done deal. Dave oversaw the due diligence and scored extra points on tenant relations; he had consulted to Wells Fargo in the past, and they welcomed us as the new property owner. I could only focus on the fact that I had not met, and would never meet, the person who supposedly would entrust his money to our care.

A week before closing, my worst fears were realized. The investor had gone quiet on Jack, right at the time that signatures and money were required. Q: "Jack, what's going on?" A: "Don't worry, I'll handle this." Jack confessed that his dealings had been with the investor's financial advisors. Ever the pro, he hopped on a red-eye from Kennedy to somewhere—I suspected Riyadh. Upon his arrival, Jack called and assured us he would immediately meet with the client. Two days later, Jack still waited for his fifteen-minute audience. He remarked that, after witnessing a public beheading in the square, things could always be worse.

Dave and I assured Adrian that everything was right on track as we privately rent our garments. Later that day, we received an email from Jack that his meeting was on for tomorrow; I tersely replied that he should call us immediately whatever the outcome. The following morning, Dave and I sat silently in the conference room at 6:00 a.m. Soon, the phone rang ominously; I immediately punched the open line.

"Jack?" I said over the garbled connection.

"You sitting down?"

"What happened?" Dave asked.

"Well, I walk in, and he seems confused," Jack said. "Apparently, the deal slipped through the cracks with his advisors."

Dave laid his head on the table.

"I remind him we're scheduled to close in two days," Jack continued. "But he just shrugs, says he doesn't know enough about the investment to move forward."

Ruination.

"I am literally being escorted to the door when I glance at a big-screen TV on the wall," Jack said. "CNN is doing a piece on the US financial markets."

Now I detected Jack's breath quickening.

"They're panning the San Francisco Financial District, and suddenly there's One Montgomery Street!"

What?!

"I'm pointing and yelling, 'That's our building!' and now everybody in the room is staring at the TV. By the way, it looked great, a symbol of strength and stability."

Dave bolted upright.

"The client jumps up from his chair and waves me to come back," Jack said. "Now he's hot to do the deal, starts giving out orders."

Fate!

"Gotta go back in with his people and finish up the paperwork. See you boys at the closing dinner."

I thought of cheering and congratulating my partner, but that would only have diminished the moment. I shook my head and listened to the hum of the dead phone line.

In the summer of 2001, Lydia's condition worsened. She had been diagnosed with lung cancer years earlier, probably the result of secondhand smoke from Dad's habit or perhaps a capricious gene. I flew back frequently to Prairie du Chien and, invariably, Lydia would lead me down the narrow stairway to the basement, which was chock-full, floor-to-ceiling, with all the possessions she had amassed since alighting at Ellis Island.

A two-foot-wide aisle allowed us to traverse this myste-rious space where, despite her frailty, she could identify the location of every last item. She pointed to a shoebox and we ascended to the living room and pored over old photographs. Over the years, she had channeled her nervous energy through a Kodak Instamatic, constantly chasing us for pics as we tried vainly to escape. She would then deliver the film to Farrell's Drug Store for processing and, days later, trium-phantly obtain the treasured 3.5" square prints.

"Here's one where you cut off my legs," I said.

Mom managed a smile.

"On this one you got rid of a neighbor," I laughed. Mom would cut out or cover up individuals whom she later deemed did not belong in the shot. "It looks like a doctored photo of the Communist Politburo after one of Stalin's purges."

She punched me playfully.

I dabbed my eyes in mirth and then in sadness, reflecting on the ways we try to create a more perfect world. As the teapot whistled, I kissed her cheek.

Back in California, I would call her nightly. At times, there was not much to talk about, but that was fine. Eventually, it came down to pain control and tender loving care; my brother, Greg, and I agreed to move her to hospice.

I now intensified my efforts to find Charlotte in hopes of effecting a reunion. Anita enlisted the aid of a contact at Social Security who scoured the database to no avail. I hired a private detective who came up empty-handed, declaring, "She's off the grid if she's even alive." I queried Mary Jo in a session, who flatly stated, "She is alive but does not want to be found." I finally accepted that my mother would never see her daughter, or I my sister, again.

By the time Lydia succumbed the following spring, she had outlasted all her colleagues in chemo and radiation therapy as well as several contemporaries in apparent sound health. I tracked her ordeal according to the five stages of grief[31] she was presumably supposed to experience, and finally confessed to the oncologist that Lydia hadn't moved beyond the first stage of denial. He replied matter-of-factly that people in denial tend to last the longest. Apparently, the will to survive cultivated in Ukraine during the war years served her to the end.

One morning, I had forgotten my briefcase and drove back to the house, where I found Anita transfixed in front of the TV. "Hon, I think you should see this," she said. One of the twin towers at the World Trade Center in New York belched flames and smoke from a tremendous gash in the upper floors. Rapt, I slid in beside her.

We soon watched both towers crumble and more death and destruction unfold on September 11, 2001. The singular impact of the event—nearly 3,000 souls pulverized—lay in the fact that it occurred in real time on digital screens before a world audience, and, especially, in a land where things such as this weren't supposed to happen. The terrorists had carefully chosen a target that not only maximized the body count, but which also symbolized the triumph of capitalism and the actualization of the American dream in a city of immigrants. "I guess no one knows the day or the hour," I weakly offered.

Six months later, another shock hit closer to home. I was strolling along College Avenue in Oakland on an idyllic day, half-caf in hand, when my cell phone rang.

"Hey, Nat."

"Dad, you'd better sit down," she said, breathless.

"What's wrong?" Too many such calls over the years had not inured me to a sense of apprehension and dread.

"They found Betty Jo's killer!"

The Alameda County DA's office had just informed Wanda that they had identified the man who butchered her sister twenty years earlier. Using previously unavailable DNA testing, they discovered that the murderer was not her husband, Ken, but an itinerant handyman who had now proven to be a serial killer, implicated in the deaths of at least six other victims in the East Bay alone.

"That's unbelievable," I said. "Where do they have him in custody?"

"This is what's really crazy," Nat said. "He died of a heart attack in Folsom Prison a month ago while serving life for another crime."

That evening, the story broke on the local news. A reporter interviewed Ken, who appeared quiet and relieved that his innocence was at last proven.[32] Wanda's extended family reacted with obvious shock, and in the ensuing weeks, wondered whether they had been led too far by the detective. Natalie and David and Alice conferred on the possibility of reestablishing contact with their cousin Jennifer and reintegrating her into the family.

What meaning to derive? Perhaps only that we never know what's coming around the corner.

On a lazy Saturday afternoon, I watched the waters of San Francisco Bay shimmer in the light haze as Anita and I drove eastbound on the San Mateo Bridge heading back to Oakland, accompanied for a moment by a gull. Most of the seven-mile span consisted of an arrow-straight causeway that hovered only a few feet above the Bay, creating a sensation of cruising on the water toward a far-off horizon point and thus producing a soporific effect on the motorist.

I am fairly certain the soothing landscape contributed to my sense of well-being as we reminisced about our life together, especially the past two years. The daughters were fully grown and doing well; the friends that remained were good friends. Stability had replaced emotional chaos; the elephant in the room—my past infidelity—made fewer appearances, although the restoration of trust was a long journey. Under her tutelage, I had determined to become a better man.

Anita broke the reverie by reminding me of our dinner engagement that evening at Scott's Seafood restaurant, causing me to start lapping cars and the East Bay hills to grow in perspective.

CHAPTER 13

No Last Words

I had dressed quickly for dinner and sat at the desk in my home office, absently perusing a real estate market report. Abruptly, I glanced at the desk clock—engraved with a faded plaque commemorating brokerage production from years gone by—and called out, "Anita, we're gonna be late." She had sequestered herself in the master bathroom to bathe and put on makeup; I pondered whether to notify Scott's that we were running late.

Suddenly, I heard a loud thud as if someone had dropped a box of books. Rather than yell to Anita again, I stepped out of the office and into the master bedroom, rapping gently on the bathroom door: "Pooh?"

No response. I knocked more forcefully, and then grasped the doorknob. *This doesn't make any sense—why won't she answer me? Did she fall asleep in the tub?* With a vague misgiving, I tried to ease the door open and then pushed harder, but it only yielded an inch or two, blocked by something. I applied my full weight and squeezed in. The vanity lights, amplified by the wall mirror, seemed too bright, while the only sound was the whir of the exhaust fan.

My wife was sprawled naked on the floor. The outline of her lustrous brown skin against the antiseptic white tile resembled a crime scene sketch. *Oh . . . surely she fainted, but from what? The steam of the bath? A glass of wine?* I knelt by her side and, with effort, turned her over. *Why is she so heavy?* I lowered my ear to her lips but heard no air.

Frantic, I grabbed her wrists and dragged her into the bedroom. I started to administer CPR, then stretched to reach the phone to dial 911, my legs split wide, as I could not let my other hand abandon her. I soon heard a faint siren that grew louder and now flashing lights flooded the window. The EMTs, very courteous and professional, took over the resuscitation effort, moving me off to the side. I phoned Natalie and blurted that something terrible had happened and please call Sonja and Betty.

The paramedics declared a code blue, then applied the defibrillation paddles, then shook their heads. Two Oakland PD officers materialized and assessed the scene, anxious to interview the sole witness. By then I was sobbing uncontrollably while alternately pummeling the carpet and clutching at its nap.

I have never cried like that, before or since. My guttural gasps for air ascended and descended an octave, then reached a crescendo, releasing demons that thrived unnoticed under cover of the illusion that we actually have control over our lives. Once the utter impermanence of existence marks you, there is no going back.

The policewoman touched my shoulder, then nudged me gently, then more forcibly—a practiced sequence. As she questioned me, Natalie rushed in, followed shortly by Sonja and Betty, wailing and confused. The coroner arrived, and the weeping stopped for a moment and a horrible gloom filled the house as his presence signaled the terrifying finality of death.

As he went about his business, more relatives came, and the weeping escalated. An hour later, he zipped the body bag with a single motion, crisp and final. The cops helped him hoist the weight on a gurney and wheel it out the front door into the darkness.

Anita was gone . . . just like that.

PART II

CHAPTER 14

Postmortem

"Precious Lord, take my hand . . . "

Napata's voice rolled over the meadow and echoed off the tombstones of Mountain View Cemetery, a 226-acre park designed by Frederick Law Olmstead and snuggled in the Oakland hills. The sun had finally pierced the morning fog and sparkled off the faces of the gathered: over 150 people of many ages, races, and faiths. Seated on white wooden chairs symmetrically arranged on the groomed lawn, they came to pay respects to Anita at her "homecoming" memorial service.

The evening prior, I had gazed at my wife, or more accurately, the remains of her physical body lying as if asleep in the casket. People had streamed in for the wake, and then it was just Natalie and I. Still in a coma of disbelief, I couldn't process much of anything. As the funeral director closed the lid, my daughter gently led me away.

Since Anita left no instructions, I had preoccupied myself with the making of arrangements in the week after her death, which proved to be a useful distraction. I selected the non-denominational Chapel of the Chimes,[33] which conveniently abutted the cemetery. Barely three months since my mom passed, I once again conferred with a dignified sales representative as to the array of dispositive choices and opted for traditional subterranean interment.

I selected a casket after arduous consideration, forgoing the tasteless and the profane, such as an Oakland Raiders coffin adorned with the icons of the Silver and Black. I reserved a chapel for the vigil and deliberated over sundry details before crossing the street to the cemetery offices where I purchased the best burial plot available and reserved an outdoor area for the memorial service and prayed for nice weather.

Natalie and I composed the obituary and the program in which she included a photo of Anita and me hugging in front of an Irish pub in Montmartre in the 18th arrondissement of Paris. We organized a post-memorial reception at Bethel Temple Pentecostal Church (of which several of Anita's sisters were members) and the burning of a CD with a playlist of Anita's favorite songs. Now, as my daughter and I left the vigil, I had only to write a eulogy.

"Take my hand, precious Lord, lead me home . . . lead me home."

Napata concluded her solo and passed the mic to the officiator. Stepping down from the platform, she gazed at me sadly. I sat in the front row next to Sonja, who in turn sat next to Anita's mother, surrounded by Anita's four sisters who lived in the Bay Area, as well as other sisters and brothers who had made the trip from Mississippi along with their families. Beyond them sat Natalie and my brother, Greg, with his wife, and a multitude of friends and colleagues.

While many wept openly, I remained focused, and when it was my turn, delivered the last words. I spoke of how *Anita would engender immediate trust* and how she *was the glue that held us together*. I remarked that a key aspect of Anita's legacy was that *she called us on our bullshit* by never pushing a personal agenda but rather *guiding us down the path*. I confessed that *she always gave me plenty of rope*. I concluded that for Anita, life on earth in the physical body was *almost like doing time*, and that *she was now very much where she had wished to be*.

After the service, as the closest of family gathered for the procession to the burial site, I spotted my partner, Dave, waiting patiently to express his condolences. He shook his head sympathetically.

"Are you holding up?" he asked.

"Yeah, I'm okay."

"If there's anything—"

"No, I'm fine. Just trying to sort through a few things."

"If you need a little time . . . "

"Well, yeah, I may need a little time."

Neither of us knew that I would need a *lot* of time.

The procession wended its way to the uppermost reaches of the cemetery, where we disembarked at the crest of the highest hill. The family murmured at the magnificent, unobstructed views of the entire San Francisco Bay Area. I reasoned that Anita would appreciate the gesture, and perhaps it would lure loved ones to visit more often than they might otherwise. The men assisted the women in navigating down the steep slope to the gravesite, and some women simply discarded their heels.

We huddled in a tight group as the sisters formed a protective circle around Anita's mother. Her failing health and thus the potential for more tragedy generated heightened concern. The cluster of mourners followed the pastor of Bethel Temple in prayer. As the groundskeepers lowered the casket into the vault, the crying intensified.

But I was cried out. I glanced at the flow of land and water traffic in the metropolis below, the populace oblivious to the fact that Anita had died, unaware of the shock to the cosmic order. I tossed a bouquet atop the casket and closed my eyes.

Finis.

After the memorial service, I felt like a cork bobbing on a dark sea, a speck in an immeasurable void. The coroner suspected a heart attack (she was only 50 with no symptoms; how is that possible?), but the autopsy results would take several weeks. For now, I decided to stay indoors with drapes drawn, unsure of what to do except await the night.

In the gloaming, I would ritualistically position a hard-backed chair in the middle of the living room, stare at the wall, and reflect on how I had treated Anita. While we had started to put our relationship back together, I could only focus on the hurt I had caused her and wonder why I should still be here while her life had been cut short.

Increasingly, my thoughts turned to suicide, first the idea of the thing and then its implementation. I could easily swerve off the freeway near Altamont Pass and careen downward hundreds of feet. Or I could park on the Great Highway at Land's End in San Francisco and wade out into the Pacific. Or I could wander into a forest in the Sierra Nevada and surrender to the elements, and thus heighten and prolong the act.

My reverie would be broken by a visit or call from Natalie, who, sensing something obviously amiss, continued to check in daily despite my protests, forcing me to recognize that I had responsibilities beyond my own self. I reached the point where my mood grew more despondent and I felt compelled to make a decision at that very instant: to live or die. I chose not to take my life, perhaps later but not then, not at that time. The next morning, after a week of confinement, I showered, shaved, dressed, and stepped out to buy groceries.

I drove along Claremont Avenue in Oakland to the supermarket. I maintained a normal traffic speed, but the sensation was one of going slightly slower, of feeling the press of the atmosphere. The sky resembled a sepia print, a sensation I recalled before the earthquake in 1989, a vague sense that something was not quite right, moments before the ground trembled.

I pulled into the Safeway parking lot, a mash-up of vehicles and pavement. Upon entering the store, I noticed that the people appeared as wraiths, gliding down the aisles, occasionally speaking to one another but making no sound. The scene resembled a silent movie without musical accompaniment, the projection speed deliberately slowed by a few frames per second. I remained unexcited and clearheaded.

At no time did I construe the episode as hallucinatory. To the contrary, I was a camera recording an illusory world, and I was the reality.

In the ensuing days, I cataloged my experiences. For example, I would be driving and would happen to look *up*. The intensity of the sunlight astounded me, and the cobalt sky bristled with energy. While paused at a stoplight, I tipped my head out and discerned for the first time the variety of trees lining the street, not only elm and oak, but also an incongruous cluster of coast redwood. I listened to the birds, probably jays and robins, embedded deep in the branches, arguing vociferously. The power lines appeared with intense clarity, as if drawn with fine-point black Sharpies. *Where had all this been before? Why hadn't I noticed?*

On another occasion, as I flipped on the car radio, the DJ introduced the next tune, "You're My Latest, My Greatest Inspiration," as performed by Teddy Pendergrass, and which happened to be Anita's favorite song. Startled, I turned up the volume:

"I've been so many places

I've seen so many things

But none quite as lovely as you."

Had I never known Anita, I would have smugly dismissed all these moments as either coincidence or neurological trickery. But now I fully trusted my experience: the scales had fallen.

And then the phone call, and I rushed to pick up a copy of the autopsy report. I located the Alameda County Coroner's Bureau, an exceedingly undistinguished two-story structure flanking the Nimitz Freeway opposite the Oakland Police Department. I ran in, exchanged five dollars for the document, and then bolted back to the car. With trembling hands, I read and reread it carefully.

The cause of death was listed as cardiorespiratory failure due to hypertrophic cardiomyopathy, or HCM. I drove home and immediately researched the term online: a congenital condition more commonly known as an enlarged heart, which can result in sudden unexpected death. I vaguely remembered hearing about the occasional collapse of a promising young athlete for no apparent reason. No one knew Anita had this condition, not I, nor her family, nor possibly Anita herself. I now knew *how* she died, in medical terms, but not *why*. And for that, I reached out to the other side.

After several days of inaction, anxious at the prospects of what I might hear, I finally summoned the will and scheduled a reading with Mary Jo. At the appointed time, I phoned the intuitive and shared the fact that Anita had passed but provided no information as to the circumstances. Mary Jo expressed her sincere condolences and counseled that it is often better to wait a bit to have a reading after such a loss in order to process the grief. I persisted, and she asked if I wanted the reading "in trance" or via normal conversation. I opted for trance, and soon her voice transformed into the now familiar Irish brogue.

"She has a light around her . . . she was a very good person but hard on herself . . . it was almost like a blood clot . . . she was short of breath all day."

I grimaced but remained silent so as to not interrupt the flow.

"There was no struggle when she crossed . . . her vision blurred for a second . . . so quick . . . she didn't realize what happened."

For that I was grateful, a painless transition, a reward for a life well lived.

"She took her rings off . . . something unique and special about her rings . . . she didn't want to be buried with them."

Startled by this specific information, I remained mute. I now realized that neither the police report nor the autopsy mentioned any jewelry. How odd that she wasn't wearing her rings and odder still that I hadn't noticed . . .

"She had a choice at that moment . . . of whether to come back . . . and she hesitated . . . you were her project on the earth plane . . . and not quite finished."

I muffled my sobs.

"She has found a hat that fits."

The reading abruptly ended. I concluded that my wife was offered the option to move on to the next realm or return to the carousel of earthly existence. I felt grateful for her happiness but also disconsolate. She had a choice but didn't choose me—was the love still there?

Now out of trance, Mary Jo urged me to take care of earthly business. She confirmed that loved ones who have departed always urge the living to move on with their lives, as hard as that might be. She counseled that I should start the healing process and achieve some level of emotional stability . . . and that I would know when it was time to talk again.

CHAPTER 15

A World Without End

I now faced the toughest challenge of my life: to prove to Anita that her calling on earth, and particularly her work with me, had not been in vain. The long-term question was how best to be a better man; the immediate concern was how to deal with grief and depression. Since the funeral, I had been offered bromides by well-meaning friends urging me to eat well and exercise and not to make any major decisions. This caused me to avoid contact with people in general, other than Natalie and of course Sonja, devastated and incredulous as to how her mother could have just vanished.

I decided to consult with a grief counselor, notwithstanding my suspicion of psychologists and psychiatrists.[34] In postwar America, I believed, as did many, that there were demonstrably "crazy" people who required institutionalized

confinement, and then there was everyone else who suffered, in the words of maverick psychiatrist Thomas Szasz,
"problems in living." By now, Freud had been largely discred-
ited, and I met with suspicion the exponential proliferation
of pathologies in the Diagnostic and Statistical Manual of
Mental Disorders (the DSM), dismissing most of them and
particularly the notion that bereavement could equate to
major clinical depression.

After screening a number of candidates, I finally chose a
practitioner who perfectly fit my stereotype: a middle-aged
woman whose photograph evidenced a knowing smile and
with an office located in a bucolic setting in Marin County
(perhaps the global leader in therapists per capita), and who
accepted insurance. She greeted me warmly with her two
hands clasping my one and directed me to a comfortable
chair. I provided my intake information while concentrating
on the intricate patterns of the Persian rug.

"What have you been doing to take care of yourself?" she
asked.

"Reading grief literature," I said.

"And what have you learned?"

I paused. "All of the standard tips for how to get my life
back to normal are bullshit. This assumes that normal is
appropriate, proper, sane. No, things will never get back to
normal, things will never be the same . . . nor should they."

"What do you plan on doing?" she said.

"Study death and find out for myself."

After some additional probing, she concluded that I
wasn't acting irrationally and seemed to be coping on a self-
directed basis. I thanked her for the session and continued on
my path. I decided that a one-size-fits-all approach—whether

prescribed methods and time intervals for the bereavement process or adherence to formulae such as the five stages—did not match up with my assessment of coping with loss. The experience was unique to each individual based on the depth of the relationship and the circumstances of the death. I was in no rush to "get over it."

But to figure things out would take time and focus. Dave had been tolerant for the past few weeks in running Urban Realty by himself, with the now daily expectation that I would show up and pack the freight. Yet business was farthest from my mind, so inconsequential when compared to the reality I was experiencing. I phoned my partner.

"Dave, this has been a little harder than I imagined," I said.

"Yeah, I gathered as much."

"I'm going to need some more time, and it's not fair—"

"Life happens."

"The best I can do right now is check in periodically and backstop you on strategy and new business," I said. "You tell me how you want to balance the scales." I knew he would be within his rights to suggest an amendment to the partnership agreement or reconsider our venture altogether.

"How long—?"

"I wish I knew."

Dave hesitated and then cleared his throat. "Do what you have to do. I'm always being approached to handle major rent arbitrations, and I still have the valuation business. Just keep me posted."

I thanked him sincerely and assured him I would.

First, I took up meditation to deal with the voices in my head, the endless loop of self-reproach. After evaluating the various forms of practice, I settled on *zazen*, the method of the Soto school of Zen Buddhism. The objective was not to focus on a mantra but rather to detach from thoughts in general, allowing them to come and go, and thus quieting the "monkey mind," the Buddha's analogy of our head as a playground for agitated simians jumping from branch to branch. I admired the simplicity of zazen and the coincidence that my dad was called Zen.

After achieving the benchmark of being able to sit still for half an hour, I felt ready to attempt group meditation and found a practice center that also happened to be located in Marin County. Expecting to mingle with stern Japanese monks, I discovered that many of the monastics and attendees were in fact Jewish men and women. Curious, I consulted with Adrian, who by now had embraced Orthodox practice.

"Adrian, what's up with you guys?" I said, admitting my perplexity.

"Boychik, what can I say . . . we like to start religions."

I found solace in this community and discovered that I was not unique, as many gravitated to meditation after a tragic event.

On the subject of death, I read philosophers and theologians, scientists and mystics, and quickly stumbled onto the writings of Ernest Becker, a cultural anthropologist whose influential book *The Denial of Death* was honored with a Pulitzer Prize in 1974.[35] Becker theorized that human action was primarily motivated by the dilemma we face of having conscious self-awareness accompanied by the knowledge of certain death. As an antidote to obsessing constantly over our dismal fate, we "deny" death by creating symbolic meaning in our lives.

Becker reasoned that humans individually and collectively create "immortality projects," whereby we become heroes in our own stories and/or surrender our will to people we deem even more heroic, pining to become part of something eternal, something that will never die. When the stories conflict, then strife results, whether a schizophrenic's response to the outside world or a nation's call to war with an enemy. This theory made sense to me, at least from a secular perspective. So I joined the Ernest Becker Foundation and became an active contributor.

I regularly visited Anita's gravesite to lay down cut flowers. The monument company finally installed the headstone, inscribed with a cameo photograph of Anita, along with the words, "A Child of God." I stared at the day of death, June 15, 2002, and envisioned a red, vertical line in the chronology of my life, a demarcation of extreme significance, much like the day a small group of men exploded the first atomic bomb, in the timeline of human history.

I investigated the surrounding markers in ever-widening rings, discovering life spans that ranged from infants to nonagenarians. I also discovered that the choicest burial spots were claimed by the Chinese, and so I familiarized myself with their burial customs. I read the obituaries, occasionally contributing to the favorite cause of a deceased whose life was particularly uplifting. I donated to the Hypertrophic Cardiomyopathy Association.

And I tried to emulate Anita: How might she respond to this person? What difference could she make here? What would she do in that situation? How would she react to a particularly difficult moral dilemma? Guided by Anita's spirit and character, I found the ground I stood on slowly shifting as I reflected on what it meant to live an ethical life.

But mostly I prayed. My prayers in the past had been either of the petitionary variety, imploring the Almighty to reach down from the clouds into the natural world and somehow intervene on behalf of myself or loved ones, or of the bargaining sort, negotiating with the Big Guy much as I would with a business titan.

Now humbled, I turned to prayers of awe and gratitude, and if I had to ask for anything, it was for strength to make it through the day and strength for others who endured far worse suffering and hardship than myself. The prayers mingled with sighs (I had been sighing a lot since Anita dropped dead), such that the experience became more breathing the thought rather than mouthing words to myself.

At last, I was ready to call Mary Jo.

I immediately expressed the hope to the medium that I might be able to speak to Anita directly. Mary Jo chided me that I should know better; a competent intuitive could never guarantee who among the discarnate would show up yearning to communicate and urged me to moderate my expectations. I pressed that if Anita did appear, could I at least make some inquiries? Mary Jo reaffirmed that she was only a channel and there was no script. As she fell into trance, my anxiety soared: Would I be able to "talk" to my wife? And then, what might she say?

To my amazement, Anita not only showed up but also pushed all the other voices and spirits out of the way (sorry, Mom!). I couldn't help myself. "Is Anita happy?" I asked.

After a beat, Mary Jo replied, "She says she feels like a sunflower, open and bright . . . if you could only see the light as she sees the light, feel the peace as she feels the peace."

"Where is she?"

The psychic hesitated, straining to decipher the imagery in her mind's eye. "Right now, she's surrounded by beings with skin like slick suits. She's quite busy, plenty to do. She's asking you to spread the rings, to give away all her jewelry. And something else."

"What? Anything," I whispered.

"She wants you to know she 'fluffs the pillows of you.'" Mary Jo paused. "She wants you to know she left you a rose petal in her Bible."

I broke down—she still loved me.

After the call, I braced myself amid muffled sobs and proceeded to the master bedroom. I had slept in the guest bedroom since that dreadful night and left Anita's possessions untouched, deeming it sacrilegious to tamper with her personal effects. I located her Bible in the drawer of the nightstand and laid it beside me as I sat immobile on the bed.

What is left to be said or thought?

I gently opened the Good Book and flipped through the pages, where I found the red flower and also discovered a number of passages highlighted by Anita for my future benefit accompanied by her pointed commentary.

Later that afternoon, I rummaged in the closet and under the bed and through boxes of memories and finally discovered the rings stashed in several compact organizers at the back of a dresser drawer. I later distributed the rings, as well as necklaces, earrings, and bracelets, to the immediate female family, offering first choice to Sonja, then Betty, and finally to the other sisters. I stored the wedding diamond and gold band in a safe deposit box, intending to give it to Sonja but not just yet.

It was time to move on.

I determined that death is something not to be denied but acknowledged as foundational to existence and a trigger to insight. The philosopher and psychologist William James noted over a century ago in The Varieties of Religious Experience that "there is no doubt that healthy-mindedness is inadequate as a philosophical doctrine, because the evil facts which it refuses positively to account for are a genuine portion of reality, and they may after all be the best key to life's significance, and possibly the only openers of our eyes to the deepest levels of truth."

Through prayer and meditation, I was able to get outside of my head, appreciating the dictum that you can't solve the problems of the mind with the mind. Hardened materialists and antitheists may scoff at the necessity of invoking a god, explaining away not only consciousness but also love as mere epiphenomena arising from the operation of three pounds of soft nervous tissue encased in the human skull.

To me that never rang quite true. I suspected that any closed system required a source code, and therefore a programmer external to the system to furnish the creativity and imagination, to give it "life." Otherwise, it would just run on and on like an automaton, on a deterministic, self-referential basis.

And I recognized that the only sensible strategy to deal with loss is to live each day as if it were the last, because, evidently, it very well might be. To live not in the hedonistic sense but with the vow to take the good and do better and take the bad and not do it again. I recollected the words of Saint James: "Whereas ye know not what shall be on the morrow. For what *is* your life? It is even a vapor, that appeareth for a little time, and then vanisheth away." And I aspired to go to sleep without regrets or resentments and feel fortunate to awaken to a new dawn.

My wife and I would communicate once or twice a year, with Mary Jo moderating our conversations. Anita would relate what she was up to, offering guidance and reassurance, and referencing intimate moments and objects that no one else could possibly know.

However, my old skepticism resurfaced, questioning whether this could all be true. As a test, I contacted another intuitive of international reputation and arranged a phone session, in effect to get a second opinion. I nervously pressed the buttons, uncertain if this was even a wise idea and ever fearful of what I might hear.

I'd had no previous contact with this psychic medium whatsoever and specifically made no mention of Anita or furnished any other background information. But he had barely begun to speak when Anita appeared, moving the other communicants to the side and effectively resuming our prior conversations.

"She's teasing me, thought I was full of it and had a good racket going," he said, laughing. "But she's glad I'm the real McCoy."

That's Anita, never hesitant to tell it like it is.

"She's like your guardian angel, helping you to help yourself," he continued. "You loved her for the person she was and is."

He casually mentioned that she was supporting a former friend of ours who had tragically committed suicide many years ago, astounding information that I had come to expect from a skilled intuitive.

"When your time comes, she will be there to walk you over," he said. "It will seem as if she passed in one moment and you in the next."

Through the human channel, Anita talked further of her life on earth and of life on the other side. As the communication started to wane, the psychic said, "She wants you to know that you are never alone."

After the call, I sat with eyes closed for many minutes. I had obtained virtually identical results to my sessions with Mary Jo, validated by secrets only Anita and I shared. At first I felt guilty for being a doubting Thomas and then utterly appreciative for a love that would not die.

One night, years after her passing, as I lay in bed restless, my wife appeared to me. She manifested as a luminous white light, not exactly in her human form yet not totally discarnate. She absorbed me into herself in an act I can only equate to physical love, but infinitely more satisfying, a total sensory experience I felt with my whole body, my whole being. No words were uttered, nor definable thoughts exchanged. I felt unity with her and with all beyond her. After a moment, she disappeared.

This was no dream but a qualitatively different event, a glimpse of a more sublime reality that awaited me. Anita may have made the choice to transit to the other side, but she never left me. Not in life and not in death.

CHAPTER 16

Rebirth

When I finally returned full-time in late 2002, Urban Realty was struggling badly. My absence had only aggravated a deteriorating situation. The company had not closed a new acquisition since One Montgomery Street eighteen months ago; several small consulting assignments had helped to keep the lights on, but now we were hemorrhaging cash.

Additionally, Dave was a year deep into what would become the world's longest divorce proceeding. I felt guilty for the time when he had covered for me, and so I put in extra hours to compensate and, candidly, to avoid an empty house.

Our investment strategy had been straightforward: The bursting of the dot-com bubble had produced a cyclical trough in the commercial real estate market that should have produced a wave of bargains, as had occurred in the early 1990s subsequent to the savings and loan crisis. I had reassured Dave that, in a quote attributed to Mark Twain, "History doesn't repeat itself, but it often rhymes." In our case, however, history wasn't even rhyming.

We had courted various institutional investor partners to buy vacant and underperforming properties, particularly in the Silicon Valley, at prices that should have been well below replacement cost, ensuring healthy profits down the road when the rental markets recovered. But few foreclosures had occurred, for two reasons. On the equity side, enormous sums of capital had rolled out of the stock market, with much of it converging on Bay Area real estate, thus inflating prices.

On the debt side, commercial mortgage securitization— the bundling of loans into pools that were then sold off to investors—had dominated the financing landscape. Unlike a bank that was obligated to move a bad loan off its books, these less regulated entities could play shell games with the nonperforming loans and avoid wholesale write-downs, creating a freewheeling environment and harbinger of things to come.

We bid on all manner of assets—real property, senior loans, junior loans, mezz pieces, partnership interests— looking for any kind of edge and routinely getting outbid. In September 2003, we offered what we deemed a ridiculously high price for a neglected, half-empty office park and waited anxiously to hear back from the broker who had collected bids on behalf of the seller. Frustrated, I tracked him down.

"So we have a deal?" I said.

"No, we picked another horse."

"Why didn't you call and at least let us improve our offer?"

"It wasn't close—there were three buyers ahead of you."

I couldn't speak.

"I know you guys did your homework," he said. "It's crazy . . . just too much money out there."

I sat down with Dave for our weekly strategy meeting and quietly informed him of the latest strikeout. For the first time, we talked openly of dissolving Urban Realty, scarcely more than two years after its formation. As I rose to leave, Dave casually mentioned that an asset manager with Commonfund, our former investor partner on 799 Market Street, had called earlier and inquired if we could meet with Don, one of their senior real estate executives, on his trip to San Francisco the following week.

Their asset managers periodically called to pick our brains on local market conditions and tactics to attract tenants to 799 Market Street. More recently, the talk turned to the bigger picture. They confided that Commonfund was encountering the same problem in buying properties as Urban Realty: an oversupply of capital driving up prices and driving down yields to ludicrous levels.

In the world of money management, I long knew that being cautious and staying in cash was a bad thing. Eventually, clients would withdraw funds and hand them to competitors who would "put the money to work" with glowing promises of heroic returns somewhere in the future. Nascent bubbles grow not from stupidity but from self-interest; if you don't drink the Kool-Aid, plenty of others will.

To address this crisis, Commonfund was about to roll out a new investment program. Instead of continuing to acquire existing leased properties, they now intended to pursue the much riskier proposition of ground-up development. This necessitated forming joint ventures in half a dozen "gateway" cities with experienced developers who would do the heavy lifting. Could we recommend any developers in San Francisco?

"Interesting," I said. "Give me until lunch to think it over."

I cloistered myself in the conference room and dimmed the lights. The hottest days in San Francisco occurred in the fall, and that day the city was sweltering.

"So got any ideas?" Dave said, walking in an hour later, toting an environmentally conscious paper bag.

"I know the perfect developer," I replied.

Dave was a vegan and took especial care in overseeing the preparation of anything he ingested. He had returned from a trendy eatery around the corner and now solemnly lifted out a garden salad for himself. He then produced a ham sandwich and potato chips, which he slid toward me with measured revulsion.

"Who? Hines? Tishman?" he said, probing the salad for trace evidence of meat or dairy.

I compressed the bag of chips—POP!

"Urban Realty."

"Sure," he replied, testing a mouthful of kale (?), ever suspicious.

"Wait while I get something," I said.

I returned with a sheet of paper.

"I printed this out from that new website Wikipedia," I said, munching. "To quote: 'There is no specific credential required, nor license necessary, for a person or company to call himself a real estate developer. A real estate developer is not a professional designation; there are no schools or associations who recognize or protect the term as a trademark.'"

Dave glanced up from the kale, intent.

"You know what this means?" I said, jabbing the paper with my index finger. "*Anybody* can be a developer. All we need to figure out is exactly what we want and how to get it."

We invited Don for lunch at the storied Sheraton Palace Hotel, a historic landmark rebuilt after the great earthquake and fire of 1906. The Garden Court restaurant consisted of a voluminous open space with a stained-glass domed ceiling, Corinthian columns, Austrian crystal chandeliers, floors of polished marble attended by leafy palms in colossal pots, all unified by a theme of gold, gold, and more gold. While admittedly more appropriate for dowagers gathered for afternoon tea, I loved the place for its relaxed, unrushed ambience and the fact that the tables were generously spaced and we could discuss business without talking in code. Of course, the food was excellent.

"Gentlemen," Don said, extending his hand after nimbly negotiating the expanse of floor area to our table. Tall, with an air of hubris, he struck me as a quick study and savvy to human motive.

"Don, we have a nice little walk planned after lunch," I said. "Let's enjoy."

Interspersed with small talk, I described to Don our air rights scheme at One Montgomery Street and thus our real-time familiarity with the city staff and entitlement process.

I slipped in my prior experience as an urban planner and, before that, as a student of architecture in Chicago. I opined on the design flavors of the day and then glanced at Dave, who spoke authoritatively on construction costs, having spent the morning with a close friend who happened to be a prominent general contractor. By the time I grabbed the check, I *felt* like a developer.

We strolled out and proceeded up Market Street, soon passing 799 Market, which Don snidely admitted had proven an excellent investment. We reached San Francisco Centre, a vertical urban regional mall anchored by Nordstrom. The Australian shopping center company Westfield had just acquired the property and immediately announced plans for a major expansion into the adjacent structure, a vacated Emporium department store. The end result would be one of the top malls nationally, attracting hordes of shoppers.

At the corner of 5th Street, I paused and squinted up Market Street.

"That, Don, is the future."

Fifth Street and its northerly continuation, Mason Street, demarcated two legendary San Francisco neighborhoods: Union Square to the east, defined by luxe stores and fabulous hotels, and the Tenderloin to the west, the epicenter of crime, narcotics, prostitution, homelessness, and general human misery. Crossing the eighty-two-and-a-half feet of 5th Street to the 900 block of Market meant engaging with a substantively different reality.

Except for several monumental structures, the majority of the block was occupied by nondescript, two- and three-story buildings housing stores that served the subsistence needs of the neighborhood. Dave and I had reasoned that if this key block could be properly redeveloped, then the entire neighborhood—identified in local parlance as the "wine country"—and the city as a whole would benefit. The significant job creation and an enhanced tax base could fund critical social service programs.

I expected Don to roll his eyes and execute an about-face; instead, he determinedly crossed the street against the light. We followed in his wake and proceeded up the block, dodging panhandlers and stepping around the doorway occupants of vacant storefronts.

"Why this? Why now?" Don asked, the singular questions preparatory to any great undertaking.

"Look, Don," I said, "you can play the development game in this town like everyone else, and bid like crazy for high-rise office and residential sites and compete with the big boys head-on—"

At that moment, a hulking, unkempt man wielding a two-by-four and cursing wildly pursued an associate amid the cars and buses on Market Street.

"—or you can do what no one else is doing and build a retail-oriented transformative development with little competition."

Don scanned the area in a 180-degree sweep, visualizing the extension of Union Square into this single, long block—like a salient, or bulge, on the military battlefield—and the quantum difference that could result.

"Who are your tenants?" he asked.

Dave jumped in, fully prepared. "Value retailers requiring a lot of space and cheap rents. They're scattered among old warehouses South of Market. Here we can give them space at half the rents of Westfield; new functional space with high ceilings, parking, and adequate loading, right over BART and Muni."[36]

"What's the risk besides the obvious?"

The moment of truth, when a savvy investor wants to know what he or she is missing, how they can get screwed in unforeseen ways, why somebody else hasn't done this already.

"Two things," I said. "One, San Francisco is probably the toughest jurisdiction in the nation to get entitlements. We're going to have a new mayor and—how should I say—a more 'outré' Board of Supervisors, if that's even possible. Do not believe what others say—any project in this town *will take years* to get entitlements."

Don didn't wince.

"Two, we're going to have to buy the land piecemeal from individual owners in order to assemble a site or sites sufficient to change the critical mass of the block. We're going to have to do it secretively and painstakingly before the market is on to us and holdout owners demand unrealistic prices."

Don remained impassive, then glanced at his watch. He stepped into the street to flag a cab, only to be blown back by a cyclist doing at least 30 mph.

"A future customer," I offered.

Don snorted, then shook our hands, and eased into the taxi.

"Gentlemen, thank you for your time," he said and disappeared.

Days passed, and Dave and I went about our business, which now pretty much involved winding down our business. We could simply not compete with deranged buyers with boatloads of cash intent not only on overpaying but also in conducting minimal discovery and not asking too many questions. Commonfund had gone quiet on us, and I resisted pestering them and appearing desperate.

And then Don phoned and said we had a deal and that their attorney would call our attorney to negotiate the partnership documents, but in the meantime, could we get busy and start buying properties? I recited to Dave the words of Winston Churchill, "Land monopoly is not only monopoly . . . it is the mother of all other forms of monopoly." He ignored me and wondered aloud what other developers Don had talked to and what other projects he had considered, and frankly, why had he picked us?

I replied it didn't matter.

We had no sense what the ultimate development would entail since it depended on the size and number of properties we acquired; our mission was simply to buy all we could. We engaged the services of a veteran broker skilled in land sales and swore him to secrecy. He identified all the owners in the 900 block of Market Street and researched their backgrounds. We then prioritized the essential parcels and the optimal sequence of purchase and registered a variety of entity names to cover our tracks.

Our first acquisition was a shabby office building with a sizable land footprint leased to the Social Security Administration. The seller assumed we were buying it for the rental income and was none the wiser. We hopped across the street and bought several contiguous parcels from Chinese individuals who were off the grid in terms of the gossipy real estate community; this proved vital in terms of maintaining the secrecy of the operation. As an extra precaution, we kept them on as property managers to conceal the change in ownership.

We next tried to buy a strip club and anxiously awaited the broker's report on his meeting with the owner.

"So who's this guy?" I asked.

"Well, he did time on a weapons charge," the broker said.

"That's it?"

"And the doorman told me he goes to Vegas every month to meet with his . . . mmmm . . . investors."

"Anything else?"

"Yeah, the worst part," he confided. "He used to be a commercial real estate broker."

I groaned. True to form, the owner asked four times what the property was worth and then raised the price every month for good measure. We did not make this deal; fortunately, the parcel was desirable but not critical.

We re-crossed the street again and acquired a property owned by a dozen relatives as tenants-in-common, necessitating twelve signatures. For the last signature, we sent a notary to San Quentin to secure the approval of the family's bad seed, who groused at the deal but eventually relented.

And then we closed on a key parcel that we had pursued since day one. The owner, a wealthy Asian investor with lofty aspirations, bluntly informed us, "I know what you're up to because I was going to do it myself. But I'm going to use the money to tie up a high-rise office site near the Transbay Terminal." We paid him a fair price and he did not publicize the sale.

Over the course of eighteen months, we had acquired seven properties from individual sellers without the knowledge of the real estate community, an extraordinary feat. We had already engaged an architectural firm to knock off concept plans as we went along to ensure that we understood all of the zoning particularities. Now it was time to conceive the master development plan.

While Dave and I surreptitiously assembled land on Market Street, we continued to pursue our development scheme at One Montgomery. We had created an exciting design for a residential/hotel tower over the existing banking temple. Our structural engineer had devised a super-truss system hidden in the mezzanine to support the high-rise, so as not to alter the fabric of the historic structure.

However, the investor viewed the property primarily as a vehicle to park money and grew increasingly reluctant to finance the speculative entitlement costs, despite our assurances of the value-add. The call from Jack did not surprise us.

"He told me to put it on the market right away," Jack said. "Oil's over $65 a barrel and moving north—wants to redeploy the capital."

"Too bad," I said. "Best site in town."

"Absolutely—listen, I have this other investor who . . . "

We sold One Montgomery Street at a hefty price abetted by the air rights discovery and let it be known that the investor obtained a return of over 25 percent on his money, exceptional for a single-tenant, net-leased passive investment property.

Our stature grew and we landed a lucrative assignment to create a $100 million commercial property portfolio for a local family. The patriarch had committed to sell a tract of land to a homebuilder for $60 million, and engaged us to create a family office for his eight adult children and seed it with premium assets.

Armed with cash and moderate leverage, we bought six buildings in highly visible markets such as Union Square, Century City, and Orange County, all in a matter of months, since we were constrained by the time deadlines associated with a tax-deferred exchange. Now Urban Realty had achieved total credibility within the commercial real estate fraternity as guys who could perform and were true to their word. And obsessed with detail.

In the course of an acquisition, I would mercilessly grill sellers, brokers, and other participants in an effort to expose both building and human flaws and get at the truth. One of the top investment brokers in San Francisco would routinely send his rookies to tour their listings with me on a dry run before going to market, ensuring there would be no question or objection that they couldn't handle, on the theory that what didn't kill them made them stronger.

Unexpectedly, we augmented our holdings months later in 2006 with the acquisition of 901 Market Street, a 200,000-square-foot office building directly opposite Westfield San Francisco Centre. Unlike the stealth purchases, this property was widely marketed, which placed us in a competitive bid situation.

We conceived a plan to repurpose the lower floors for retail, which significantly enhanced the income and supported an aggressive offer. After the predictable effort of the seller to squeeze us, we bumped up the price slightly and won the bidding.

Our master development project in the 900 block of Market Street now consisted of three phases: a to-be-built 250,000-square-foot shopping center; the Northside Block, a proposed mixed-use development of residential and retail uses across the street; and the repositioning of 901 Market. The most transformational of the components was the ground-up vertical mall on over an acre of land; no significant retail development had occurred downtown since San Francisco Centre opened fourteen years earlier.

And this project we named CityPlace.

We had executed individual agreements with Commonfund as we serially closed on properties. With the full scope of the project finally determined, we consolidated them into several master partnership agreements. On the eve of signing, Dave and I reviewed the documents for the last time on a call with our attorney.

"So how did we do?" I asked.

"Not bad," he said. "You have your equity and participation in the profits upon completion, as well as your monthly fees and performance incentives."

"What about our partner?"

"Commonfund will still have final say on major decisions such as a sale or financing, but considering you guys haven't put any money in—and I don't know how you pulled that off—that's to be expected."

I estimated the total project at over 700,000 square feet, with a finished potential value of $400 million, a number that filled up almost all the spaces on the screen of my HP-12 calculator. For the first time in my life, I faced the prospect of real wealth. Verily, this was the American dream. I high-fived Dave and leaned over the speaker.

"Print the docs, counselor."

CHAPTER 17

Capricorn Rising

Before Christmas, I flew to the Virgin Islands for a week of relaxation. I had not traveled since Anita's passing, preferring seclusion to the ordeals of the post-9/11 world. The Caribbean held happy memories, but Jamaica was now the murder capital of the world. Other locales I had visited, such as Trinidad and Caracas on a trip with my old girlfriend Ruby, had also spiraled downward: the former a victim of gang and drug violence and the latter a societal collapse under the socialist policies of Hugo Chavez. So I opted for a fresh destination.

Upon deplaning at Charlotte Amalie, I immediately discovered that Saint Thomas proved a major port-of-call for monstrous cruise ships that disgorged swarms of tourists into the town center, so I stayed holed up at the Marriott. I had packed a copy of The Odyssey (R. Fagles translation), the epic Greek poem composed nearly three millennia ago by one or more authors identified as Homer and which recounted the decade-long wanderings of King Odysseus after the Trojan War. The foundational monomyth of Western literature, this classic has served as allegory for many journeys: the spiritual quest, the stages of life, and particularly, the challenges faced by a man.

That night, I opened the patio door and let the curtains billow horizontally into the room. With lights off, I reclined on the bed and reflected on my personal circumstances. I had yet again navigated the shoals of financial ruin and would now be embarking on a business adventure more challenging than any I had previously attempted.

Admittedly, I wasn't sacrificing my life on the field of battle or even curing cancer. But I rationalized that in the role of developer, I was at least making a positive contribution by creating new things and not merely acting as a financial intermediary, a panner for gold in the river of capital.

My thoughts turned to Natalie and her boyfriend, Solis. They had first met onstage at a fete for accomplished Native American high school graduates ten years earlier. They met for the second time in an ethnic studies class at Cal Berkeley, a reunion that blossomed into a friendship and then an on-again, off-again romance. The entire extended family now waited expectantly for the engagement announcement.

Solis had recently persuaded Natalie to join him at the Native American Health Center in Oakland; she had once considered law school but grew disenchanted with the profession, much to my relief. His father had been an activist in the day, supporting the Native American occupation of

Alcatraz[37] thirty-five years earlier and still wearing the mil-
itancy of yesteryear on his sleeve. He had raised Solis alone
from childhood until remarrying and had instilled in his son
a respect for the old ways.

I drifted off amid visions of grandfatherhood.

The following morning I ventured into town and duti-
fully visited Blackbeard's Castle and strolled the stone-paved
streets lined with pastel wood-shuttered buildings fabri-
cated by Danes in the colonial era, lunched on callaloo, and
otherwise acted the visitor. Yet the enthusiasm of the solitary traveler exhibited in my youth eluded me, replaced by
a vague loneliness. I returned to the hotel, plunged into The
Odyssey, and read into the night.

Discontented, I checked out of the hotel in the morning and caught a ferry to the less-populous island of Tortola,
where I elected to finish my trip at a secluded beachfront
lodge. Isolation came at a cost, alas, as that evening I was
incessantly bitten by "no-see-ums," vicious sand flies imper-
vious to repellant.

At daybreak, the flies took a time-out, so I sauntered in
the surf and watched my footprints disappear and examined my life after Anita. Engulfed by the emptiness of our
house, I had moved out several months after her death, first
renting an apartment and then finding an idyllic cottage in
Piedmont, with weathered siding and a magnificent picture
window overlooking a sumptuous garden. I invested my long
days in Urban Realty and my nights in reading and executing
my calming rituals. Gradually, I re-entered the social scene.

Napata would periodically host salons (aka house parties)
on Sunday afternoons. Session musicians would set up in
the living room while she laid out food platters meticulously

prepared the night before. Soon the place filled, and invariably a "special guest" would materialize to rock the house. At times, a brother would eye me suspiciously, to which Napata would interject, "Oh, that's just Martin . . . he black." Later, a regular confided, "You know, you're the only white man I've met that when we're talking, I'm not conscious of talking to a white man." I took that as a compliment.

And I usually connected with Glen and Cynthia when they flew back to the Bay Area to visit. On one such trip, Glen informed me that the 5th Amendment might be closing; he still gossiped with his Oakland posse and had heard it through the grapevine. We immediately vowed to pay our last respects and drove solemnly to the venue the following evening.

The joint was half-full on a Saturday night. We spotted the owner sitting solitary at the end of the bar. As Dennis bought us a round, the owner confided that it was time to cash in the chips and shutter the fabled institution, recently rendered smoke-free by force of California law. Glen and I wistfully tapped our drinks to her glass.

At that moment, four women entered, laughing and joking, and seated themselves at a nearby table. As they debated what to order, I looked at Glen: Gnarled with arthritis and forced to use a cane, he hadn't lost his game. He had already assessed the situation and grunted at me with a smile, then motioned with a sidelong glance to one of the women.

"I'd like you to meet my friend here . . . "

The days at the lodge found me continuing to plow through The Odyssey, reading at leisure and calling to mind the meter.[38] At night, I lolled with the other guests, particularly entertained by a Canadian couple, who regaled me not with tales of the Northwoods but with exploits of fleeing socialized medicine and gratefully finding health care across the border. They asked me if I had a special someone and I said no, not exactly.

I thought of my dates since Anita's passing. One, with an actress from LA, ominously named Tina. I should have heeded this flagrant portent and instead succumbed at a vulnerable moment and mistook her acting for the real thing, and of course she dumped me as if snipping a small branch from a tree.[39] Two others, with kind, decent women, led to relationships that lasted for months and which I abruptly terminated, resulting in their tears and disbelief and my feeling like a wretch, which in turn led to prolonged periods of abstinence on my part.

I argued with myself that I had not been naively searching for "another Anita," since our relationship had survived her passing three and a half years earlier and continued in good form. Rather, if I were ever to marry again, I had to be absolutely certain: The third time would be the charm . . . or the last strike.

The night before my departure, I nursed a Red Stripe, imprisoned inside my room by the sand flies and more than ready to leave. I savored Christmas the following week at the home of Wanda's older sister, who had succeeded their mother as clan matriarch. Natalie, David, Alice, and all the family, including the periodic batch of new babies, gathered every year, having drawn names at Thanksgiving, and cheering when Santa—a position rotated among the men and this year rumored to be David—entered to distribute the gifts. For the first time, Natalie would take responsibility for making the fry bread and, I predicted, would eventually assume the mantle.

I finished The Odyssey on the plane somewhere over the Bahamas and imagined Homer's wine-dark sea and the Greek islands with their mysterious inhabitants who tested his hero in unforeseen ways. I reflected on Odysseus alternately incurring the favor and wrath of the gods, conferring with the dead, gaining advice from shape-shifting strangers, and being constantly battered but never broken.

I cautiously anticipated 2006 and what Fate might have in store.

On New Year's Eve, a "wink" appeared in my email box.

I deemed internet dating an efficient tool, if selectively deployed and accompanied by caution. Typically, I would review hundreds of women's profiles and then respond to perhaps one but usually to none; I rarely posted my own profile, concerned in the manner of indigenous people who did not wish to be photographed for fear of having a bit of their spirit stolen.

Today, I had inadvertently left my profile exposed for viewing on Match.com, and when I returned from the store, I discovered the wink, an indication of preliminary interest without any sort of personal message.

The sender was a woman from Nantucket, Massachusetts, which I calculated to be as far from Piedmont as is possible in the continental USA. Her terse profile revealed she was black (interesting—I had expressed no racial preference), beautiful (if the pic was to be believed), and a Capricorn (a not unfamiliar sign). The wink led to an exchange of abbreviated emails, where misstucketwinks@talkmatch.com admitted that she couldn't exactly explain how she had found me or what prompted her to tap send, and I conceded that in this day and age, heck, what was 3,000 miles anyway.

Three days into 2006, I ceded my phone number, still alert for a scam and the possibility that she in fact was an acne-laced male hacker from Moscow. The following day, the phone rang, and I noticed a 508 area code.

"Hello?"

"Hi, Martin, it's Virginia—from Match!"

"Wow, it's really you," I said.

"I'm at Logan waiting for my flight to New Orleans. Visiting Mom. But I wanted to say hello. Can I call you when I land and get settled?"

"Sure, have a nice flight, Miss Virginia."

"Oh, you can call me Ginger."

Late that night, she phoned from somewhere deep in the bayou and spoke in hushed tones. Apparently, her mother was shocked and appalled that her daughter had met a man on the internet and insisted that I was surely a maniac and that she should call the police. Ginger whispered that, weeks ago, she had planned a trip to the Bay Area.

"I get in next Saturday evening . . . "

Interesting . . . Anita's birthday.

" . . . the day after my birthday."

Whoa.

"I know you'll probably be tired," I said, "but I'm going to a party that night. It should be fun; maybe you'd like to join me?"

"I wish I could," she said, "but I've been invited to a party that night too. A friend's picking me up and we're driving straight to downtown Oakland."

I paused. *My* party was in downtown Oakland.

"Listen," I said, "this may sound a little strange, but do you know Carmen?"

She screamed, and I heard her mother awaken and cause a commotion. Ginger apologized and put me on hold for a bit, and I knew it was the same party. Fate the Dealer had just slipped us an ace from the bottom of the deck.

This revelation changed the dynamic of the connection. The threads of our lives, spun and measured, had now touched, like two hot wires. Ever wary, I insisted we make a pact on the spot not to tip off our mutual and unsuspecting host so if things didn't work out between us, no one would be the wiser. Ginger reluctantly agreed; we would meet "by accident."

That Saturday night, I nervously trod up the stairs to Geoffrey's Inner Circle, a private club located in a historic building. Geoffrey Peete, a politically connected business-man and cultural mainstay, ran a classy establishment that Carmen had rented for her husband's birthday. After passing framed photographs of the proprietor with Ali, Belafonte, and other celebrities, I encountered probably 200 celebrants who milled about the dignified premises, featuring arched windows and faux Doric columns.

I greeted Carmen at the door and then removed my eye-glasses for reasons of vanity just as the DJ lowered the house lights. Visually impaired, I stumbled toward the no-host bar, where I squeezed between two thickset individuals and ordered a Heineken. I squinted in the dim light. If there was another white face in the crowd, I couldn't detect it, so I calculated that it would be easier for Ginger to find me than vice versa. I casually leaned against a column and waited.

"Hi, Martin."

I turned as Ginger played peekaboo behind the pillar. The camera of first impressions recorded an alluring angular face with high cheekbones and hair braided in a tight weave to her mid-back, accompanied by a slender frame displaying stunning cleavage and compressed into a little black dress, all perched confidently atop five-inch Christian Louboutins.

Damn, who looks *better* than their internet photo?

"Hey, Ginger," I said, with mustered nonchalance. I reached forward to hug her lightly and whispered, "Remember, we're strangers."

"Totally," she said.

I scored her a Chardonnay and suddenly Beyoncé started belting "Crazy in Love," and Ginger pulled me to the dance floor for the first of many, which later included a slow dance of imperceptible movement. The chemistry was immediate and undeniable and led to a walk at midnight along nearby Lake Merritt with its Necklace of Lights,[40] in retrospect a well-conceived romantic interlude, although questionable from a security standpoint. We agreed to meet for dinner on the morrow.

I picked Ginger up at her brother's apartment. Marvin— reserved, fastidious, gay—was appropriately protective. His sister and I repaired to the Claremont Hotel, a landmark resort oddly nestled in a residential neighborhood in the

Oakland-Berkeley Hills and which had narrowly escaped destruction from the firestorm. Tonight, a mantle of fog cloaked the San Francisco skyline and now threatened to engulf downtown Oakland, the lights of the office towers twinkling innocently, oblivious to their impending doom.

We touched wineglasses and toasted serendipity.

"So it was probably a long road from Jackson to Nantucket," I said.

Indeed. Raised on her grandparents' farm in rural Mississippi, Ginger observed her father administer regular beatings to her mother, who cut and ran one day, never to return. Years later, Ginger herself endured one shit kicking too many from her boyfriend and fled with her two sons to Oakland and resolved thereafter to back down from no one. Through pluck and determination, she talked her way into a position of household manager, finding employ with the ultra-rich, and raised her sons as a single mom.

"My last position was with a family in Palo Alto," she said. "They would summer in Nantucket and eventually asked me to manage their properties and yacht on the island year-round."

Her occupation piqued my curiosity. I had negotiated with real estate titans in a business environment but did not get to know them *like that*, in the most intimate setting of their personal residence with all the family secrets exposed.

"Ever work for an oligarch?" I asked, envisioning outsized profligacy.

"I've been lucky," she said, "mostly old money. There's a ninety-day trial period—if it doesn't feel right, I walk."

"Like it?"

Ginger fingered the chain of her Gucci clutch. "Pay's good." Her knowledge of shoes and handbags proved encyclopedic. She admired Jackie O. and confessed to an obsession with fashion even as a child.

We finished dinner and the mutual vetting process. The fog had consumed downtown Oakland and approached menacingly, moving phantasm-like up the hillside. Neither of us had broached the topic of age: In a few days, I would turn 56 to her 43, and she looked at least ten years younger. As we waited for the parking valet, I nudged her in the ribs.

"You know, they'll accuse me of robbing the cradle."

"As well they should, you dirty old man," she said, hooking my arm.

We drove down the hill in quietude, and then Ginger remarked that she would like to see my cottage and I executed a sharp U-turn, tires squealing. The next morning, we swung by Marvin's to get her roller bag—his raised eyebrows now relieved—and proceeded to the airport, where we hugged and kissed and Ginger melted into the TSA line.

I had scarcely returned home when my phone vibrated.

"Hi, Dad."

"Hi, Nat, what's up?"

Pause. "I have a surprise . . . "

Oh, this is it, they're engaged!

"I'm pregnant."

I strained to minimize the interval of my stunned silence.

"Wow," said the frog in my throat. "When—?"

"The doctor thinks early August."

"I mean . . . when is the wedding?"

"Dad, I just found out. We haven't had time yet—"

"Look, I can start calling around for a venue," I said.

"Dad!"

"Okay," I conceded, "but tell Solis he better do the right thing." I visualized the shotgun stored on a high shelf in my bedroom closet. "Nat, I love you, and let me know what I can do to help."

Which turned out to be the stereotypical role of the father of the bride: provide financial support and otherwise stay out of the way.

Six weeks later they married. Natalie and Solis selected the Monterey Plaza Hotel, constructed on piers over a rock outcropping on the waters of Monterey Bay. The fifty or so attendees—the closest of family and friends—luxuriated in the Pacific sun on a capacious deck and watched otters frolic.

Soon Nat's girlfriend appeared with a mic and launched into "At Last," the Etta James standard. I walked my daughter down the stairs to the waiting groom while the officiator, a Native ecologist/herbalist/minister, performed an abridged Pomo ceremony amid the scent of wormwood.

Afterward, I helped usher the guests inside for the reception: David and Alice, now with spouses and children; Sonja, always a part of the family; Wanda, complaining to anyone who might listen that Natalie should have had a formal Cinderella wedding; Solis's parents, his father looking remarkably mellow.

I lingered outside, peering over the railing, observing the waves punish the pillars. How remarkably lucky I was, realizing the immigrant dream in a world where little is assured, watching the child succeed the parent by not only doing better but being better.

Ginger and I had agreed to proceed cautiously like mature adults, but these efforts proved feeble in the face of the formidable cosmic forces that brought us together. Of course, I had discussed the matter in a session with Mary Jo, and Anita approved the relationship, urging me as usual to remain fully engaged with the material plane.

I had disclosed to Ginger my prior marriages and the event that made me a widower, and that I was ready to move on. I vowed to myself to minimize discussions of Anita and to remove any display of photographs and memorabilia lest Ginger believe she was competing with a ghost.

By springtime, Ginger had quit her job, left Nantucket, and quickly landed a position in San Francisco with an iconic venture capitalist. We moved to a home in the fire zone, which I had hastily rented after surrendering the cottage. It happened to be located about 200 feet above the house that I had abandoned four years earlier, a fact I attributed to mere chance: Most newly constructed homes—modern and spacious—were located in the firestorm area, and this was the only one immediately available.

We later flew to Jackson, Mississippi, where I met her sons, Napoleon and Tory, 24 and 20. I learned Napoleon was a hard worker, often holding down two or even three jobs, while training for competitive bodybuilding. But life had dealt Tory a different hand. A car accident rendered him paraplegic at age 3 when his father tried to outrun the law with the family in the car. As a teenager, he endured an epic surgical procedure that left him with a metal rack installed across his back and fused to his spine.

After high school, he tried his hand with college for a year, and then left and moved in with his brother and coped with life as best he could. In constant pain and dependent on others for most of the things we take for granted, his routine consisted of staying up until dawn tinkering with his computer and playing video games. Then he would desperately seek sleep, assisted by a cocktail of meds. I determined to help Tory in a meaningful way, but the mechanics would elude me for years.

Meanwhile, Ginger and I settled into domesticity. Soon we bought a house two doors down the same street where we'd been renting, and as the months passed, Ginger coolly informed me that I had best make her an honest woman lest the neighbors talk. I bobbed and weaved for more than a year and then went down for the count.

"Ginger, give him an uppercut!"

The photographer directed Ginger to simulate a punch to my chin. Wearing oversized fire-engine-red Everlast boxing gloves and her wedding dress, she enthusiastically complied. I grimaced in faux pain, careful not to wrinkle my black tux with eggshell tie and vest.

"That's a wrap," he said.

At Ginger's insistence, I had commissioned John to do our wedding photographs a week before the event. He ran a modeling agency in a loft warehouse in the Dogpatch neighborhood of San Francisco and had lined Ginger up with a few gigs; we respected his skill, quirky but inventive. John plied us with a respectable Chardonnay as his assistant attended first to Ginger's hair and makeup and then to the bridal gown: a two-piece champagne satin affair featuring a boned lace bodice with a minimal scoop neckline complemented by a ruched A-line skirt.

He then directed us (by now, more than relaxed) through a sequence of improvised shots. For example, me with aviator goggles perched on my forehead, pursuing Ginger on a Bajaj motorcycle while she gamely fled on a silver Razor scooter. She, posed like *The Thinker*, regarding my dress shoes worn on her bare feet. Me, coaxed to execute a jumping heel click. John added a number of traditional shots and later presented us with a commemorative album.

Given our ages and station in life, Ginger and I opted for a micro wedding involving only the immediate families: Nat, Solis, and my grandson, Dasan, now a year and a half; and Ginger's sons, brother Marvin and a close girlfriend. (I mused that even this spare attendance would exceed my prior weddings.) We selected the nondenominational Piedmont Community Church for the ceremony. The minister, tall and boyish, guided us through the preparation in the weeks prior, including a 115-question Premarriage Awareness Inventory, which we both completed in a satisfactory manner.

On a glorious spring morning, we gathered in the church's splendid courtyard. Ginger's sons had flown in the night before and arrived with Marvin.

"'Sup, homes?" I said, grazing Tory's palm as he executed a wheelie with his wheelchair.

Tory rolled his eyes and sniggled.

"Papa, Papa!" a voice interrupted.

My grandson sprinted past his parents, and I scooped him up in a single motion. Nat had outfitted him in a tuxedo and bunched his long hair in a bun. Solis and his father insisted on letting Dasan's hair grow unbridled in the Native tradition; I favored a shorter, more traditional cut, and our amicable contention prevailed for years.

The minister arranged us in front of the fountain and administered traditional vows in a concise service. We proceeded to the Claremont Hotel for a luncheon and cake cutting, and then Ginger and I flew to Los Angeles for our honeymoon, a weekend in an executive suite of the Beverly Wilshire Hotel at the foot of Rodeo Drive (Ginger's favorite destination) and the setting for the movie *Pretty Woman.* My new wife gifted us with matching Rolex Oyster Perpetual timepieces—his and hers.

CHAPTER 18

CityPlace

Our relationship evolved alongside CityPlace.

The developer of a major real estate project is a lot like the director of a tent-pole movie, assembling an enormous cast and marshaling vast resources while overcoming innumerable obstacles, all in the hope that once the dream is converted to reality, people will come. For the lead actor in the CityPlace movie, we selected Gensler. While known initially for interior design, the company had grown rapidly and would later become the largest architectural firm in the world. We had longstanding relationships with several of the principals and thus felt we could control matters.

Commonfund pushed back. "Don wants a black cape," Dave said, referring to a renowned designer with international name recognition. "Oh, hell no," I said. "The sonuvabitch architect will double the fee and take a cut of the action as well—that's our money!" *No siree bub, Gensler and I will put our heads together and do just fine!* We prevailed.

We retained Dave's contractor buddy to advise us from the get-go, which also gave him a leg up on winning the construction contract when it was time to bid the job. I challenged him to keep Gensler honest, and most important, to spot the unknown unknowns. We recruited a bright young man to run financial calculations and interface with the digital world.

To deal with the city and the opposition, we hired a land-use attorney who spoke faster than I could think, a PR firm with close ties to the mayor, and a lobbyist who, as a condition of her engagement, extracted our promise to do exactly what she commanded at all times and without hesitancy. We did.

The supporting cast included an environmental consultant, a transportation consultant, a historic preservation consultant, a structural engineer, a civil engineer, a geotechnical engineer, a surveyor, a retail-leasing broker, a marketing consultant, and others who escape memory. Commonfund asked if we were finished hiring. We were.

In a typical municipality, there exists a zoning ordinance that outlines the rules and regulations as to how a property can be developed; if a developer conforms to these standards, then he or she is entitled to build "as of right." While San Francisco had nominally adopted a zoning ordinance, it meant little since nothing was guaranteed and everything could be challenged. I cautioned Don: "The word *entitlements* is a misnomer—we aren't entitled to jack."

The first step in the process consisted of filing an environmental impact report. I had written EIRs thirty years prior as a city planner when environmental regulation, arising out of well-intended efforts to protect nature, was in its infancy.

As usual, California was at the forefront of progressive legislation that invariably would later collapse under its own weight. EIRs had swollen into multi-hundred-page documents and pounds of backup studies prepared by a cottage industry of consultants to hammer developers into submission. The process had devolved into spectacle, a sport contest. But at least I understood the game, poring over every draft of every analysis, searching for damaging subtext in seemingly innocuous findings of fact.

We then focused on perfecting the design. Since the building envelope for our shopping mall was basically a box sandwiched in the middle of the block, we were limited in our choices as compared to, for example, a skyscraper surrounded by an open plaza. We searched for a hook, a high concept, and eventually focused on the façade.

The typical regional shopping center resembles a windowless fortress, designed so as to facilitate the display of merchandise with controlled lighting and also, like a casino, to minimize distractions and thus concentrate the customer's attention on parting with their dollars. We decided to violate this canon and conceived a monumental glass curtain wall for the length and height of the building, which would reveal the excitement within, most notably a ninety-foot-high atrium with scissored escalator banks and tons of shoppers.

I examined a variety of glass types with Gensler and was particularly intrigued by fritted glass.[41] The architects presented us with examples obtained from the manufacturer, but I couldn't trust this sizable investment to a few hand-held samples. Gensler admitted that the material had not yet been used widely in the US and that the only built prototypes were a couple of high-rises in Manhattan and, oddly, a public library in a small town in Iowa. I told Dave we were going on a little trip.

We caught a red-eye to New York and then doubled back to Chicago, driving from O'Hare to Iowa.[42] Later, with our mission accomplished, we sat on the tarmac for our leg back to San Francisco. Three hours passed as we waited for thunderstorms to abate. Well after midnight, as the plane finally moved on the cleansed runway and Dave snored, I doodled the fritted glass façade on a napkin and nodded approval.

We next turned our attention to the most critical element of our production, to wit: appeasing the authorities and silencing the critics. Obviously, the failure to obtain entitlements is a terrible fate, but even worse is an "approval" with so many concessions and exactions and payoffs and deleterious design changes that the project is effectively rendered uneconomic, an outcome I had often observed as a broker. The goal was to get it done *on our terms.*

I thought back to my Chicago summer of '68 in the waning years of Richard J. Daley—the last of the autocratic big-city mayors—when life was much simpler for a real estate developer: You were told how much to pay and where to pay it. Now, in twenty-first-century San Francisco, we faced hostile fire from politicians, neighborhood activists, special interest groups, political gadflies, and crazed bloggers, to name a few. And our actions would be scrutinized in the local business press and in the blogosphere.

Urban Realty took proactive steps to build goodwill, particularly with respect to our existing tenants, a number of which were nonprofits. We cut rents for some, forgave back rent for others, and assisted all in the relocation process. Our most visible tenant was an organization serving 500 low-income and homeless psychiatric patients. After detecting that a prominent hospital subsidized a portion of their budget, we bought and modernized a nearby building for their use by persuading the hospital to guarantee the new lease, thus using their credit to finance the transaction.

We addressed the clamoring of preservationists who sought to stop the project by declaring several of our existing, dilapidated structures worthy of preservation. We produced meticulously researched reports proving in one case that the building had been remodeled so many times that there was little left of the original fabric, and in another, that the property was not in fact the site of a clandestine gay bar in the 1950s.

And we otherwise did what was necessary, particularly in recognizing the concerns of key neighborhood groups such as the San Francisco Bicycle Coalition, which wielded considerable influence and whose likely member almost ran Don over on that stroll down Market Street. Of course, we cultivated the favor of politicians by contributing to their reelection campaigns and otherwise wrote personal checks as directed by our lobbyist.

Our feature film was now well into principal photography.

By mid-2007, with our Mid-Market development humming smoothly, we looked to grow our business and take on new projects. We saw virtually every major commercial real estate acquisition opportunity in California, offered on a number, and again gaped in disbelief at the winning bids. I happened to call a leasing pro to discuss rents, and the talk soon turned to the financial markets.

"My son's three years out of college," the broker offered, "and he's having a better year than I am."

"Really," I said. This made no sense. "What's he do, run a tech startup?"

"No, he works in a boiler room in Irvine originating home loans. What they call liar loans—borrower has no income, no savings, and no credit."

"Isn't that like, uh, fraud?"

"Not if everybody's doing it."

Intrigued, I researched the matter further and discovered that the lending excesses in commercial real estate paled before the machinations in the residential mortgage market. Individual loans were being packaged into pools by investment banks and assigned fictitious credit ratings, then sold to institutional investors either too lazy to research the underlying mortgage quality, or worse, deliberately negligent. I quickly called a commercial mortgage agent whom I could rely on to speak the truth and met him at Starbucks.

"Break down some of your recent deals," I said between sips of half-caf. He described highly leveraged acquisitions with unrealistic underwriting originated by lenders who didn't keep the loans on their books but quickly shed them after extracting lucrative fees.

"These loans should never have been made," I said.

He laughed. "My deals are pretty good—you should see the bad ones."

I imagined these goings-on repeated all across the country. "This is unbelievable—what happens when the bubble bursts?"

"It's worse than you think," he said, proceeding to school me on derivatives—opaque financial instruments bought and sold privately in an unregulated marketplace—which amounted to "insurance" side bets on the original mortgage pools. I envisioned people three and four deep at the craps table who were betting on the *player* holding the dice, their bets far exceeding all the chips on the table.

"What's the size of the derivatives market?" I asked.

The broker shrugged. "No one knows . . . trillions?"

I almost fainted, thanked him, and rushed back to Urban Realty's headquarters and directly into Dave's office.

"You will not believe what's going on out there," I said.

Dave looked up, startled.

"We're right in the middle of the biggest Ponzi scheme of all time."

I clumsily tried to explain how Wall Street was unloading unprecedented financial risk across the globe. Dave calmly referenced what he'd read in the trades, that the problem pertained only to the so-called "subprime" residential loans, and that it was being contained, i.e., the quarantine of a minor component of the overall market. I replied that it looked more to me like a pandemic and that shit had just not yet hit the fan.

"Well, we're in good shape on our projects," Dave said. "We have quality assets at a low basis. Commonfund's balance sheet is strong. And the main thing, we're modestly leveraged. So we should weather the storm."

I studied the traffic streaming down Bush Street. "You're probably right."

In January 2008, I sat in our conference room next to Stephen, the broker who earlier had sold us 901 Market. He worked for Eastdil, the dominant brokerage firm for the sale of the most substantial properties, and therefore was a credible source, as much as is possible for a broker. We had persuaded Don to fly out for this critical strategic planning meeting and invited Stephen to opine on the market.

For months, we had warned Commonfund of pending disaster in the mortgage industry, yet they remained remarkably unconcerned. I knew they had access to the same or better information than we did, and so I could not figure out why. Dave and I hoped to convince Don to take steps to further limit our collective exposure.

I heard footsteps trudge up the stairs. Dave walked Don in and we immediately got down to business.

"Things are a little choppy out there," Stephen said. "Prices are starting to soften; no one is sure all the bad news is out."

"How's San Francisco?" Don asked.

"Still strong, but we're advising owners that if they're thinking of selling, to do it ASAP."

"What about 901 Market?" I said. We had just secured the City's approval to convert the lower floors to retail and implement a shopper-friendly façade. Since the building was listed on the National Register of Historic Places, which by statute precluded almost any alteration, our proposed renovation amounted to a coup and had instantly created value.

"We can get $100 million, maybe more," Stephen said. "Considering you paid $65 million—what, eighteen months ago?—not too shabby."

I strained to maintain a poker face as my left brain furiously calculated the size of the estimated profit to accrue to Urban Realty as capital gain, many millions of dollars. I glanced at Dave, who appeared to be performing the same mental arithmetic, and then at Don, who remained impassive.

"That's a nice round number," I stammered.

We discussed the details of a potential sale and then I ushered the broker out, closed the door, and sat back down opposite Don.

"This is a gift," I said. "We may not see that pricing level again for many years."

"The sale will validate the whole block," Dave added, "and prove out our concept."

Don shifted in his chair.

"You two have done a helluva job on 901 Market," he said. "But—"

I moaned.

"—we're not a seller today. We want to keep the assemblage intact, and besides, it would just reduce our assets under management."

Don resisted our impassioned pleas. We finally gave up and turned to updating him on CityPlace, unrolling an impressive timeline of tasks and milestones of accomplishment, confirming we were on time and on budget. After an hour, he nodded approvingly and rose to leave.

"By the way, gents," Don said, "Commonfund has decided to refinance most of its properties nationally, including all of the Mid-Market properties, in a portfolio loan."

What???

"You mean a single loan with cross-collateralization?" I said. This was the worst of all possible worlds: If one property defaulted, the lender could go after the others.

Don nodded.

"Who's the lender?" I asked.

"Anglo Irish Bank."

My face must have resembled the anguished creature in Edvard Munch's painting *The Scream.* Anglo Irish Bank did not lend to hardworking Dubliners but was a high-flying commercial lender, with a rumored $9.5 billion exposure to the US real estate market alone.

"I'll need you guys to sign a few documents later this month," Don continued. "Appreciate it."

He shook our hands firmly and strode out. In our minds, Commonfund had dealt Urban a vicious one-two punch: They refused to sell 901 Market for a spectacular price and then threatened the entire venture by including the assets in a dangerous portfolio loan.

Dave and I considered our options. Perhaps we could force a sale of 901 Market by exercising the buy-sell clause, but that would be resisted and we would miss the window of opportunity. Also, the joint venture agreement did not expressly prohibit a portfolio loan, which frankly had never even entered our realm of thought in the negotiations. To challenge our partner at this critical stage with a low probability of success would only strain the relationship.

We resumed our labors under a pall of apprehension, and two months later, Anglo Irish Bank funded the loan. Our fortune, and the fortunes of many, would soon change.

CHAPTER 19

Awakening

As I sat in my office cradling the phone, the partially closed door burst open. Bob, eyes wild with excitement, entered holding a book aloft, which he then laid reverentially on my desk. I had hired Bob to perform incidental plan checking for our various buildings. Annoyed by the intrusion, I rebuked him with a glance, pointing at the handset and waving him off. Sensing the faux pas, he retreated and disappeared.

We were getting significant pushback on our proposed parking garage at CityPlace, and I was in the middle of a consequential call with our lobbyist, discussing options for mounting a counter-offensive. After hanging up, I threw the book on the credenza, noting in passing its title: *The God Delusion* by Richard Dawkins. This trivial event should have been immediately deleted from the hard drive of my memory. I left to get a Starbucks and thought no more about it.

Circa 2:00 a.m., I woke and deemed the incident decidedly weird. My relationship with Bob was casual and purely business. What had compelled him to breach protocol and barge in unannounced without an appointment? And especially with the aim of engaging me at a highly personal level? My first instinct was to scold him the next time we talked. But what if he was only the messenger?

I adjudged his manifestation to be a sign and therefore significant and even perhaps an opportunity to alter my personal trajectory. I committed what little free time I had to investigating the matter further and, in the ensuing weeks, I read the book and examined this latest incarnation of the science versus religion debate.

While I deemed myself a fallen-away Catholic in terms of practice, I had never "not believed." Dawkins, a British evolutionary biologist, had reinvigorated the argument. I regarded his conjecture—that belief in God is a delusion and that religion is pernicious—as old as the hills. However, by adopting a stridently anti-theistic stance, exploiting his credentials, and appealing to a popular audience, Dawkins converted the thesis to cash.

As book sales soared, Dawkins was joined by like-minded individuals soon dubbed by a journalist the "New Atheists." They marketed themselves skillfully, debating men of the cloth[43] and even that rare scientist with religious leanings in lively encounters typically held on college campuses; videos were easily accessible on a burgeoning website called YouTube. The skirmishes reminded me of the boxer versus wrestler bouts of yore.

I made no mention to Bob. Self-identified as Jewish, he had clearly experienced a secular epiphany of some kind. I resisted the urge to chide him: *Bob, how could you give up your power, cultivated over millennia?*

Instead, I focused inward: Who was I to talk, and how could I proactively weigh in on the debate? More important, what was I doing to advance my own religious and spiritual development?

During the 1960s, it seemed like my generation—the baby boomers—had been blasted through a portal into a new world of freedom and license, accompanied by a loss of religiosity and other anchors of meaning. Today, not only religious belief but theology and philosophy had been deemed irrelevant and pushed to the side. And for those still aligned with a faith tradition, how many committed to ongoing practice?

I attributed this falling away not so much to the hard sciences, whose ideas had become so abstract as to be unintelligible not only to the layperson but even to other scientists outside the field of specialty, but more so to technology, which had wrought wondrous magic, resulting in spectacular advances in communications, health care, and other areas.

One commentator dubbed this phenomenon *techno-secularism*, which "has an ethical vision that focuses on healthful living, self-fulfillment, and avoiding the struggles of human life and the inevitability of death."[44] In terms of material comfort and amazing gadgets, the average citizen enjoyed a lifestyle previously unavailable to kings. Why worry about God?

The allure was particularly persuasive in the Bay Area, with San Francisco the irreligiosity capital of America[45] and Silicon Valley the global epicenter of technological innovation. Small wonder that I rarely encountered serious dialogue of a religious or spiritual nature, especially in the world of business. At home, Ginger believed in the Almighty and said her prayers but also was not an overt practitioner.

I considered various avenues and then settled on the Ernest Becker Foundation, the organization I joined after Anita's death and to which I contributed over the years. Several of its members were enjoying international recognition for crafting psychological experiments influenced by Becker's ideas and thus re-energizing his name.

Yet other members, in my opinion, merely proffered a personal agenda with minimal self-awareness and little regard for Becker's actual thought. I called Neil, the founder and president of EBF.

"Martin, so good to hear from you!" he said. A retired internist and endocrinologist, Neil tirelessly promoted the foundation and enthusiastically supported all of the members, even non-academic irritants such as myself.

"I've got an idea, Neil."

"Excellent!"

"Let's do a symposium on Becker," I said, "to discuss his thinking on science and religion." Born to Jewish immigrant parents, Becker helped liberate a Nazi concentration camp during his military service. He considered himself a scientist and remained an atheist for much of his career. However, in his mature writings, Becker rediscovered his belief in God. He conceded that humans couldn't think their way out of their mortal dilemma and that genuine religion represented the highest level of meaning.

"Wonderful!"

"We'll fly in the foremost Becker scholars," I said, "and have a civil dialogue."

Neil paused. "We're a little stressed on our budget right now."

I mentally computed the costs of travel, accommodations, and hall rental. Perhaps $5,000–10,000, and well worth it to get the right people.

"No problem, I'll sponsor it," I said.

"Terrific!"

We agreed to name the symposium "Religion: The Quest for Ideal Heroism," the title of the last chapter in Becker's *The Birth and Death of Meaning*. The preparation required months to find a suitable venue, coordinate the scholars' schedules, agree on a format, and market the event. I reread Becker's published works and his private papers as well as relevant academic journals.

Becker, reportedly the most popular lecturer on campus, had taught at Cal Berkeley in the sixties during the height of the free speech movement. Forty years later, we welcomed him back. On November 15, 2008, five experts on Becker convened for a private afternoon salon at our house, followed by an evening panel discussion open to the public at the Church Divinity School of the Pacific in Berkeley.

Ginger did not share my interest in Becker but proved a gracious hostess. The guests sat relaxed in our living room, several on the sofa under a framed oil painting of the child Puyi, the last emperor of China, which I had acquired in Hong Kong years ago; the others by a console table with an ornamental vase holding dozens of dried roses, the remains of bouquets presented to my wife on special days, which she saved.

The most notable attendee was Sam Keen, an author and philosopher who had interviewed Becker at his bedside in March 1974 just days before his death, and which experience he described as a "holy event." I opened the salon with Becker's own words from the deathbed transcript:

"I think the major thrust of my work is to go frankly in the direction of the merger of science and religious perspectives . . . I don't think one can really be a hero in any really elevating sense without some transcendental referent like being a hero for God."

The participants defined religion in broad terms, not the punching bag caricature of Christian fundamentalism adopted by the New Atheists but whatever power source a frail human being attaches to in the quest for meaning, akin to German theologian Paul Tillich's "ultimate concern." The attendees shared a Judeo-Christian upbringing, from Mennonite to Canadian Baptist, and varied in their current outlook, from agnostic to Buddhist.

Sam felt strongly that humans do not live only in the world of science[46] but in a world of symbol and myth: not myth as a false idea or delusion but rather myth as a vehicle to explain the unexplainable, specifically why we as insignificant creatures have been put in this predicament of having conscious self-awareness of our inevitable physical demise.

And we discussed what it meant to be a hero for God and therefore authentic religiosity. One of the scholars spoke of Becker's religious reawakening at the birth of his child, and quipped, "There are no atheists in neonatal wards."

I restated Becker's assertion that we all maintain our own immortality projects (as described earlier) and posited that we often yield to the false rhetoric of others at either end of the political spectrum, and that without a reflective self-awareness of this issue, it is very difficult to move forward.

I had planned the evening program to attract as many "Beckerites" and curiosity seekers as possible, especially students and other young people who might keep Becker fresh and alive for the next generation, energized by the scholars onstage. Fifty or more attended, most of whom had some familiarity with Becker.

The panelists spoke of their first encounter with Becker as a "bolt of lightning" and as being aroused from a "dogmatic slumber," to quote Kant. Several audience members admitted to discovering Becker after a personal tragedy. Becker himself opined on the suddenness of catastrophe and the irony of his pending demise: "...the thing which people try to banish most from their minds with their character armor, which...is the suddenness with which terror strikes life on the planet, the fact that people are really so fragile and so insecure. There is nothing they can do."

Two of the scholars spoke of startling "coincidences" in their lives, "taps on the shoulder" and "signals of transcendence" that they could not dismiss, and which prevented them from "closing the door and saying I'm an atheist." Another expressed concern as to how humans make every effort to live as if they are immortal—with no limits and the ensuing over-consumption and environmental degradation. And Sam finally confessed, "I believe in a God who encompasses all, but of whom I know very little."

After the event, Natalie and Solis congratulated me and avowed that they found the discussion interesting and they weren't just saying that. As the hall emptied, I ushered Neil outside.

"Think Becker's ghost showed up tonight?" I said.

"Martin, you know I'm not into that woo-woo business," Neil said, chuckling.

"Yeah, well . . . maybe we created a little ripple in the cosmic field."

"You performed a real service for the foundation," he said. "Thank you."

We shook hands for several seconds and diverged in the night.

Reflecting on the symposium, I tried to locate myself in space and time and make sense of my adult life over the past forty years. I was attracted to Becker's theory of death denial as the best explanation for why people do what they do. However, most of the hours in my day were still concentrated on business and the pursuit of material gain . . . success. With Anita's help, I had turned the corner but then stagnated. Life had again become comfortable enough; any sense of urgency that it could all be snatched away had been forgotten.

I struggled to determine how to reinvigorate my practice, which had peaked in my teenage years when I attended

Campion Jesuit High School. I regarded my cohort as one of the last beneficiaries of a classical liberal education. The Jesuits taught me not only religion but also how to think and write; under their tutelage, I learned far more than in college.

Over the centuries, the Jesuits promoted intellectual rigor, theological debate, the teaching of science, and similar pursuits, which ofttimes resulted in tension with the Holy See. To me, they were not only scholars but also men of action and resolve.[47] With them I would start afresh.

The Jesuit Retreat Center of Los Altos—El Retiro San Iñigo—consists of thirty-eight wooded acres overlooking Palo Alto and surrounded by the secluded estates of Silicon Valley's technology entrepreneurs. Presciently, the Jesuits bought the initial parcel in 1925 and converted the structure into a retreat house to serve the contemplative demands of Bay Area residents. In the ensuing decades, they acquired adjacent properties and built more buildings.

I admitted to Ginger that I needed to escape the press of business—if only for a little while—and signed up for a self-directed weekend retreat at El Retiro. Unlike a group retreat, which involves structured activities, my only obligation was to leave electronic devices and other distractions at home and maintain strict silence throughout the entire stay. I had the option of meeting with a spiritual director but otherwise would be on my own.

As I exited Freeway 280 and meandered through lush residential neighborhoods, I thought that three days of not talking could be a long, long time. Lost in reverie, I twice missed the unassuming entrance. I proceeded slowly up the driveway and encountered a group of buildings designed in the Mission Revival style, featuring burnt-orange clay roof tiles projecting over wide eaves that sheltered cream-colored stucco walls.

After registering, I located my room, furnished with a bed, writing table, and chair. And a Bible and wall-mounted crucifix. I tossed my duffel bag in the corner and lay on the bed and unintentionally fell asleep.

I awoke at dusk and strolled to the refectory for dinner and lingered to enjoy the view, which included glimpses of San Francisco Bay. I stopped to peruse the well-stocked bookstore, procrastinating against the solitude that awaited me in the monastic cell.

At a section marked "Spirituality Has Many Paths," I beamed upon noticing a copy of *The Autobiography of a Yogi*, a favorite book of mine.[48] Paramahansa Yogananda, a Hindu monk who introduced yoga and meditation to "Westerners" in the early twentieth century, recounts in engaging English his meeting saints of both Hindu and Christian faiths and witnessing miracles.

Before leaving, I purchased *The Spiritual Exercises of Saint Ignatius*, the prayers and contemplations written by the founder of the Jesuit order in 1522, which, according to the retreat center's website, "provide the spiritual and intellectual foundation for all that happens at *El Retiro*." In the room, I cracked open the book and found the saint wasted no time in getting to the heart of the matter. He directed me to first "bring to memory all the sins of life, looking from year to year, from period to period . . . "

Which I did into the wee hours.

Let me say I have no problem with the word sin. Better to call it by name than explain it away as biologically maladaptive behavior or mere error or otherwise excusable relative to culture or situation. My sins were varied and many, acts of commission and omission over the decades. As I recalled the people I knew, the places I'd lived, and the things I had done, one thought led to another, and thus did the sins multiply. Did Saint Ignatius draw on inspiration, I wondered, or on personal experience in devising these exercises?

I had sloughed off professional misdeeds throughout my career on the rationale that commercial real estate involved sophisticated parties who presumably knew how to take care of themselves and for whom business ethics represented a contradiction in terms. I called to mind my hidden regrets: not doing enough for my parents after moving beyond their reach, and, especially, ignoring Natalie's spiritual and religious development as a child. Perhaps it would have been a matter of the blind leading the blind, but to not even try?

I tied my maximal shame and moral recidivism to my relationships with women. The permissiveness engendered by the '60s facilitated superficial love and sex without commitment. And my increased financial success created a false sense of power and control. I thought of the moment when I left Ruby for Tina, and of other sweethearts and their hurt when I walked away. Of course, nothing matched my betrayal of Anita.

Awash in guilt, I finally dozed off.

In the morning, I ventured out clear-eyed, adjusting my senses to nature. El Retiro occupied its own hilltop consisting of dense forest cover, including stands of California live oak, deodar cedar, and Monterey cypress. I meandered along a path that featured hand-carved Stations of the Cross—fourteen images of Jesus Christ on the day of his crucifixion—interspersed with holly and poppy and thistle.

I edged down a steep trail labeled "Labyrinth," startling a mule deer and espying a raptor (which I judged to be a red-tailed hawk) weaving among the treetops. Somewhere below in Palo Alto and the Valley, I mused, in the place where it all started, tens of thousands labored to create a more efficient mechanical world.

Emerging from the woodland, I passed the chapel and checked the schedule, noting a Mass late in the afternoon. I spotted a bench and sat to rest. As I closed my eyes, I glimpsed my child-self trudge through the snow and the dark on a frigid winter morning to St. John's Catholic Church for weekday Mass, undeterred in my commitment as altar boy . . .

In the sacristy, I donned a floor-length black cassock, and over that, a white surplice. I located the candle lighter, taller than myself, and marched piously into the sanctuary. I noticed a smattering of the devout ensconced in the pews.

Wobbling on tiptoes, I strained to light the towering candles atop the altar, attempting to touch the flame of the lighter to each wick, the piercing eyes of the congregants stabbing my back, anticipating my failure. I retreated to the sacristy and awaited the priest, who soon materialized and followed me out in procession.

"*Dominus vobiscum,*" he boomed.

"*Et cum spiritu tuo,*" replied the flock.

I proceeded to serve a flawless ceremony. The Latin rite, the incense, the hymns, the burden of guilt but also subsequent redemption, were powerful motivators. But most wonderful to me was the belief in Jesus Christ and a personal God who I could talk to in my head, who would listen and offer encouragement in times of trial.

Oh, the memory!

I slowly rose from the bench and returned to the room and delved deeper into the *Spiritual Exercises.* Saint Ignatius now directed me "to weigh the sins" and then "to look at myself, lessening myself by examples" and finally "to consider what God is, against Whom I have sinned, according to His attributes, comparing them with their contraries in me." As I acceded to the instructions, my heroic self-image crumpled further.

I later entered the chapel and found a half-dozen individuals sitting on folding chairs grouped in a cluster. The spiritual director, Father Bernie, clad in civilian attire, directed me to an empty seat. I surmised that the congregation tonight consisted of a few stragglers from the group retreat and myself. He checked his watch and then launched into the service.

Father Bernie celebrated the Mass in twenty minutes as compared to a typical Sunday ceremony of an hour or more. At this pace, rather than lapse into daydreams, I found myself focused on the key components of the liturgy: the Word, the Eucharist, and the Communion rites. Stripped to its essence, the Mass represents the common language of Catholics around the world and through the millennia.

When Father Bernie distributed the communion wafers, I raised my palm to decline. He nodded and, minutes later, concluded the rite. As the other souls trudged out of the chapel, he cornered me.

"Everything okay?"

"It wouldn't have been right for me to take communion," I said. "I haven't been to confession for a while, and the sins have sort of piled up."

"We call it reconciliation now," he said. "How long has it been?"

I simply shook my head.

"Meet me tomorrow morning at eleven," he said. "I'll be in one of the parlor rooms by the conference hall—we'll go to confession."

"But, Father—"

He gripped my arm, patted my back, and sent me off.

That evening, I finished my condensed enactment of the *Spiritual Exercises*, hoping to progress to the point of expressing "an exclamation of wonder with deep feeling, going through all creatures, how they have left me in life and preserved me in it." Yet I dwelt on the scheduled reconciliation and trembled at the idea of divulging decades of sins aloud to a stranger, especially face to face, without the curtain of anonymity available in a confessional. I decided to leave a note of apology and check out early.

With my packed bag, I emerged in the late morning, passing two women not chattering but rapt in thought, fully adapted to a mute world. As I moved past the refectory, the tinkling of silver betrayed the setting of table service. I arrived at the registration desk and faced the program coordinator, a genuinely pleasant lady.

"Mr. Sawa, are you leaving already?" she said. "You know that lunch is included in your stay."

The wall clock read 11:00 a.m. I reached into the duffel bag and withdrew the note.

"Could you please give this to—"

I paused and then excused myself. Turning the corner,
I peered into doors lining the hallway until I located Father
Bernie, relaxing in a small wood-paneled room unadorned
save for a handful of chairs. I closed the door behind me and
proceeded to confess my sins of the past forty years. Father
Bernie listened patiently, dispensed a penance of prayer and
good works, and granted absolution.

Of course, this was not the end of the matter with a
snap of the fingers. I had reconciled with the Church and
with God, on the promise of avoiding sin and offering restitution for past misdeeds by my future acts. While an enormous burden had been lifted, I also assumed a proportionate
responsibility going forward.

As I motored down the driveway past a gauntlet of olean-
der, I mouthed an exclamation of wonder and a silent prayer
of gratitude.

I had returned to the roots of my faith and Catholic practice. While recognizing there may be different paths up the
same mountain, I felt it important to commit to one road
and avoid too many switchbacks. I intended to continue my
study of Buddhism and Judaism but didn't want to lapse
into a cafeteria approach to religion. In the words of Huston
Smith, perhaps the foremost scholar of religious studies in
the twentieth century, "Christianity has been my central
meal. But I'm a strong believer in vitamin supplements."[49]

I recognized that institutionalized religion, as with any
human endeavor, is populated by flawed and even reprehen-
sible individuals. I grieved the sexual abuse of children by

Catholic clergy and more than once retrieved memories of myself as an altar boy, imagining the utter vulnerability of a child not only to an authority figure but also to a corrupted man posing as an agent of God. These individuals and their co-conspirators should be prosecuted to the fullest.

Yet I was unprepared to discard an entire faith tradition that had survived for millennia in the face of numerous crises—spiritual survival value, if you will—because of the heinous behavior of a few. I simply couldn't ignore religion at its best, especially the saints and prophets and martyrs whom I admired more than anyone.

And so, I committed to a simple plan of more active participation:

- Mass attendance on Sundays and holy days (a weekly reprieve from postmodern insanity, and typically surrounded by nice people);
- Regular confession (a gut check of how I'm doing and free as compared to talk therapy);
- Prayer (more of it, and particularly the Rosary, plus a weaning away from the more flagrant varieties—"God, do this and do that for me");
- Support for Catholic organizations (such as the Ukrainian Greek Catholic Church, with its rock-solid tradition, married priests, and explosive growth);
- Mindfulness (in the classic sense versus the commercialized, contemporary version severed from religious moorings).

I regarded these action steps as unimpressive when compared with the practice of the truly observant, but for me, a doable start. Many months had passed since Bob threw down *The God Delusion* and fired a salvo for atheism. Surprisingly, or maybe not so, neither of us ever mentioned the incident, chatting occasionally on business matters but not "going there." In the cosmic order, he had accomplished his mission, and I the same.

Fortuitously, my awakening occurred at the precise time the financial world imploded.

CHAPTER 20

Detonation

By mid-2008, the subprime mortgage market self-destructed, and the contagion spread to the financial universe. The Commonfund loan demonstrated how vigorously Wall Street fought to squeeze out the last deals. As the investment bank Bear Stearns folded, the Federal Reserve facilitated its bailout by JP Morgan Chase, promptly drawing criticism for rescuing private companies deemed "too big to fail."

The summer witnessed the ongoing collapse of more financial entities and the increasing injection of federal tax dollars to stem the tide, drawing the further ire of taxpayers and a handful of honest politicians. Over my career I had seen my share of bubbles, but none this big. And what particularly riled me was the arrogance of so many in perpetrating the fraud. I sensed that the pendulum had reached the point

of unstable equilibrium and was about to start its descent
and go too far, too long in the other direction.

While continuing to pursue the CityPlace entitlements
and develop the concept design for the Northside Block, we
urged Commonfund to commit to the renovation and re-
tenanting of 901 Market, so as to produce immediate income.
We had strong interest from a number of value retailers who
would lease all or most of the ground floor, the most valuable
space in the building.[50]

I arranged a tour of the premises with the real estate
manager of the tenant we most coveted, accompanied by her
retail-leasing broker. After walking the surroundings and
every inch of the space, the two conferred for more than ten
minutes. Finally, the broker drew me aside behind a building
column.

"Look, Martin," he said. "She thinks the location is perfect and the space lays out really well."

I found such candor refreshing—typically, a tenant
would point out the deficiencies in hopes of securing a stronger bargaining position.

"But . . . "

I noticed the paint peeling on the pillar—we'd better test
for lead.

"She's just not sure you can get it done in time. Their
existing lease expires in a year—"

"No problem."

"And you have a lot of demo and code work to do—"

"We'll push this hard. Our partner's on board, and—"

He drew closer to me.

"*That's* the problem," he whispered. "She heard that
Commonfund might be having some problems."

Before I could issue an emphatic denial, he continued.

"She made some calls. Everybody is nervous about the economy right now. Making the wrong decision could end her career. She just can't take the chance. Sorry."

They thanked me graciously and faded into the crowd on Market Street. Dave and I immediately called Commonfund, who professed shock at the inference and reaffirmed that we could start the renovation . . . as soon as we signed a major tenant, which landed us squarely in a catch-22. Our relationship with our partner continued to deteriorate.

The hammer officially fell on September 15, 2008, when Lehman Brothers filed for bankruptcy, the largest ever in the United States. The stock price of the investment bank fell 93 percent in one trading day on the heels of precipitous declines in the prior weeks. What became the defining event of the global financial crisis created a panic due not to the size of the losses involved (immense) or to the venality of its executives (greater still) but to the fact that this time the government did not step in.

The game was rigged no more.

The world's major banks could no longer conceal that they were holding IOUs of questionable value. Unsurprisingly, one of the first dominoes to fall was Anglo Irish Bank. In January 2009, the Irish government effectively nationalized the institution, and a year later, the books revealed the largest loss in Irish corporate history. Hidden loans to insiders heightened the intrigue, with the debacle quickly labeled Ireland's version of Enron.

But Dublin lay 5,000 miles from San Francisco, which faced its own problems. The fall of Lehman creamed the value of commercial real estate companies nationally and particularly roiled the Bay Area markets. Rents plummeted, vacancies soared, and property sales evaporated, as no one could figure out how to get a deal done. For the next two years, Urban Realty continued its efforts to secure entitlements for CityPlace and advance its other projects on Market Street amid the chaos: a surreal, Sisyphean task.

During this time, I felt an underlying sense of dread. No matter what Dave and I did, success lay outside of our control, influenced by strangers in faraway places. Outwardly, I displayed the utmost confidence to our team; a man does not whine about misfortune, especially from a situation voluntarily entered into. Anita's passing illustrated how capricious life can be. And my newly found religious practice provided respite.

Yet, what gnawed at me most was all the time invested that I could never recover . . . and to what end?

In January 2010, Don left Commonfund, followed shortly by other executives. Later in the year, Commonfund Realty Investors announced that the real estate fund had lost 87 percent of its value over the prior twelve months. The cat was publicly out of the bag, and much worse than Dave or I had imagined. We braced for the meeting with Don's replacement.

Jim, with a freshly scrubbed face and Irish to boot, met us on Market Street on a drizzly Monday morning. He had been quickly elevated after the hasty exodus of key executives and charged by Commonfund to keep his personal impulses in check. I discovered he had attended a Jesuit college and therefore deemed him credible until disproven. As we walked, Dave brought him current on all the properties and especially CityPlace, now under review by the Planning Commission.

"When do you think it will go for a vote?" he asked.

"Probably June or July," Dave said. "Once we have the approvals, it'll take another year for working drawings and permits, and then we can be out of the ground."

Jim had not brought an overcoat, and droplets rolled down his forehead. I tried to shelter him with my umbrella.

"I'm going to be honest with you guys—we're having cash flow problems."

I had suspected as much, but the words spoken aloud brought the reality home.

"Once we have the approvals, we can find another partner, even in this environment," I said. "Just force Anglo Irish to accept a payoff and release the lien."

"The new regime at the bank has dug in," he said, "and the attorneys are running the show."

The rain intensified and the neighborhood denizens scurried for cover. I nodded at Dave and we guided Jim back down Market Street.

"We want to keep pushing ahead," he said. "But we need your help."

Help like how?

"We'll keep paying your monthly developer fee but need to restructure your performance fees."[51]

"What does restructure mean?" Dave asked.

"Commonfund will give you promissory notes for amounts owed."

We knew instantly that we would not see a cent for a long time, if ever. The three of us walked mutely for the next block, ignoring the shoppers streaming into Ross at 799 Market and the tourists stolidly weathering the elements at the cable car terminus.

Coincident in time with Jim's visit, Ginger quit her job as a house manager. Since we had first met, she'd used her income primarily for the purchase of luxury items for herself and the home. At the time of our marriage, I had assured her that when she "retired," I would provide a stipend so that her lifestyle would not suffer.

Occupationally, Ginger's worldview had focused on the material. She had not only leapfrogged her origins but landed in the homes of the super rich, exposed to everything money could buy in the twenty-first century: multiple estates, private aircraft, megayachts, and gargantuan staffs constantly on call, 24/7. Now with plenty of free time, she fully committed to enjoying life in the present.

Except in the most general of terms, I had not discussed the intricacies of my commercial real estate business with Ginger, as I hadn't with Anita or Wanda. I played down the financial crisis while it flashed on the news every night and determined to keep my promise to Ginger for as long as I could. But it wasn't easy, particularly when she would breeze in laden with shopping bags.

"Had a good day?" I asked.

"Wonderful," Ginger said. "I had lunch at the Rotunda, and you know, they always find a great table for me even when they're full." The Rotunda was the top-floor restaurant at the Neiman Marcus store on Union Square, and Ginger was on a first-name basis with the host staff.

She set the bags down and pulled out the now familiar Christian Louboutin shoebox. Nothing provided Ginger with greater visceral delight than this particular label.

"What do you think?" she asked, dangling a pair of stiletto Pigalle Follies with the trademark red-lacquered soles.

"They're, uh, really nice," I said, estimating their cost and wincing. "How many does that, uh, make now?" Ginger had already slipped on the celebrated footwear and pranced to the bedroom to conduct a more formal assessment as I stared into the middle distance.

Our love had grown since our auspicious encounter, two people alike in so many respects, fueled by the drive to succeed and the power of will and personal responsibility. Surprisingly, the ardor quickened even after the initial chemistry should have waned. But states of high passion are oft accompanied by states of high dudgeon, and the emotional swings intensified. Our marriage increasingly became a battle of wills, and I sought to avoid spending my nights in combat as I did my days.

After intense deliberations with myself, I vaguely suggested to Ginger that a little belt-tightening might be in order and let it go. Who knew? Perhaps Urban Realty would weather the financial turbulence.

Dave and I furiously set about to develop new business and discovered half the world engaged in the same enterprise. The crisis ripened into the Great Recession, the most significant economic decline since the Great Depression of the 1930s. The unemployment rate in America hit 10 percent as over eight million jobs disappeared. The impact was felt across the board, unlike the aftermath of the dot-com bubble and its concentration in the technology sector.

I wrote to California's senators, urging them to punish the wrongdoers, noting that fines and censures meant nothing to mastermind criminals and only hard time for the most senior executives might alter downstream behavior. I suggested withholding a percentage of recovered funds to hire the best legal talent in the land to assist federal and state attorneys and thus counter the excuse that the cases were too complex to prosecute. I waited and waited for *anyone* to be nabbed, even as a symbolic gesture. The appalling lack of action reaffirmed to me that it was no crime if everybody was in on it.

Urban Realty celebrated briefly when the Planning Commission certified the Final EIR—the defining approval— for CityPlace in July, and then keened when a dissident faction appealed the decision to the Board of Supervisors. Our immediate fortune now hung on the mood of eleven women and men, elected by a rabidly progressive populace that had recently crushed Walmart's efforts to locate in the city, and who were now asked to cast their lot with a developer intending to bring corporate retail tenants to beloved Market Street.

Dave and I strode across the plaza to San Francisco City Hall, a Beaux-Arts monument built in 1915 and taller than the US Capitol. We entered the fabulous rotunda and skipped up the thirty steps to the second floor, which housed the chambers of the Board of Supervisors, the supreme legislative body of the City and County of San Francisco. Inside, the room reeked of gravitas: An ornate rail separated the dais from the pews of the audience, with chandeliers suspended from an intricately carved ceiling, almost like in a church.

We greeted our team and then secured excellent seats for the coming spectacle. At 2:00 p.m. on the Tuesday afternoon of September 14, 2010, the supervisors convened for their weekly meeting to consider, among other items, an appeal of the CityPlace EIR by the dissident activists. If we survived the appeal, we would have finally secured entitlements for our centerpiece project and the catalyst for the block's transformation. If not, we would be sent back into the mire of redesign, more concessions, infeasibility, and eventual ruin.

The clerk of the board had placed us as number twenty-five on the agenda. Three hours later—an interval that vividly brought to mind why I'd left the planning profession—the board's president finally announced our item.

Immediately, Chris, the supervisor in whose district CityPlace lay, blurted, "I have some not-so-good news." He had tried to broker a truce between Urban Realty and the appellants, which had failed the night before. Significant weight was given to the opinion of the local supervisor by the other board members. I shot a glance at our land use attorney, who urged calm with downward pressed palms.

The spokesperson for the dissidents seized the momentum, protesting our parking garage and the traffic the project would generate (duh), predicting the indiscriminate killing of bicyclists and pedestrians by crazed capitalist shoppers. What he failed to mention was that our project, to be tenanted by value retailers, would serve the needs of lower- and middle-income residents, primarily female shoppers handling bulky items and not lithe young men on ten-speeds. He beseeched the board, "Don't rush to judgment! Don't make a decision the City will regret for generations to come!" I gained the attention of our political consultant, who silently rebuked me for showing fear.

The appellant then trotted out a number of "concerned citizens," fellow activists, and eccentrics, including one who sang a song lambasting CityPlace and another who criticized the design as "suburban," the most crippling insult possible in the City by the Bay. I stifled a moan, as Dave remained stoic.

The board president now summoned our supporters. A line of speakers formed, snaking to the rear of the chamber. Carpenters, electricians, plumbers, and others from the trades implored, "We desperately need the work." Representatives from Tenderloin neighborhood groups acknowledged, "The developer has bent over backward to accommodate us." A longtime resident recounted that relatives visiting from overseas described this neighborhood as "the worst they've seen in any American city," and how CityPlace would turn things around. And last in line, Bob—my atheist instigator—waxed eloquent on the exceptional design.

With the public input finished, Chris refused to relent, declaiming that CityPlace "was kind of an ugly building." I started to rise but was restrained by my partner. Chris then surprisingly softened his stance and praised our willingness to assess a parking exit surcharge—which happened to be his idea—to be used to fund pedestrian and bicycle improvements in the surrounding block.

When the president called for a roll call vote, I closed my eyes; all of Urban Realty's effort over the past five years was effectively reduced to the next minute.

By the time Dave and I finally exited City Hall, the fading sun glowed amber on the monumental dome of Madera granite encrusted with gold leaf. The Board voted 9–0 in our favor, with two of the eleven supervisors absent. The CityPlace team had effectively laid the groundwork behind the scenes. Chris had demonstrated his progressive creds to the end but ultimately did the right thing.

Our victory was total: not only with the exceedingly rare unanimous vote—which telegraphed to the opposition that any future appeals or litigation would be futile—but with the fact that we had held firm to our design and our principles, particularly with respect to the 188-space parking garage, which *everyone* had assured us would never happen.

We had created immense value in probably the toughest jurisdiction in the country. The question remained as to how we would realize it. Dave and I wearily shook hands and agreed to take tomorrow off.

CHAPTER 21

Lost and Found

"Marty, you're not going to believe this . . . "

My brother, Greg, revealed on the phone that a couple in Florida had called him and asked if he "knew a Charlotte Brown who might have used the name Sawa?" Over twenty-five years had passed since we lost contact with our sister. Could this be real? I immediately called the family, and after extensive questioning, provisionally satisfied myself that the woman they knew was in fact Charlotte. They volunteered to set up a meeting but cautioned that she had been home-less for many years and suffered from mental illness. Could I handle it?

On the flight to Orlando, I reminisced about our salad days, sitting cross-legged on her bed as Charlotte tuned the portable tube radio, picking up the top forty hits on mighty WLS Radio in Chicago—with 50,000 watts of power, the seminal purveyor of culture to teenagers across the Midwest—and then standing and gyrating to Elvis or perhaps demonstrating the Twist. I reflected on my efforts to locate her over the years. Online search sites didn't exist, and so the process involved phone calls and snail mail to this agency or that. I had ramped up my efforts after Dad passed, and when Mom died, I gave up. Now I faced the guilt that I should have done more.

That evening, Greg and I drove to a subdivision of contemporary homes mysteriously carved out of an older neighborhood in central Orlando. We found the dwellings clustered around a pond—I discovered such natural bodies of water were prevalent throughout the region—outfitted with a small fountain. We located the residence and were warmly ushered in.

Probably in their early fifties, Bill and Susan were as saintly a couple as I had ever encountered: he a sportswriter, firm but kind, and she a teacher, persevering and eternally optimistic. I later learned they denied themselves superfluities, not for lack of acumen or effort, but because they kept giving away their time and money to help others.

Greg and I immediately noticed that an entire wall of the living room was dedicated to framed studio photographs of their three sons, now teenagers: Each son had his own row of yearly photographs taken since birth. I thought of Natalie and enviously admired the display.

We sweltered in the August heat, as Bill did not like to max out the AC. While their sons bounced in and out, Bill related how he had first encountered Charlotte ten years earlier at St. James Cathedral in downtown Orlando, the diocesan seat that also functioned as their parish church.

"Nobody knew what to make of her," Bill said. He related how Charlotte would sit for hours in the back of the chapel, enveloped by a stillness punctuated occasionally by arguments with herself.

"She became affectionately known as the bag lady," he said with a chuckle, "not because she was homeless—which she clearly was—but because she swung her handbag incessantly in wide circles."

"It took two years before Charlotte spoke to us," Susan added. With the support of the Catholic congregation and the St. Vincent de Paul Society, they guided her through the process of qualifying for government assistance and found her a small apartment. They gained Charlotte's trust and persuaded her to see a doctor, who quickly diagnosed paranoid schizophrenia and prescribed antipsychotic drugs.

"Once she started on the meds," Bill said, "her episodes pretty much stopped." The family continued to help Charlotte with shopping and chores, and most significantly, picked her up each Sunday for Mass, followed by breakfast at a downtown café. I was stunned at this display of loving-kindness.

"She was very guarded about her past," Susan admitted, "and it took us a long time to tease out that she even had two brothers. Also, she used her married name, 'Brown,' and this led to a lot of dead ends."

I now shared my childhood with Charlotte and the years that followed. After the incident with the biker, my parents consulted with the family doctor, who wrote it off as adolescent angst and convinced them she would mature out of it.

Which it appeared she had. She moved to Chicago, landed a secretarial job, and got engaged.

Mom, Dad, Greg, and I had boarded the Twin Cities Zephyr and lounged in the dome car of the streamlined passenger train, bound for Chicago for the wedding. I recall dancing with my sister at the reception and congratulating her husband, Richard, believing she had found happiness. By the time I moved to Chicago two years later in the summer of '68, she had borne a son, Ross.

"How did she seem at that time?" Bill asked.

"The anger had gotten worse," I said. "She would really lay into Richard . . . totally unwarranted. I blamed it on the stress of motherhood and tried not to think about it."

"Because of the age difference, I barely knew her," Greg said. "I saw her for those few times when she, Richard, and Ross came to Prairie du Chien to see the family. I mostly played with my nephew."

Charlotte and Richard divorced in 1978 after a horrendous fight, just weeks before Natalie's birth; he retained sole custody of Ross, then 10, and afforded him a stable home life. Charlotte later married a man named Brown; from what little we knew, that marriage fared even worse. It produced another son, whose existence I discovered upon receiving a baby picture in the mail, the last contact I had with my sister.

And then the incident at the Schooner Bar.

We all sat silent. Bill finally punctuated the quiet by restating the game plan. They would bring Charlotte to the diner after Mass as per their custom, mentioning along the way that she would have visitors. Susan explained that Charlotte would not speak unless spoken to, if then, and urged us to temper our expectations, cautioning, "She's not the same person you knew."

On a sunny Sunday morning, Greg and I fidgeted with our coffee cups at the retro diner, replete with Formica tabletops, checkerboard black-and-white floor tiles, and throwback waitresses in open-collared nylon dresses and white aprons. Soon Bill and Susan arrived with a grayed, weather-beaten older woman sporting an ill-fitting wig, whom they seated opposite me. The woman immediately grabbed a menu and surveyed its contents. I regarded her, not wholly the sister of memory but not wholly a stranger either.

"Charlotte, you know these characters?" Bill asked.

As she lifted her gaze, I said, "Hey, Charlotte."

My sister stared at me for a moment, then replied, "Hey, Marty. So . . . what are you guys doing here?" Her tone suggested that we had arrived mistakenly, perhaps an hour early for a scheduled appointment. We all simultaneously struggled to suppress a laugh. Fortunately, a genial waitress materialized to take our orders.

"So, Sis, what looks good?" I said.

"I always get the number four," she replied without hesitation.

Charlotte and I picked up where we had left off decades before and slowly inched toward each other over the aroma of bacon and eggs. She displayed a surprising acuity, and I addressed her forthrightly and without caregiver talk, sensing that she could gauge authentic versus feigned behavior. I thought not of our fights but of happier moments.

"Remember when we would play Mass, and I would get to be the priest and you the server?" I said. "And you would always forget to bring my cap at the recessional, and I would have to sing its Latin name—'bi . . . ret . . . ta'?"

Did her eyes twinkle for a nanosecond? I waited until Charlotte polished off the number four and swiped the last of the runny yolk with a fragment of toast.

"I'll be flying back to California and Greg to New Orleans," I said. "Can we come visit you again sometime?"

"Yeah, sure," she said without looking up.

As we parted, Bill pulled Greg and me aside and remarked on how animated Charlotte appeared. I offered my sister a hug, which she resisted, and then patted her back as she walked away. On the plane, I reflected on the dichotomy of our lives, how my world had enlarged while Charlotte's had shrunk as she wandered the streets of who knows where, her feet logging countless miles every day, her purse tracing innumerable arcs, her ego forfeiting all powers of agency.

With considerable regret, I realized I could never duplicate what Bill and Susan had accomplished, effectively adopting her in the hour of need. But perhaps I could make her life a little easier and broaden her experience. And I would engage with her as I had with so many others, at eye level. And perhaps love would grow.

Months later, on my next visit to Orlando, I addressed the matter of immediate consequence, and that of course was . . . to visit theme parks! What better way for Charlotte to taste the expansion of America that had eluded her throughout those lost years? Without forethought, I opted to take her to Disney World.

I pulled up in the rental car at Charlotte's residence in downtown Orlando and counted the third unit in an attached row of four wee apartments. Bill had described the location as less than a mile from church and therefore ideal. Her daily route commenced down leafy streets shaded by canopies of live oak and southern magnolia, through a district of historic homes, past Lake Eola Park, and ultimately to St. James Cathedral.

I knocked but once and Charlotte appeared in the doorway, ready to go, dressed in a simple pullover shirt, black slacks, and sneakers, and, of course, a green canvas bag slung over her shoulder. I peeked inside and noticed a compact living room, kitchen, and neatly kept bedroom. She locked her unit and with measured, deliberate steps, approached the car and waited for me to open the door.

We sped off excitedly and soon exited Interstate 4, to be immediately funneled past Epcot and other Disney attractions, which tempted us like sirens in The Odyssey until I slowed for a bank of tollbooths. I muttered at having to fork over for parking, and Charlotte nodded in agreement. We found a space at the periphery of a ginormous surface parking lot, then acquiesced to a stiff entry fee, boarded a monorail that deposited us at the park entrance, endured an interminable wait for two rides under the torrid Florida sun, searched in vain for a drinking fountain, and then, exhausted, we left, but not before being hustled for a photo in front of the Cinderella Castle.

Embarrassed, I vowed to do better.

The next day, we discovered the Holy Land Experience and struck pay dirt. A Christian-based, non-denominational theme park, the website boasted that it "recreates the architecture and themes of the ancient city of Jerusalem in first-century Judea." We viewed exhibits such as *Martha's Kitchen* and *Lazarus' House* and live stage productions of Biblical stories including *Jesus at the Temple* and *The Story of Maria Magdalena*. Whereas she couldn't wait to escape Disney World, Charlotte sat enthralled, watching a reenactment of a Crucifixion scene in the Orlando drizzle. The HLE became a staple of my visits, and we came to know all the attractions and shows by heart.

I would fly out to visit Charlotte several times a year as well as send her money and coordinate her budget with Bill. This financial assistance enabled Charlotte to cautiously extend her boundaries—for example, treating herself (albeit reluctantly) to lunch at IHOP. While shopping for groceries, Susan convinced Charlotte to improve upon her diet of frozen dinners but later admitted, "She still won't eat her vegetables."

I bought Charlotte a phone, and our calls matured from long periods of listening to each other breathe to active conversation.

"Hey, Charlotte."

"Hey, Marty. Thanks for the birthday card."

"Watching TV?"

"Uh-huh."

"What's your favorite show?"

"*Dancing with the Stars.*"

"Did you get out of the house today?"

"Susan took me to CVS."

And so forth. Bill confirmed that finding her brothers had emboldened Charlotte to the degree that she would approach parishioners, rather than hover in the shadows, and actually *speak first*, much to their amazement. I chalked up another victory.

Future visitations focused on more serious concerns as we endeavored to help Charlotte obtain a passport and identification card. I hoped to fly her out to California to meet all the family, but we would first have to get her proper ID and then convince her to board an airplane. Bill and I entered the Byzantine world of the Department of Homeland Security, ill-prepared for what lay ahead.

After I helped Charlotte fill out and file countless forms, the immigration officials informed us that she existed in a netherworld of being a naturalized citizen but unable to prove it. I hired an immigration attorney, who advised us to obtain copies of her marriage and divorce certificates, but these proved insufficient. With the help of another attorney, I spent the better part of a year negotiating with Austrian authorities for a copy of her original birth certificate, which they finally relinquished after satisfying themselves that Charlotte had no plans to re-enter their country.

To no avail.

My failure in not being able to help her regain her identity was exceeded only by my frustration in not reuniting Charlotte with her son. Ross and I had stayed in loose contact over the years, which accelerated when he and his wife flew out to California in 2006 and we had a reunion of sorts that led to periodic email exchanges. He made it clear that Charlotte had been abusive, and when his dad remarried, he embraced his stepmother.

I contacted my nephew shortly after finding Charlotte. Shocked by the news, he nonetheless resisted my attempts to bring them together. In his forties, he still could not overcome the final memory of his mother and the dreadful scene that triggered the divorce.

Now several years had passed, and I felt I had developed enough trust with Charlotte to bring up the subject. On one of my visits, we went to the movies and saw *Cowboys and Aliens*, agreeing that it was a preposterous mash-up. Then I coaxed her to dinner at a Thai restaurant near her home, four blocks beyond IHOP, and thus, uncharted territory.

"How do you like the food?" I asked, biting into an imperial roll.

"It's good."

"I'll get you a gift card so you can come regularly," I said. "I don't know if I told you, but I talked to Ross the other day. He's still up in Chicago."

Charlotte concentrated on the pad thai.

I reached into my billfold and produced a photograph. "Here's a recent picture with his wife and daughter," I said. "They were talking about maybe coming to Disney World. It might be nice for all of us to get together."

Charlotte studied the photo.

"Should I see when they're coming out?" I asked.

"Sure."

Later that night, I conveyed my accomplishment to Greg. But Ross and his family didn't visit Orlando that year or the next. Life's exigencies always seemed to get in the way. My negotiating skills had proven inadequate, but still I reasoned we had plenty of time.

"Martin, Charlotte passed away."

Five years after his first call, Bill stunned me again. He phoned from Charlotte's apartment, and I heard the police and paramedics in the background. I could visualize the scene, and thoughts of Anita flooded my mind.

"How . . . did it happen?" I asked feebly.

"Susan came to pick her up for the class," Bill recounted. "You know Charlotte is always ready waiting at the front door. When Susan got no response, she used her key and found Charlotte lying on the floor by the bed."

My latest project with Charlotte involved registering her for computer classes for senior citizens at the local neighborhood center. This would constitute Charlotte's first foray into a community outside of St. James Parish, and I was convinced she could succeed.

Today was the day Susan was to pick her up for the first class. Thinking positively, I had already arranged for a shuttle to pick her up for future classes. I had waited expectantly for a call from Susan to obtain a debriefing.

"Was she sick?" I asked. "I mean, did you have any idea?"

"No, she had a hard life, but we didn't see it coming," Bill said. "I'm sure the coroner will do an autopsy. She looked peaceful, no signs of any struggle."

I thanked him for everything, then set the phone down and compressed myself into a ball.

The next day I flew to Orlando for probably the last time. I located a competent mortuary and met with the funeral service professional, a sincere and empathetic woman. I robotically made the arrangements, wrote the obit, selected the newspapers for the announcement, ordered the flowers, and coordinated the sundry details.

Greg and I again convened at Bill and Susan's house as we had five years earlier, sweltering in the July heat. (Bill had not relented with regard to the AC.) Susan announced that their three sons, now all young men, would be attending the memorial service. We reminisced over lasagna and Italian wine.

"The boys loved Charlotte," Susan said. "They would sit next to her at church, bake her cookies, make Christmas gifts for her."

"At first, we were hesitant," Bill added. "You know, was Charlotte capable of violence? How would she deal with our sons?"

"But it all turned out better than we could have hoped for," Susan said. "Our sons learned to treat all people as human beings. She was a gift to our family."

We toasted Charlotte.

"It's a shame we weren't able to get her an ID," Bill said. "Probably will show up in the mail tomorrow."

"Did you talk with Ross?" Susan asked.

I nodded and then shook my head, obviating further discussion.

That night, alone in an Orlando hotel room and cooled by three beers and powerful air-conditioning, I penned my eulogy and mused about how Charlotte had shifted my perspective. I had dismissed most clinical designations of mental illness, but now recognized in hindsight the classic onset of schizophrenia in Charlotte's teenage years. I had also ignored the connection between mental illness and homelessness. I now could no longer look at a homeless woman without seeing my sister, without thinking about the chain of circumstance that leads one to become lost to the world.

But mainly, I thought of Charlotte's courage in the face of suffering and realized how puny my life challenges were in comparison. I wondered how she could have survived all those harrowing years, and could only surmise that, as the result of her Catholic upbringing, Charlotte summoned a deep and abiding belief that led her not only to find meaning but also to seek physical refuge inside churches: Literally, her faith had saved her.

At the memorial service, forty-four people honored our sister, which surprised even Bill. In his sermon, the rector praised all those parishioners "who had embraced and loved her in life, a love that was great enough to unlock the inner sanctum of a soul hidden away for so long in those vacant stares." He wondered, "How many other Charlottes are yet to be found?"

I ended my eulogy with the same sentiment I had offered at Anita's memorial. "Live each day as if it's the last, because it very well might be. Go to sleep without regrets or resentments, and feel fortunate to awaken to a new dawn. And don't wait until tomorrow to show love to those who enter your life. When it's time for a memorial service, it's too late."

Several weeks later, I obtained the autopsy report, which considered the manner of death "natural" and caused by diabetes mellitus. I arranged for Charlotte's ashes to be transported to Prairie du Chien and interred with Mom and Dad; fortunately, the back of their headstone was blank, which allowed for the added inscription.

Together again in death, if not in life.

CHAPTER 22

Forest Dweller

The approval of CityPlace by the Board of Supervisors energized our efforts to find a new financial partner as Commonfund continued to fend off redemption requests from its investors while negotiating with Anglo Irish Bank to reach a settlement and thus the potential release of collateral. Which excitement proved short-lived.

Late in 2010, after failing to restructure its fund, Commonfund announced that it would cease direct real estate investment, effectively throwing in the towel on all its development projects across the country. In February of 2011, Anglo Irish Bank filed notices of default—the first step in the foreclosure process—on the Market Street properties we had so arduously acquired years ago. But the bank had no desire to own the assets; it was merely following legal protocol in preparation for selling its entire $9.5 billion US book of business.

Dave was furious and phoned our counterpart developers in other cities and discovered that several were preparing lawsuits against Commonfund. "We have a strong case!" he declared, which assertion I recommended verifying with a litigator.

I had not sued nor been sued by anyone in my professional life. A hardened businessperson would argue that, rather than being virtuous, I had merely left too much on the table. Perhaps, but in my reckoning, peace of mind and productive use of time counted for more.

The attorney confirmed that our case was not a sure thing and would likely take years and substantial dollars to prosecute to conclusion. I contemplated the matter for a week and then suggested a compromise to Dave, which he warily found acceptable in principal. We called Jim to test Commonfund's receptivity.

"Look, Jim, life is short," I said. "Our litigator is champing at the bit, but we've got an idea that might be good for you, good for us."

"I'm all ears." Promoted to essentially clean up a mess and work himself out of a job, Jim would embrace suggestions to make his life easier, I calculated.

"You know that building down the street?"

"You mean 799?" For reasons unknown, they not only still owned the building that had initiated our relationship but had also excluded it from the Anglo Irish Bank portfolio loan.

"The asset could use a little attention," I said, "and the Ross lease is expiring soon—that's, what, most of your net income for the property?"

"So what do you have in mind?"

"We'll take over the building, renegotiate Ross Stores and the other leases, and get paid monthly management and periodic success fees," I said. "In cash."

"In return for?"

"Waiving any prospective litigation."

Jim paused. "That seems fair—I'll bring it up at the next committee meeting."

"And one last thing," I said. "If you ever sell the property, we share in a piece of the profits."

"No way."

"I don't mean profit from the $35 million we paid way back when. What's it worth today, maybe $60 million?"

"Yeah, probably."

"We'll set the bar there. The market sucks; it'll probably go down in value. What do you have to lose?"

"Let me think about it," Jim said.

A month later, we signed our deal. Commonfund had bumped the threshold up to $70 million, to be on the safe side lest they should have to pay us anything. On a sale over that price, we would share in the profit on a negotiated percentage basis.

The vultures circled the carcass of the Anglo Irish Bank's loan book. Hedge funds and private equity firms called us regularly to suck information on our properties and the overall market. They offered vague promises of "making it worth our while" and "utilizing our expertise" if they won the bidding, assurances I informed Dave were utter bullshit.

These were the apex predators, and they didn't achieve that status through acts of mercy.

I knew the drill well from my brokerage days. The hyenas had no intention of building CityPlace or entitling the Northside Block or repurposing 901 Market. They would immediately lay off the performing loans to a money center bank and then tee up the sale of the assets underlying the nonperforming loans as quickly as possible after obtaining title through foreclosure or deed-in-lieu—the successor buyers could do with the properties what they wished. Arbitrage of this sort, especially if properly leveraged, produced substantial returns.

Dave was anxious to pursue new business. While the major stock indices had by now recouped most of the losses suffered from the 2007 peak to the 2009 trough, nationally the real estate markets remained moribund. The effects of the nascent economic recovery had not yet rippled through the system, and investors were particularly wary of the asset class that created all the problems in the first place. Yet, in every cycle, the strongest markets recover first, and the commercial property market in San Francisco showed signs of life.

Moreover, the reputation of Urban Realty remained intact. A reporter with the local business press summarized the saga of CityPlace with the observation: "[T]here are two guys you have to feel sorry for in this story . . . ," noting our achievements and the demise of our financial partner. Yet I didn't feel sorry for myself. My mother had cautioned me, as I'm sure a few other moms from Eastern Europe had warned their children: You make your bed, you lie in it.

Nor did I feel angry. I recalled the lesson of a man diagnosed with terminal cancer who raged at his rabbi, "Why me?" To which the rabbi replied, "Why not you? When you amassed great wealth, did you ask, 'Why me?'"

My foray into commercial real estate development was only one more improbable occurrence in a life I had ceased trying to predict. I had relentlessly pursued financial success under the rationale that it provided a "better life" for myself and loved ones and bought me personal freedom. But in terms of achieving true success as a whole, integrated man, I was still Anita's unfinished project.

Now I felt oddly serene, perhaps due to my improved spiritual practice which I had maintained since the retreat, or maybe attributable to the enhanced perspective one attains at 61 years of age or to some undetectable biochemical reaction in my brain. I had nearly walked away from the business life when Anita passed a decade earlier but for loyalty to my partner and the ever-present lure of adventure. But now I asked: *Will my legacy be no more than a series of real estate deals?* The juice no longer sustained me.

The BART train was crammed at peak morning commute. Pressed by the throng, I tumbled out at Montgomery Street Station and promptly jogged to the escalator, up the fast lane, through the turnstile, and into the open air. At Starbucks, I joined the orderly queue of young men and women clad in the tech uniform of black jackets, tees, jeans, and sneakers. When suits fell out of favor in the Financial District, I briefly considered adopting the "dress like you don't care" style (having still maintained my college body size) but quickly opted for polos and khakis after calculating that the Silicon Valley prole garb cost more than my formal attire.

I proceeded up Montgomery Street with half-caf in hand and hung a left on Bush Street, counting sixty paces before trudging up the stairs to the headquarters of Urban Realty. I poked my head into Dave's office and found my partner obscured by piles of documents. He motioned me in, and I gently shut the door. Only my wife knew what I was about to do.

"Dave, it's been a fun ride," I said.

He regarded me quizzically.

"It's time for me to get out of the game."

He shook his head in frustration and sadness. He knew me so well—the years of reading a partner in tense situations with high stakes—that he didn't ask for an explanation or even attempt to haggle.

"When?"

"We'll finish out 799 Market and close our business with Commonfund and then dissolve our partnership. But effective today, I won't be involved in any new projects that Urban Realty takes on—it's all yours."

Dave regarded me squarely.

"You can have my shares and the rights to the name," I said, musing on the weeks of deliberations leading to *Urban Realty Co., Inc.* (we even offered a reward to colleagues who might come up with a winner) and the ensuing, nail-biting legal search for copycats.

"You sure about that?" he asked. The standard industry practice for partnership dissolutions was to vigorously renegotiate each and every point of a long-forgotten agreement thick with dust. But I felt bad walking out on Dave and refrained from pursuing any financial gain from claims on the goodwill or prospective deals.

"Yeah, and you don't have to worry about me competing with you."

"So what are your plans?"

"I have no idea."

We broke legal ground by engaging one attorney to represent us both with the aim of avoiding the protracted combat fundamental to both partnership and marital dissolutions as well as minimizing legal fees, surprisingly unaffected by the Great Recession. The attorney admitted to never being asked to do such a thing and remained uncomfortable even after we executed numerous conflict waivers. On most points, we directed him to fill in whatever was normative in the market or commercially reasonable. Finally, he gravely announced that consideration must be paid for my shares; I demanded ten dollars, and Dave quickly agreed.

Finis.

I had earlier discussed the matter with Ginger, who accepted without fanfare my decision to quit, after I assured her that we had enough to live on for a while. She had softened her stance to a degree as the Great Recession cloaked much of the world and the hard-luck anecdotes of colleagues abounded. And surprisingly, she conceived her own strategy.

One morning, as I fumbled with a pot of coffee, eyes half shut, Ginger bounded into the kitchen and blurted, "Let's move!"

"Huh?"

"Let's move!"

"Where?"

"To Texas!"

"Texas?!"

"I've got friends in Dallas," Ginger said, "and I can be closer to my sons."

"Well—"

"And it's way cheaper, and we can get a McMansion—"

"I don't know about *that*."

"And Tuttie can run free," Ginger pleaded. We had just adopted a dog at the Alameda County Fair named Tuttie Fruttie, who was fast becoming a surrogate child and whose name we dared not change lest she suffer an identity crisis.

Such a move—unthinkable on its face—would be met with derision by the progressive liberal community that constituted most of the Bay Area. While conceding that one could buy a better home for a fourth of the price, they could not imagine any other reason to consider the Lone Star State.

After cursory research, I discovered a number of economic and demographic similarities between the two states, which culturally were light-years apart.[52] I called several business associates who either lived or invested in Texas, and they laughed at my questions, assuring me that the major cities were in fact quite cosmopolitan, with robust transportation, health care, and other infrastructure.

Candidly, I needed to sell myself less on Texas than accept my disillusionment with California. I deliberated whether my reflections were that of a grumpy old man, befuddled and confused in the face of sweeping social change, and determined that I still possessed clarity of thought and the ability to judge objective reality.

I then evoked the memory of driving across the Bay Bridge at twilight in 1973, my trunk packed with my worldly belongings, gazing at the San Francisco skyline and the incredible opportunity that awaited me. Had I turned into an ingrate? No, I concluded that I had contributed at least as much as I got and was therefore qualified to hold an opinion.

I conferred with my ex-protégé, Steve, who left Cushman & Wakefield shortly after my exodus. He moved to LA and achieved prosperity running a one-man brokerage, and then married Beatrice, a Haitian woman, which union produced two offspring, one of whom is my godson. Steve confided that they would soon be moving from Laurel Canyon to Pasadena. Like San Francisco, the culture of the Westside had run amok, and no, I wasn't crazy.

The Bay Area had swollen into a technology and financial services behemoth, growing by more than 50 percent in population, altering the conduct of human affairs throughout the world, and becoming the domicile of unimaginably wealthy people. Yet this success came, as success is wont to do, at a cost, not only the oft-mentioned exorbitant housing prices and unmitigated traffic congestion, but a deterioration in overall life quality for many inhabitants.

Over the decades, California had become a one-party state, and San Francisco and Oakland one-party cities. Without the tension of opposition, a progressive orthodoxy asserted increased control over more and more aspects of peoples' lives, driving out those who either disagreed or couldn't afford it. San Francisco now led the nation with the lowest share of households with children. Oakland suffered a continuing loss of its black population, harking back to 1960s levels.

By 2010, the Oakland police force had been decimated,[53] perhaps on the theory that the rule of law inhibited social progress. At a neighborhood watch meeting, a cop from the racially diverse police force privately confided to me, "If you face a real threat in your home, call the fire department— they'll respond in a few minutes, but we may not get there for a while." I later winced as I watched these dedicated men and women humiliated by their own administration in the Occupy Oakland protests.

But perhaps the most telling incident for me involved Walter Hoye, a soft-spoken black pastor concerned with the impact of abortions on the black community.[54] Accompanied by two elderly parishioners, he saw fit to peacefully protest a for-profit Oakland abortion clinic. Predominantly older white women shielded him from talking to predominantly young black women, and later, with a complicit administration, aggressively fostered his arrest and incarceration.

I tried to avoid thinking about thorny issues such as abortion, but the case intrigued me on free speech grounds. I studied the filings and talked to the attorneys and concluded that his rights had been egregiously violated by the City of Oakland. Apparently, tolerance did not extend to diversity of thought or speech. Civic actions once unthinkable had become commonplace.[55]

I finally concluded that little anchored me to the Bay Area except family. Natalie had just given birth to daughter Tenaya at Kaiser Hospital in Oakland, as she had with Dasan and as Wanda had with her. I studied the *ashrama*, the four stages of human life in Hindu tradition: student, householder, retiree, and renunciate. I realized that with the birth of my grandchildren, I provisionally qualified to enter the third stage of *Vanaprastha* or "forest dweller," whereby an individual retires to a forest hut and engages in nonmaterial pursuits in preparation for the final stage of total renunciation and the realization of *dharma*.

Upon further examination, I found I met the other criteria for this transition: All of the children had established lives of their own, and I had discharged my social and professional responsibilities. I thus fulfilled the preconditions of *Vanaprastha* and resolved to become a forest dweller in the solitude and isolation of the Texas plains amid mesquite and sagebrush.

Except that I had one last obligation to first fulfill, a journey that I had repeatedly planned and canceled over the years and which grew more urgent as living witnesses disappeared and, with them, the truth told firsthand.

After meticulous preparation, I flew to Ukraine.

CHAPTER 23

The Bloodlands

Blocking the sun with my hand, I glanced up at the bronze statue of a bewhiskered gentleman who gestured to me broadly. On May 27, 2011, I stood on Ukrainian soil for the first time. I thought it fitting to pay homage to the most famous Ukrainian: Taras Shevchenko, a nineteenth-century poet, writer, painter, public figure, and the father of Ukrainian literature. He lorded over me and the central square in Lviv, the largest city in Western Ukraine.

Travel to Ukraine prior to the collapse of the Soviet Union in 1991 was pointless. The visitor's itinerary would be tightly regulated and any contact with locals scrutinized by the KGB. I had planned a trip in the 1990s with my parents, who were decidedly less excited than I'd been; they might have found a relative or two and perhaps would have extolled the virtues of America without the worry of reprisal by the Soviets. But Dad succumbed to a stroke, and then Mom announced her cancer.

Ginger initially planned to come but then began having doubts. "What's it like over there?" she asked. I checked the usual travel advisories and found isolated instances of violence by xenophobic fringe elements against foreigners of all stripes—including highly visible black folk—not uncommon in the former Soviet states. "The data's a little sketchy," I said, "but it's probably real." Ginger wished me bon voyage.

Now it was day one of a journey I'd contemplated for more than two decades. Glancing around the square, I inhaled the cultural richness of Lviv, especially the magnificent churches dating back to the thirteenth century. However, this was no sightseeing trip. I had come to uncover my parents' past. They were both born in 1922 near Ternopil, a medium-sized city about eighty-five miles east of Lviv, and lived there until 1944 when they fled to points unknown until materializing two years later in an Austrian refugee camp after the end of World War II.

I reasoned that if I could locate their birthplaces and other sites of consequence, if I could talk to living witnesses, if I could visualize historic scenes, if I could hold the rich black earth and feel the ghosts, then I would know my parents better and so myself.

As I strode briskly back to the hotel, I anticipated the evening event at the Ukrainian Catholic University. I had supported this institution since Pope John Paul II[56] blessed the cornerstone in 2001. The university was holding a fundraiser to honor benefactors at its burgeoning campus. Several of the graduate students had been instrumental in conducting advanced reconnaissance for my trip, traveling to Ternopil and cajoling the archivists to produce whatever information on the Sawas might have survived destruction during the War and subsequent Soviet suppression. Tonight, we would coordinate logistics for the days to come.

"Mr. Sawa, so nice to meet you."

Clad in jeans and wearing wire-rim spectacles, Taras escorted me into the banquet. I would soon discover that what seemed like every third Ukrainian man was named Taras. The crowd represented donors from Ukraine, Europe, and North America, as well as teachers and students, everyone clothed in a mix of casual and dressy dress but virtually all wearing traditional Ukrainian shirts or blouses.

"Please call me Martin," I replied. "Actually, please call me Markian, my real name." For some reason, my parents had christened me Markian but then never uttered the name again, instead pulling Martin out of the air, probably in an effort to speed up my assimilation. With my billowy white collarless linen shirt, hand-stitched with a pattern of brilliant red, gold, and green, I wallowed in my Ukrainian-ness.

Taras complied. "Mr. Markian, please to let me introduce Father Borys." Tall, balding, with a white beard, and ascetically thin, Borys Gudziak was a seminal force behind the reestablishment of the school as well as the reinvigoration of the church. Taras positioned me for a photo op and whispered that the priest would soon be elevated to bishop.

An attentive female student seated me at a table where I was presented with the cuisine of my youth: *borscht, varenyky* (pierogis), *nalysnyky* (crepes), and the like. I made small talk with an attorney visiting from Chicago until the tinkling of spoon against glass announced Father Borys at the mic. Surveying the audience, he spoke in flawless English.

"In the twentieth century, some 17 million inhabitants of Ukraine would be killed or die an unnatural death due to world wars and Soviet and Nazi extermination policies," he said, recounting how the communists confiscated church property; criminalized the Mass; and murdered, imprisoned, or exiled the priests, which only served to drive the church underground. I imagined how my parents might have huddled furtively in the forest with their neighbors while a priest distributed crumbs of bread as communion.[57]

"Under the Soviet Empire, the Ukrainian Greek Catholic Church was the largest illegal religious body in the world," Father Borys continued. "Per capita, no other church produced more martyrs during the Soviet era." He concluded by expressing his hope that the university would be a center for cultural thought and the formation of the new Ukrainian society based on human dignity.

As the crowd milled, I felt a tug on my sleeve.

"I will be your interpreter for trip," Taras said. "We will look for villages of your parents tomorrow. I have found capable driver."

"Another student?" I asked.

"No, Ivan . . . formerly Red Army. He has nice car, knows roads good."

I smiled. With no Cold War to fight, Ivan now fought traffic.

Upon exiting the hotel the next morning, I immediately spotted Taras and Ivan standing next to an aquamarine VW van. I had expected Ivan to sport a beer belly, bushy eyebrows, five o'clock shadow, and a Prima cigarette hanging from his lips. Instead, I found a tight-lipped, fit, neatly dressed man of my age. Extending my hand, I drew from my limited repertoire and wished him *dobry den.*

Taras cheerfully opened the door. "Mr. Markian, we will sit in back. I will show you my research."

We drove off into the summer sunshine along a busy two-lane highway, occasionally buffered from the rolling farmland by stands of ash and alder. I spontaneously decided to make a side trip that would cost us the better part of the day. I had heard of a town called Hrushiv, a speck on the map famed for a wee church that was the site of two Marian apparitions: one in 1914, which portended the rise of communism three years later, and the second in 1987, which presaged the fall of communism three years later. The latter apparition, repeated over a few weeks, drew hundreds of thousands of visitors and overwhelmed the KGB.

Ivan located the church with ease, and Taras and I admired the structure: a burnt sienna wooden octagon with a gold cupola. We entered a fabulously restored interior. The faithful placed offerings in a silver bucket suspended over a faux well. "What do you think?" I asked. Taras shrugged. "The Vatican did not approve this miracle, but who knows?" We crossed ourselves, made an offering, and quietly withdrew.

As we reached the outskirts of Ternopil well into the night, Taras spotted a hotel and motioned Ivan to pull in. We checked into our rooms and agreed to meet for breakfast. Although the hotel appeared to be recently built, it was constructed to the standards of a Motel 6 circa the 1960s with skinny walls, fickle HVAC, and temperamental plumbing. Too tired to object or hunt for food, I fell asleep.

I awoke ravenous, quickly dressed, and scooted to the restaurant for breakfast. Perhaps ten customers—all men—sat mutely or spoke in muffled tones as a solitary waitress stood impassively by the food service window. Spotting my comrades, I mouthed *"pryvit"* (hi) and sat next to Taras. I then politely asked the waitress for coffee, a gesture which she utterly disregarded. She continued to wait for a plate to be handed to her by an invisible cook.

Some ten minutes later, she brought coffee and took our orders without a word. A half hour later, she retrieved several plates from the window, only to deliver them to a couple of businessmen nestled in the corner. As the other customers continued to wait meekly, I couldn't restrain myself.

"Taras, why doesn't anybody *say* anything?" I fumed. Even Ivan, clearly a tough guy, smoked passively and looked away. Taras bowed his head.

"Mr. Markian, is different here, not like USA," he said. "People learn not to talk because it only produces trouble. KGB was always spying. Even children would denounce parents, send them to Siberia. Hard to change overnight.

"Ukrainians are very educated but very poor," he continued. "Average person makes $150, maybe $200 for a month. Old joke about the communists—they pretend to pay us, and we pretend to work—still true. We are trying."

I felt awful. I knew times were tough here, but not in any real-world sense. The dissolution of the Soviet Union forced Ukraine to move overnight from a planned, state-run economy to a market economy. Most of the population was plunged into poverty, while the rate of hyperinflation resembled that of Zimbabwe or the Weimar Republic.

Savvy entrepreneurs, often unabashedly criminal, aligned themselves with corrupt politicians to acquire newly privatized assets at cents on the dollar; I had read that the combined wealth of Ukraine's fifty richest oligarchs was estimated at 85 percent of Ukraine's GDP. As the economy slowly recovered after the millennium, it was hit again by the Great Recession, resulting in a state of affairs inconceivable to the average American.

"I'm sorry," I said. As Ivan stubbed out his cigarette, I glanced at my watch and motioned to Taras. "C'mon, let's hit the road. We can buy food on the way."

Ivan eased the van off the highway and we rumbled into the countryside. I calculated that for every mile of back road, we went back a century in time. Ivan halted for a horse-drawn, two-axle wooden wagon loaded with hay as the farmer, wearing a flat cap against the fierce sun, lightly applied the whip with reddened forearms. Unlike the privatization of land in the cities, the government of independent Ukraine prohibited the free transfer of most agricultural land, instead returning it to the peasants in small, typically four-acre plots; a number were leased to agricultural conglomerates, but many were still farmed individually. Life as my parents and their ancestors knew it had been freeze-dried.

"Aha, this is where Mrs. Sawa was born!" Taras announced as he pointed to a small sign that read "Kolodiivka." Ivan skillfully avoided the ruts as we pressed on, negotiating a sharp turn to find a wooden church built atop a small hill. In the middle of the day, a throng spilled out from the main entrance. "Is today a special feast day?" I asked. "No," Taras replied. "Farmers come like this every day, too many to fit inside." Pent-up demand, I reckoned.

Taras revealed his strategy. We would first talk to the village priest and explain our mission. We hoped he could introduce us to the oldest lucid resident, who might remember my mother's family and help identify her homesite. From his previous visit with the land cadastre official in Ternopil, Taras had a rough idea of the location, but of course names and ownership had changed after the War and again after independence in 1991.

Having blessed the faithful and shed his vestments, the priest led us along a dirt path to a dilapidated masonry house topped with a corrugated metal roof. A sturdy babushka, white scarf tied neatly under her chin, ventured out and greeted the padre. She listened intently to Taras and then disappeared inside. As chickens pranced around my legs, the woman produced a gaunt, frail old man.

Her father spoke of my mother's dad and believed him to be an artist of some kind, who along with most villagers disappeared during the War. He slowly led us down another path to a wildly overgrown lot with the collapsed remains of a small stone house. Taras studied his notes and then nodded excitedly. I beheld the ruins: This was it. I noticed a cluster of cornflowers triumphant among the weeds, and imagined my mother as a girl, running barefoot through the village and into the forest, picking berries and chasing butterflies.

I thanked the villagers profusely ("dyakuyu"), then trailed Taras and Ivan back to the van, grieving for my mother and her family and all the others whose innocence had been stolen when the ground opened and spewed epic evil. I have found it nearly impossible to communicate to native-born Americans the idea that, when your homeland—the ground upon which your house stands—is overrun from all directions by murderous strangers who pluck away those dearest to you, then everyone becomes your enemy, and no one can be trusted.

The next day, we set out to duplicate our success and locate my father's village in the hinterland north of Ternopil. Ivan followed his instincts, and Taras's eyes darted about as he searched for a sign announcing Synyagivka. After an hour, hopelessly lost, Ivan pulled over and simply sat in silence. With newly found patience, I contemplated our predicament until the lightbulb went on.

I reached into my duffel bag and extracted a new Apple iPhone 4. I had resisted smartphones and other gadgets— equipped with superior intelligence and supplied with more virtual friends than I cared to have—but finally capitulated and bought the Apple model the day before my trip, reasoning that I could save space by not having to pack a separate cell phone, camera, and voice recorder.

"Let's stretch our legs," I said.

We tumbled out of the van and were promptly smacked by the white sun. Gathering under the canopy of a lone oak tree amid golden fields of wheat, we huddled around the device as if discovering fire. Amazingly, I obtained service and navigated to the map icon and descended on Ukraine. Taras and Ivan studied the map and debated for several minutes before finally achieving consensus. "No such village," Taras said. "We go back to Ternopil and ask questions."

We feared that the village had been wiped off the planet during the War but instead discovered that it had been merged with an adjoining hamlet in a municipal downsizing. The locals pointed us in the right direction and we arrived, dusty and excited. Again, the priest extended his hospitality and volunteered to introduce us to the village elder. But he first insisted we tour the church.

Inside, I whispered to Taras, "This is beautiful . . . the intricate carvings, the gold plating, the illustrated dome . . . How can these poor people afford it?" Taras whispered to the priest and translated his response: "All the faithful helped. The artisans gave their time and the farmers their labor. They restored church to its rightful glory." Stripped of identity and meaning by the communists, the village had rebounded with fervor.

We met the elder, over 90 years old but displaying amazing vigor; oddly, he sported a neatly pressed, pale-blue dress shirt rather than farm clothes. The man immediately led us to another abandoned plot of dense overgrowth and engaged in protracted discourse with Taras. "His father knew your grandpa well," Taras said. "He was appreciated by local community for his teaching practice." I prodded Taras to inform him my parents were married in Ternopil in 1943, both 21 years of age. The old man nodded. "Young people would leave village to work in city and then fall in love."

"What was it like then?" I asked stupidly. He shook his head: "Very bad. Last months of German occupation. Many Ukrainians already sent to labor camps in Germany. Red Army would come, destroy Germans and destroy Ternopil." As Taras translated, he met my gaze and stated, "Your grandfather was very smart. Probably helped resistance underground. He surely taught son (my father) how to survive."

The subsequent days found us sleuthing for relatives as we pursued leads among the grim apartment blocks of central Ternopil. We eventually found a man pottering around a garden attached to a modest house on the city's perimeter whom Taras believed to be a third cousin.

As Taras explained who I was, the man remained expressionless and made no effort to invite us inside. He remarked that a first cousin who would be much more useful to me had moved to Siberia a few years ago, and after that, their communication ceased. With not much more to say, I nodded to Taras, gratefully thanked the man, and left.

That evening, I bid Taras and Ivan farewell. I had accomplished more than I had expected. In a few more years, no one would be alive to provide a firsthand account. Witnessing the farmers huddled at the church, resilient in the face of hardship and suffering, I found a world far removed from California in the twenty-first century but perhaps more representative of humanity.

As Taras and Ivan returned to Lviv, I prepared for the second half of my trip, which would take place in Kyiv, the capital of Ukraine and one of the oldest cities in Eastern Europe. There I hoped to decipher the broader historical picture of "what happened."

My trek to Kyiv proved a triumph of miscalculation. In assessing my options, I determined that the 260-mile distance didn't warrant the brain damage of air travel. I likewise shunned train service, which still ran predominantly on the old Soviet nighttime schedules and where I would undoubtedly share hard seats at 3:00 a.m. with vodka-soused locals munching on *salo* (raw pig fat).

Taras had enthusiastically recommended *marshrutki*, or minibuses. I remarked that they sounded colorful and probably an excellent way to enjoy the landscape. I reckoned travel time using a US freeway standard and sealed the deal. What I discovered the next morning was a derelict twelve-passenger van that, instead of having been put to sleep or stripped of parts, had been merely retrofitted with more seats.

The passengers trudged aboard as the surly driver recited the house rules, none of which I could comprehend. Squashed next to a thick-necked individual, I hugged my duffel bag. I learned that there were only two scheduled stops of precisely 15 minutes each for a potty break. On the first, the driver pulled away as a frantic babushka burdened with bags stumbled behind. Only direct physical threats by several of the men caused the driver to stop and let her re-board. On the second stop, no one was late.

I balanced the guidebook on my bag and traced our route. The German horde had swept into the Soviet Union on June 22, 1941, in Operation Barbarossa, the largest military campaign in history. In a matter of weeks, the Wehrmacht had cut through Lviv, Ternopil, and Kyiv. The military casualties on the Eastern Front exceeded the body count for all the other battles of World War II—worldwide, combined. And these were themselves exceeded by the civilian deaths. Hitler redefined the concept of total war, and Stalin returned the favor, with both invoking primeval animosities and atavistic impulses with unprecedented savagery.

Of especial cruelty was the "Holocaust by Bullets." Immediately after securing a predominantly Jewish village, the Nazis would organize the extermination of the local population, typically by marching men, women, and children to excavated pits where they were stripped naked and summarily shot. Rape and other atrocities were freely exercised along the way. Then the synagogue and the rest of the town were burned to the ground. As we motored through the countryside, I recounted the place names . . . Brody, Berdychiv, Drohobych, Rivne . . . and now observed that sunflowers flourished where once shtetls had bloomed.

Some nine hours later, the marshrutki disgorged its passengers onto the streets of the capital. I checked into the Dnipro Hotel at the foot of Khreschatyk Street—an eight-lane boulevard dubbed the Champs-Élysées of Kyiv—and stumbled to my room, where I fell on the bed and slept deeply.

The next morning I awoke to the sound of sirens. Drawing open the drapes, I observed that the Hotel Ukrayina, a State-built relic from the Khrushchev era situated on the opposite side of the plaza, was on fire.

As black smoke poured out from the upper floors, I decided I might as well get up in the event that they might evacuate the Dnipro as a precaution. Also, I had softened my stance and allowed myself a day of sightseeing before attending to more serious matters, and the morning was already slipping into midday. Grabbing my valuables, I hastened downstairs and located a taxi loitering in the parking lot outside the hotel lobby. Amid the swirl of fire trucks and emergency vehicles, I hopped in.

"I'm late for a meeting with Akhmetov," I joked, making eye contact with the cabbie—a sanguine, clean-shaven young man—via the rearview mirror. "Do you know the way to his house?"

The cabbie nodded. "Of course, I go there all the time. He asks for my advice." Rinat Akhmetov was Ukraine's reigning oligarch, the *capo dei capi*.

"My name is Markian. You are . . . let me guess . . . Taras?"

"Ha-ha, you are funny man. I am Ihor."

"If you promise not to charge too much, I need a driver for the day."

"*Miy druh* (my friend), I give you my special rate saved for Americans."

I chose to first visit the Caves Monastery, a system of underground passages first occupied over a millennium ago by the monk Anthony, a solitary hermit. Dodging a gauntlet of babushkas hawking figurines and other religious tchotchkes at the entrance, I descended in a procession of locals and tourists all holding small candles, navigating the narrow passageways and a multitude of steps.

The locals deftly maneuvered through the dim corridors occasionally punctuated by relics affixed to the walls; the hefty European and American tourists, not so easily. Peeking into earthen spaces that served as sleeping rooms and chapels, I marveled at human resiliency but was glad to finally exit.

"Ihor, let's go visit the world's deepest subway station," I said as we pulled away from the Caves. Did I have a fetish for the subterranean? As we motored along Lavrska Street, I asked, "Are your parents from Kyiv?"

"No, Odessa. My mother is still there. My father disappeared when I was young; he liked vodka more than family."

"I notice most Ukrainian women are very attractive but do not smile much."

"Not much to smile about. My mother is gynecologist and makes less money than truck driver. The State still runs health care system. Most doctors are women . . . and poor."

In minutes, we reached Arsenalna Metro Station. Entering the unremarkable surface vestibule, I purchased a ticket with difficulty, and then proceeded to the polished escalator that disappeared down an arched tunnel for an interminable duration. Brightly illuminated advertising on small LED displays flashed by regularly and broke my trance.

At last, I discerned the platform below, only to discover it was merely a landing that led to another escalator. Some five minutes later, I reached bottom, precisely 346 feet below the surface. Feeling totally disconnected from the world above, unlike in any other subway station, I quickly hopped on the up escalator and eventually resurfaced.

Ihor and I spent the rest of the day driving by famous cultural sites. I noticed the occasional new high-rise office building dwarfing its neighbors, and reflexively tried to estimate its size (straining to convert feet to meters) and the rents necessary to amortize construction costs (gamely attempting to convert US dollars to hryvnia, which had replaced the accursed Soviet ruble). We returned to downtown Kyiv at dusk, driving past a TGI Friday's and a McDonald's, and then the Maidan—the central square popularized internationally by Ukraine's "Orange Revolution" in 2005—before arriving at the Dnipro.

Firefighters and *militsiya* (police) were completing mop-up operations at the Ukrayina, now a darkened hulk. I advised Ihor that I would be attending a performance of the

Stars of the Bolshoi Ballet at the National Opera House that evening, but a walk would do me good. We agreed to meet the next day.

It was Sunday morning and therefore time for Mass; since the retreat, I attended regularly on Sundays and holy days. I had located St. Alexander Cathedral several blocks away and expected a monumental edifice such as St. Sophia or St. Michael's, the spectacular cathedrals of the Eastern Orthodox Church.[58] Instead I found a modest pastel-yellow structure with four white Doric columns framing a portal introduced by a flight of eighteen stone steps.

I slipped in quietly, as Mass had already started, and seated myself near the rear. I noticed eight black congregants sitting together several pews forward, more than I had noticed in total since stepping off the plane. Aha! Perhaps I could engage them and learn of their experience firsthand.

While the faithful filed out at the conclusion of the service, I treaded down the steps and approached the group of young men and women chaperoned by an older man blessed with a kind face devoid of any wrinkles.

"Hi, excuse me, sir, do you speak English?" I asked.

He nodded.

"I'm American, visiting Ukraine for the first time," I said. "I am interested as to how people from other countries find it here."

He glanced about to determine if I was alone and then gauged my sincerity. "These are Catholic students from

Nigeria on a scholarship program. I help them adjust, get around."

"Yes, you have many Christians in Nigeria.[59] What's it like for them here?"

"They get a very good education for a low cost. However, they must be cautious. Most Ukrainians are respectful, but the skinheads will do them harm. During the day, we travel in groups. Rarely do we go out at night, and certainly never alone."

"Do you notify the police?"

"Of course, but they look the other way or say, 'Oh, it's just a few hooligans.'" By now, the students had clustered around us.

"That is not good."

He shrugged. "You seem to know a little about Nigeria, so you know that the persecution we suffer as Catholics in our own country from Boko Haram and others is much worse." Eyeing his charges, he said, "I tell them: Wherever you go, be strong in your faith."

Exhausting all ten of the essential Ukrainian phrases I had committed to memory, I beamed encouragement to the students and then returned to the hotel where my tour guide patiently waited.

"Ihor, take me to Babi Yar."

We drove to the historic Lukyanivka neighborhood northwest of downtown and pulled curbside next to a heavily wooded, twenty-seven-acre park. I left Ihor and joined the others who strolled along the rustic paths. Occasionally, a visitor would stop at a memorial plaque and whisper prayers.

On September 29–30 of 1941, *Einsatzgruppe C*, one of the Nazi paramilitary death squads that followed the

German army, murdered 33,731 Jews in the largest shooting massacre of the Holocaust. The victims were herded into a ravine known as Babi Yar and executed as they lay naked upon the already dead. Over the subsequent months, the Nazis murdered another 100,000 Ukrainians—partisans, POWs, Roma, patients of mental hospitals, and other unfortunates—in like manner.

Two years later, the Red Army repelled the Germans at Stalingrad, the bloodiest battle in the history of warfare, and drove them westward across the Great Steppe back toward Berlin. In an effort to conceal their atrocities before retreating from Kyiv, the Nazis forced prisoners to exhume and burn all the corpses at Babi Yar and scatter their ashes to the four corners, an exercise efficiently repeated at other extermination sites and death camps.

While rock pigeons and turtledoves flitted among stands of towering birch, I perambulated past flower beds planted with salvia and roses and tried to grasp the enormity of this depravity by imagining all the souls who had passed into and out of the soil. Were any of the victims related to my family? Perhaps some were acquaintances of my grandparents? But just as language proved inadequate to describe the event, so too did my thoughts in trying to connect with the victims.

I returned to the taxi and sat quietly for a moment, as did Ihor, who undoubtedly had ferried passengers here countless times.

"Now, Ihor, let's go to the Holodomor Victims Memorial."

The word Holodomor translates from Ukrainian as "death by hunger" and refers to an act of genocide perpetrated by Joseph Stalin. The dictator orchestrated the starvation of some six million men, women, and children in the period 1932–33, at the same time Hitler was appointed chancellor in Germany.[60] Stalin ordered the confiscation of the grain harvest *and even the seeds* from Ukrainian peasants and used it as currency to advance his first five-year plan, as well as to suppress a nascent Ukrainian independence movement.

Stalin's propaganda and denial of the famine were parroted by Western journalists and intellectuals, most notably Walter Duranty and the *New York Times*. As Moscow Bureau Chief and Stalin's most useful idiot, Duranty was fully aware of the calamity in progress but instead painted a rosy picture. Unrepentant years later, he even defended Stalin's show trials, remarking, "You can't make an omelet without breaking eggs."

For the next sixty years until the dissolution of the Soviet Union and the subsequent unearthing of classified records, the Holodomor remained the greatest genocide that no one had heard of. The Holodomor was officially recognized by the Ukrainian Parliament in 2006 and the memorial completed two years later.

As Ihor dropped me off to wander about, I first noticed the verdant setting, nestled on a high bank overlooking the Dnieper River, which bisects Kyiv and the whole of Ukraine into west and east. Seated on a bench, an old man—face as red as a Ukrainian beet with wild white hair and a luxuriant handlebar mustache—strummed a doleful song on his bandura. I seated myself next to him and contemplated the Candle of Memory, a one-hundred-foot-tall white monument. I then rose and lingered at the Hall of Memory, which documented the 14,000 towns and villages that suffered through the catastrophe.

But the most poignant reminder was a bronze statue of an emaciated young girl clutching a handful of wheat, guilty of the crime of picking up remnant grain left after reaping, punishable by immediate execution. I realized I had no visceral concept of the horror of mass starvation, when people first ate leaves and grass, and then dirt, and then, at times, one another's dead bodies.

"Have you seen enough today?" Ihor asked as we pulled away from the memorial.

"Yes, I have seen enough. For today and many days." I reflected for a moment. "Ihor, what do you think of America?"

"I have comrade who lives in Los Angeles, in Hollywood area. He says not like we see in movies."

I smiled.

"My *gido* (grandfather) thinks Americans are spoiled babies. He says when some bandits knock down a few buildings with airplanes, your president tells citizens to go shopping."

Couldn't argue.

"But I would still like to move there someday . . . that is dream of many Ukrainians."

Back in the room, as I packed for my morning flight home, I thought of Mom, who demanded I finish all the food on my plate at each and every meal and who filled the basement floor-to-ceiling with evidence of her material success. I thought of Dad, closed off emotionally and distrustful of all authority, both the left and the right. I thought of Grandpa, a staunch advocate of education as a bulwark against stupidity and gullibility. And of Grandma, devoutly religious.

I now realized that Ternopil lay at the epicenter of a geography that stretched from Berlin to Moscow, an area described by the historian Timothy Snyder as the "Bloodlands," the scene of the greatest mass murder of civilians in human history. I no longer resented my dad's silence and his unwillingness to talk of the past. He spared me melancholia that I in turn would surely have passed on to Natalie and others. I got it. Quite simply, the worst imaginable conditions the Sawas expected to encounter in their new homeland would infinitely surpass the best of times they had left behind.

CHAPTER 24

Success, Truly

Over the course of a single day in January 2012, Ginger and I toured fifteen homes in a swath across the suburbs of North Dallas. We had discussed other cities and neighborhoods in Texas and deemed this locale as the most cosmopolitan. I had engaged Scott, a local Realtor, to assist us. In the week preceding our trip, we discussed recent sales and identified properties that met our criteria.

Fourteen homes later, with the sun going down, Scott suppressed his frustration and maintained an enthusiastic demeanor. None of his carefully curated residences had excited Ginger, the final arbiter. I acceded to the husband's role in such matters and remained mute. He steadfastly drove us in a spacious BMW sedan to a development still under construction at the urban edge. We passed a golf course and artificial lake and zipped into a gated community, stopping at a newly constructed spec home.

"The builder is motivated to sell," Scott enthused as he fumbled with the lockbox. "They're starting the next phase and don't want to be carrying inventory."

As he opened the door, Ginger's eyes widened, beholding spacious rooms, high ceilings, hardwood floors, modern appliances, and a staircase reminiscent of an antebellum estate.

"I love it!" she squealed, charging past Scott and shouting out the features, drawing on her professional expertise as house manager.

"Ginger," I whispered in pursuit, "what did we agree to? 'Not showing you're interested'?"

My wife disregarded me, sweeping through all the rooms and visualizing the placement of furniture. "Ooh, Baby," she said. "This is it, this is home!"

I regarded Scott's cherubic glow; undoubtedly, he had already calculated his commission.

We evaluated the exterior in the near dark, at which point Scott noticed the sales manager for the homebuilder locking up the office down the street. In an unexpected display of athleticism, Scott sprinted to the manager, persuading him to turn the lights back on and then summoning us enthusiastically.

"Let me handle this," I muttered to Ginger as we approached the pair. I motioned Scott aside. "You know what these guys paid for the land and you know what their construction costs are," I said, "so what's their breakeven?" Scott estimated the price at which they would make no profit or perhaps lose money on this individual sale. The asking price was ridiculously cheap in comparison to California, but my natural instinct was to make the best deal possible.

The manager greeted us warmly. "So, y'all interested in our project?"

While Ginger pored through a picture book of the development and nearby amenities and Scott paced the room, I conferred with the manager in his private office with the door shut and blinds open. Scott probably watched the manager's face alternately brighten and frown amid the haggling. He likely saw me withdraw my checkbook and fill in the blanks and present the deposit. He undoubtedly witnessed the shaking of hands.

And just like that, the Sawas planted their flag on Texas soil, at a price substantially less than the cost of a cramped condominium apartment without parking in a mediocre neighborhood of San Francisco.

Tuttie Fruttie strained at the harness as I opened the front door of our new home and donned my Ray-Ban Wayfarers. A snow-white female Chihuahua/terrier mix, barely eleven pounds, Tuttie exhibited a split personality in accordance with her dual bloodline: a loving and loyal lapdog favoring Ginger inside the house, and a calculating and utterly fearless hunter in the outdoors. Barely thirty days in Dallas, Tuttie had acclimated totally.

We had let her run free but once, when she went hell-bent after a bobcat in the prairie beyond our backyard. Now, I kept her tethered on a thirty-foot leash to limit what she chased while allowing her to run down and almost catch rats, squirrels, or other small mammals to satisfy her prey instinct.

I did my best thinking on these morning walks with Tuttie before the business day started back in San Francisco, and thus, the demands on my time for 799 Market. Dave and I had just renegotiated the lease with Ross Stores at a much higher than anticipated rental rate in what would be the largest retail lease of the year in San Francisco. However, the walks were reserved for more consequential matters.

Tuttie insisted on always leading and yanked me along a path that meandered by the lake. Typically disinterested in birdlife, she abruptly stopped and stared in fascination at a magnificent egret, standing indolently in the still water.

Today, my thoughts focused on Ginger's son Tory. For years, I wondered whether I'd have had the guts to tough out life if dealt the same hand: a young black man, severely disabled and in constant pain, with no college degree, dependent on government assistance and our contributions. His perseverance had been an inspiration to me, but I doubt he knew it.

I had mentored healthy, college-educated young people eager to make a mark, barking at them across the sales floor and inuring them to the realities of the commercial real estate jungle. All I knew was tough love and the world of business. But Tory's situation was orders of magnitude harder. I had wondered what I could do for my stepson, especially from Dallas, that the best-meaning family could not.

After prolonged contemplation, Tuttie adjudged the bird more foe than friend and broke out in a dead run before the leash tautened and snapped her upright. The egret beheld the spectacle lethargically, then slowly lumbered into flight as Tuttie dragged me along the shoreline in vain pursuit.

On the fly, I had concocted a plan to persuade Tory to start his own business. I beta-tested the idea on Ginger, who replied, "What can I do to help?" No sissy mom, she had raised Tory with a firm hand but regularly admitted he could benefit from male influence. I convinced her this would be a guy thing, and she agreed not to get directly involved. Now, all that remained was Tory's buy-in.

Tuttie traced the egret's flight as it soared away into a speck. Not experiencing a twinge of defeat, she sniffed vigorously for the next object of relentless tracking.

I can't rightly recall how I discovered a Ukrainian Greek Catholic Church less than ten minutes from our house—perhaps a store clerk or other local mentioned it after I boasted of my ethnicity in passing. I excitedly informed Ginger, who was equally amazed that there might be Ukrainians in our midst. Raised Southern Baptist, she now practiced privately, kneeling nightly at her bed, hands clasped in prayer. I had been attending a Roman Catholic church but she urged me to go for it. I now cleared my calendar for Sunday Mass at St. Sophia's.

At 10:00 a.m., I drove up to a squat, community-center-type structure hidden in an older residential subdivision; the only religious ornamentation was a small gold cross mounted on a roof ridge peak. How incongruous and surreal! I parked in the paved lot amid a smattering of vehicles—normal cars with not one pickup sporting a gun rack—and leaned into the unrelenting Texas wind at a diagonal to the ground.

I stepped into a bland foyer, snatched a bulletin, and then entered the nave. The room exploded with forms and colors. Banners hand-stitched in traditional Ukrainian embroidery lined the entrances to the pews. The *iconostasis,* a spectacular hand-carved wood screen rising to the ceiling for the full width of the room, concealed the sanctuary from the nave; three royal doors furnished access and visibility. Icons depicting Christ, mother Mary, and the angels and saints blazed in the spectrum of hues.

Forty or so faithful sat quietly in the snug pews. I slipped in beside a woman and her daughter, both blonde. In my pew I discovered two booklets, one written in the Cyrillic alphabet in Old Church Slavonic and the other an English transliteration. As I perused the latter, a youthful bearded priest—whom I identified from the bulletin as the Reverend Father Pavlo Popov—entered the sacristy clad in a brilliant gold vestment and opened the service.

"*V myri Hospodovi pomolimsia.*" (*In peace let us pray to the Lord.*)

"*Hospody, pomyluy.*" (*Lord have mercy.*)

The Divine Liturgy is a serious matter: no musical instruments, no singing of traditional hymns, no hand shaking or back patting. The format follows a call-and-response between the priest and the faithful, alternating between English and Ukrainian. Saint John Chrysostom, the Archbishop of Constantinople, penned the words of the liturgy—effectively a litany of prayers—in the late fourth century AD.

Now a deacon emerged, vigorously swinging a censer, the chain clanging. The fragrant incense, the sonorous chanting, and the gentle supervision of the icons combined to create a hypnotic quality. Midway through the service, the priest stepped down to the first row of pews, scanned the flock, and delivered his homily:

"Today, I want to talk about icons, the windows to heaven." He explained that we do not worship images of wood and paint—we worship God alone. He emphasized that the icons are intentionally two-dimensional, not intended to portray what things looked like or to create a graven image but to show the spiritual reality and beauty of the person or event.

The faithful stood for most of the service; I noticed that even the children rarely fidgeted. The priest distributed communion in the traditional manner: a piece of bread soaked in wine and delivered with a small spoon. He addressed each person by name as they stood before him and politely asked mine.

"Markian," I said.

Father Popov concluded with more prayers, particularly invoking Mary, known by the title Theotokis. He then dismissed the congregants . . .

"*Slava tyebe hospodi.*" (*Glory to Thee, O Lord.*)

"*Amin.*" (*Amen.*)

. . . but not before they all sang "Happy Birthday" in Ukrainian and English to a grizzled parishioner; of course, I joined in.

I pulled out of the parking lot still a bit mesmerized. The entire scene reinforced a chain of belief that stretched through the centuries unaltered, a bedrock of faith stronger than the caprice of culture. I reflected on the lineage of Ukrainian Catholic priests—extremely courageous men in service to their faith—extending from the dawn of Christianity to the Siberian camps to Father Popov, tending his flock in an unlikely outpost in north Texas. The circle of my personal journey of faith had closed.

I had come home.

Southern heat and the smell of weed. Ginger and I traveled to Jackson that summer to visit her sons. We now sat on the steps of their apartment complex nestled among the longleaf pine on Jackson's north side, bullshitting with Tory and four of his homies in the evening ritual. Offered a joint and a Bud, I declined the former and accepted the latter.

"Miss Ginger, Tory talks 'bout you all the time," cackled one of the men.

"Yeah, I bet," Ginger said, eyes twinkling, grinding a spent Marlboro Light to dust.

As the banter continued, I stepped off the stoop and edged toward Tory's apartment around the corner. "Tory, got a minute?"

Tory regarded me quizzically, then rocked back on his wheelchair and deftly spun around. "And none of you MFs better hit on my mom," he tossed out over his shoulder, only half kidding.

"Naw, we scared a her," another man teased amid the guffaws.

Inside, the apartment that Tory shared with his brother resembled the aftermath of one of those twisters that rip through Mississippi this time of year. I created a space for myself on the couch. "Tory, I have an idea . . . "

"An idea?"

"How would you like to make some serious coin, upgrade your lifestyle?"

Tory rolled his eyes. "Really."

"You're savvy with computers. I know you help your friends out when they're having trouble—you can get paid for that."

"You mean like start my own business?"

"Exactly. It would have to be legitimate, of course—no hacking. Maybe something like computer advice and repair. Look, I've done this before, piece of cake."

Tory eyed me suspiciously.

"You're not really at a competitive disadvantage," I continued. "You can work out of your bedroom, for starters. Now of course, you'll have to do everything yourself. I'll be available by phone to offer opinions and suggestions, which you can accept or reject. And you'll have to bootstrap it. Maybe I'll chip in a few hundred bucks here and there, but I'm no VC."

"Why would you do this for *me*? I mean, what's in it for you?" he said.

"Look, it's either this or go shopping all day with your mom," I said and paused for a beat. "You can believe all the bullshit you've been told as to why you can't. Race? Doesn't matter. No college degree? Doesn't matter. Handicapped? Doesn't matter. All that matters is how bad you want it."

Tory scrutinized my intentions for the longest time. He slowly rolled to the door and nudged it open. Waves of laughter pealed from the steps, as Ginger was clearly enjoying the upper hand. Pushing out, he said, "I'll think about it."

Three days later, after Ginger and I had returned to Dallas, Tory texted his acceptance.

That fall, Ginger and I prepared for a visit from my daughter and her family. Natalie had recently been promoted to Director of Human Resources at the Native American Health Center, and Solis accepted a position as a social worker with Alameda County, dealing with foster youth and child abuse cases. Dasan started first grade, while Tenaya celebrated her first birthday.

I scooped them up at Love Field and proceeded home on the North Dallas Tollway. Naturally, the immediate topic of conversation was residential real estate and the four-, five-, and six-bedroom homes that could be acquired for a song. Ginger hugged all, and Tuttie Fruttie licked all except for Tenaya, who screamed in terror, much to Tuttie's chagrin.

We dedicated Saturday to exploring Natalie's roots, which we all deemed a priority over noted Dallas attractions such as the JFK Assassination Tour and the cattle drive at the Fort Worth Stockyards. For my daughter's 50 percent Ukrainian side, I arranged a morning visit with the Popovs. While I had shared with her photos and stories from my trip, I relied on the priest to speak authoritatively on matters Ukrainian.

"Markian, so good to see you," Father Popov said at the door of the rectory, which turned out to be a small apartment squeezed betwixt the church and a preschool. "Please," he said, motioning all of us to file in.

We met his lovely wife, who held their newborn and presented a gift of frozen pierogis. After gracious conversation, the priest led us back out, and soon Natalie found herself inside a Ukrainian Greek Catholic Church for the first time since her baptism thirty-four years earlier.

"Dasan, Saint Sophia had three kids, just like the Popovs," I said as my grandson eyed the iconostasis.[61] Father recounted growing up perhaps seventy-five miles from my parents' birthplace during the twilight of the USSR and then immigrating to America while studying for the priesthood as the Ukrainian diaspora in North America was experiencing a shortage of clergy.

Father Popov guided us around the diminutive church, interspersing anecdotes of Ukraine with an explanation of the symbology of the Byzantine Rite. As we prepared to leave, he knelt before Dasan. "This is a place where we meet God."

Next, we drove eighty miles north to delve into Natalie's 50 percent Native American side, arriving in Durant, Oklahoma, the headquarters of the Choctaw Nation.[62] Along the way, Natalie recounted the grim record of the Trail of Tears and the plight of her people, one of the so-called "Five Civilized Tribes." In the period 1831–33, approximately 17,000 Choctaws were forcibly removed from their ancestral homeland in the area of Mississippi and Alabama and relocated to what later became Oklahoma. Several thousand perished along the forced march.

We visited the tribal headquarters housed in an older three-story redbrick building, perhaps once a school or a hospital, surrounded by a manicured expanse of lawn that enhanced its stature. Most of the offices were closed on Saturday, but Nat recounted meeting the chief years ago when she drove him to appointments on his visit to the Bay Area and elaborated on the workings of the tribal council.

We discussed the route Grandma Carnes followed from nearby Antlers to Oakland during the War and then meandered around town visiting tribal enterprises. Eventually, we found our way to the Choctaw Casino and Resort, an AAA Four Diamond facility and the flagship of eight casinos and hotels operated by the tribe.

As we drove home mutely in the night, Dasan and Tenaya slept at their mother's side. On approaching Dallas, I admitted to Solis my surprise at discovering a substantial South Asian population in the north suburbs. "Real Indians," he laughed.

On the third day, we rested. Ginger prepared a gargantuan meal consisting of honey-baked ham, collard greens, red beans and rice, corn bread, peach cobbler, and half a dozen other items lost to memory but which certainly did not include chitlins, whose consumption—and more significantly preparation—I abhorred.

At the dining room table, we held hands as Dasan recited grace, softly mouthing the prayer composed by Solis's dad: "Thank you, Grandfather (God), for this day, for this life, and for this food. May it nourish our mind, spirit, heart, and body. Thank you for the animals, the plants, the water, and our ancestors. A-ho (Amen)."

Later sprawling on the sofa, I felt so fortunate to have watched my daughter not only exceed her parents but resolve that her children would do the same, continuing the immigrant dream. Treading the line between tradition and modernity, Natalie and Solis committed their careers to helping the less fortunate while staying true to their marriage vows and avoiding the pitfalls of materialism.

And I gave thanks for the diversity of experience I had found through my marriages and relationships. The willingness to see past the fictitious categories of "race" required constant effort, starting with an examination of what lay in my own heart. My approach was always to look the other squarely in the eye, mano a mano, to feel neither superior nor inferior, to treat him or her like a real person and not a mosaic of slogans honed on social media. A difficult enterprise to be sure, necessitating at times a deftness akin to that of a monk disarming a samurai.

"Flight attendants, prepare for takeoff."

Since moving to Dallas, I had flown back to San Francisco a number of times in connection with the 799 Market assignment, but this trip had an air of finality. In a surprise move, Commonfund advised us that perhaps it was time to sell the building, barely a year after we had cut our deal. We pleaded that, with the market rebounding, the value would only rise with the passage of time; however, they were anxious to exit the real estate business.

That afternoon, I would be meeting with Dave, Jim, and Stephen, the very broker who had urged us to sell 901

Market years before. Yet as the plane attained its cruising altitude, my attention focused not on real estate but on Tory. What started out as a crack at business mentorship now consumed much of my time and had become effectively a new adventure.

I had counseled Tory that to compete as an entrepreneur, he had to operate with a clear head. Over several months and with amazing grit, he had weaned himself off the meds and the reefer amid excruciating pain and without complaint, and now asked, "What's next?" I questioned whether I could have mounted such courage in the same situation. Impressed by Tory's determination, I committed wholeheartedly to the enterprise, wherever it might go and however long it might take.

He had already lined up gigs for his computer business when shit hit the fan one afternoon as I returned from walking Tuttie Fruttie.

"Have you talked to Tory today?" Ginger demanded, clearly upset.

"No, we have our regular call later tonight."

"Did you know he might have to go to the hospital?"

"Huh?"

"He had to move some computers and refused to ask for help, wanted to show them he was hard. He begged me not to tell you. Do you know he'll call me and tell me things and swear me to silence? Do you know how much he wants to please you?"

Stunned, I felt like a total asshole. "Baby, I never told him—"

"He's my *son*. Barely weighs a hundred pounds . . . You want him to kill himself?" Ginger sobbed. I embraced her in silence and then slunk into the study where I interrogated myself: *How badly is he hurt? Should I pull the plug on the venture?* I nervously hit the speed dial.

"Hey," Tory answered weakly.

"You . . . uh . . . okay?"

"Yeah . . . just need to take a little time off," he offered gamely. Tory recounted that he was on a contract government job—a significant assignment that could lead to more engagements—when he forced himself to physically relocate a dozen oversized CPUs, somehow lifting or dragging them.

Relieved that he would recover, I refrained from reprimands as I imagined that he had proven himself a man. With moist eyes, I framed my response in pragmatic terms. "Look, Tory," I said, "your health comes first. You don't want to be taken out of the action and placed on injured reserve. All prudent business owners need to revisit their business plan periodically, and this seems like the right time, so get your rest and then we'll strategize."

As much as I had derived satisfaction from negotiating mega real estate deals, it did not equal the satisfaction I felt at Tory's strength of will and budding success. I sensed his would be the more improbable story, the greater reinvention, the more inspiring fulfillment of hope. I reclined my seat and dozed off.

"Please make sure your seat backs and tray tables are in their full upright position," intoned the flight attendant.

I yawned and shifted to business mode as the plane banked for its approach to SFO, and played out "what-if" scenarios in my head.

"The market is recovering faster than anyone predicted," Stephen said, "and 799 Market will attract a lot of attention."

I entered the meeting in the conference room of Urban Realty ten minutes late as Dave and Jim pored over a market study furnished by Stephen. Quickly shaking hands with all, I sat next to Dave and tried to read the broker's body language.

"How's that?" Jim asked.

"With the Ross lease extended and their A credit, there's little risk for the investor."

"Who's the buyer?" Dave queried.

Stephen paused. "A domestic or offshore institutional fund with a long view. They'll pay up to be in San Francisco. They've been through cycles before and know whatever they have to pay now, they'll have to pay more later."

We silently digested the remarks. Finally, I asked the obvious.

"So the number is . . . what?"

The broker hesitated. Too low and he wouldn't get the business; too high and the property would languish. Dave and I held our breath—was it worth more than the negotiated baseline value of $70 million in our agreement with Commonfund?

"Of course, we would recommend going out without an asking price," Stephen said, "but in terms of the, uh . . . *guidance* . . . let's say $80 to $85 million."

While Jim betrayed approval, I remained expressionless and asked many more questions and then thanked Stephen for his presentation. The number was frankly higher than any of us expected, and for Urban Realty, good enough. A week later, we signed the listing agreement.

The marketing flowed without incident. Technology had streamlined the vetting process, and we allowed prospective purchasers to peruse relevant documents in the now virtual war room. Stephen called for initial offers and then mercilessly egged on the high bidders to improve their price. Our reaction went from pleasant surprise to shock: The winning bid came in at $93.5 million.

For the next three weeks, we waited for the inevitable "haircut"—a buyer's request for a price reduction attributable to deficiencies uncovered during the due diligence process—which never came. The deal closed on October 19, 2012.

Dave and I split Urban Realty's share of the profit and formally dissolved our partnership. I no longer had to worry about how I would pay the bills for the foreseeable future.

Now it was time to live.

Epilogue

The story ends when I say it ends.

However, in real life as opposed to reel life, the movie keeps on playing. To satisfy the curious . . .

Over a two-year period, Tory overcame his inner voices and conventional wisdom. After running his own business, he accepted a position with my former employer, CB Commercial, now the largest commercial real estate services firm in the world, and without any intervention on my part. As a remote troubleshooting computer technician, he later garnered industry awards, achieved a financially and physically independent lifestyle, and bought a new house. The obstacles he faced and overcame—when everything possible that could go wrong did go wrong—would render most rags-to-riches stories paltry.

Natalie assumed the reins of the Native American Health Center as CAO, guiding the organization in expanded health care programs and even real estate development projects, while Solis continued his social work with a private foundation. Dasan was recently admitted to St. Joseph Notre Dame High School and awarded the school's Presidential Scholarship for merit. And Tenaya's athletic prowess and tenacity cause even adults to murmur. "She's on a whole different level," Natalie confesses.

Wanda died from a stroke. As with Charlotte, it was not until later in life that she was clinically diagnosed with schizophrenia and bipolar disorder, labels that belatedly served to explain the anger and mood swings that destroyed our relationship. I assisted the family with the arrangements and obit and delivered a eulogy.

I continue to keep close tabs on my other stepchildren— David, Alice, Sonja, and Napoleon— offering support and occasionally garnering snippets of family information. Being off the grid, I miss what they share on social media, but consider it a small price to pay for avoiding manipulation by algorithms and lines of code conceived by a cadre of young men, clever but not yet wise.

My business partner, Dave, suffered a horrific boating accident only months after we parted ways. A 500-passenger ferry rammed his twenty-two-foot motorboat on San Francisco Bay, instantly killing a companion and leaving him with injuries too numerous to recount. The doctors attributed his amazing recovery to his vegan diet. We stayed in touch for several more years until my emails went unanswered.

CityPlace was eventually built—true to our design—by a subsequent owner. The impact on the neighborhood proved inconsequential, as the problems of the Tenderloin radiated out to the city at large. While gleaming new office and residential towers sheltered perhaps the most privileged demographic in human history, at street level, nervous techies and tourists navigated a politically induced dystopia of brazen crime, discarded syringes, human feces, and unsupervised, makeshift encampments of the addicted, the mentally ill, and the dispossessed.

Napata, unfazed by age and following the tradition of many black American chanteuses, spent more and more time in Paris. Glen died in Las Vegas from natural causes. After the memorial service, the celebrants gathered at Cynthia's house, where late into the evening, his homies segregated themselves from the women, children, and other mourners and slipped into the garage. We drank and acted out stories of Glen and Oakland in its day and laughed ourselves to tears.

Tuttie Fruttie reached my age in dog years but has missed nary a step, still chasing fleet black squirrels halfway up trees. I tested her dog DNA, which revealed Chihuahuan ancestry but, astonishingly, no terrier, causing me to again reflect on the vagaries of ethnic identification.

Ginger and I divorced in 2014. Our relationship did not end but merely transmuted into another form. In the ensuing years, we lived apart in various cities and talked every night, tried at times to reconcile, but couldn't, and without any spoken agreement, remained faithful to each other. Physically united again, and still lovin' and fussin', we are giving it another shot.

Every morning, I look in the bathroom mirror, and if I see myself, it's a good day. I count my blessings and express immense gratitude to the Big Guy and marvel at the fortune of my life. I still wander among the tombstones and reflect on the impermanence of that which we hold most dear as I prepare for the life of the world to come.

And Anita? Rest assured she is doing just fine.

Notes

1   Alice Carnes moved to Oakland from Oklahoma during World War II. In the early 1950s, the Bureau of Indian Affairs encouraged Native Americans to leave the reservation and assimilate with the general population in large cities. With the help of the Quakers, Mrs. Carnes founded the Intertribal Friendship House in 1955, one of the first American Indian Community Centers in the nation, to assist these new arrivals.

2   Its cinematic appeal was shared by a young filmmaker from Modesto who had just released a surprisingly popular movie called *Star Wars* and shot several scenes in Death Valley, deeming it a suitable approximation of an alien landscape.

3   Over a twenty-year period, the City of San Jose completed 1,377 annexations, expanding helter-skelter throughout the Santa Clara Valley, accommodating developers who replaced orchards with subdivisions and high-tech campuses in a region dubbed by a journalist "Silicon Valley," an allusion to the chemical element used in the fabrication of integrated circuits.

4   The aboriginal population was reduced first by the Spanish and Mexican occupation and then nearly extinguished by the Anglo conquest after the Gold Rush. Due to disease, reduction of the food supply, massacre, and overall culture shock, California Indians were almost rendered extinct, leaving perhaps 20,000 souls from disparate small tribes at the turn of the twentieth century, who were ceded what was assumed to be worthless land. These survivors included the ancestors of David and Alice on their father's side, who resided at the Elem

Indian Colony of Pomo Indians on the east shore of Clear Lake in Northern California.

5   A large tidal lagoon designated in 1870 as America's first official wildlife refuge, Lake Merritt constitutes the heart and soul of Oakland.

6   I spoke with Mohamed several times in the ensuing weeks as he was drawing up plans for the house, and then our communications ceased for no specific reason other than the divergence of life paths.

7   The personal seal used to sign documents, art, and other paperwork in lieu of a signature. Dating back to the Shang Dynasty in 1600 BC, chops are still used for certain official purposes and in informal contexts.

8   Powwows are typically gatherings of people from a variety of tribes, with structured programs and cash prizes, as compared to Big Times, the much smaller get-togethers for individual California tribes.

9   The movie spawned a number of imitators, such as *Boiler Room, The Wolf of Wall Street,* and even its own sequel, *Wall Street: Money Never Sleeps.* In the highly subjective opinion of this writer, none came close to the original.

10 A few brokers had started to carry portable cellular phones for just such emergencies; however, the phones were very expensive and resembled infantry walkie-talkies, and I found them . . . well . . . rude.

11 At its height, the famed venue on the outskirts of San Francisco hosted the Beatles' final concert, as well as a Papal Mass celebrated by Pope John Paul II; the Giants, and later the 49ers, left for new arenas, and the structure was eventually demolished.

12 Ultimately, sixty-three deaths for the entire Bay Area were attributed to the Loma Prieta earthquake, of which forty-two

occurred in Oakland with the collapse of the Cypress Structure of the Nimitz Freeway.

13 Noted alumni included Vicente Fox, the future president of Mexico; George Wendt, the actor who later portrayed Norm on *Cheers*; Leo Ryan, the California congressman murdered at Jonestown; and Patrick Lucey, a future governor of Wisconsin.

14 The Sultan of Brunei, then reportedly the world's richest man, had recently purchased the hotel and intended to shutter it for an extensive renovation. I wanted to savor its storied past before it was sanded and painted over and erased forever. The property soon closed for over two years.

15 The majority of personal ads appeared in alternative weekly newspapers, which espoused a progressive agenda and zany articles, and were given away. The East Bay Express covered Oakland, Berkeley, and surrounding communities and offered a good deal: the first twenty-five words of the ad were free.

16 Later ordained as a bishop, Reverend Gordon would achieve local fame as "Mr. Tie-the-Knot," reportedly officiating at over 20,000 nuptials, including many for stateside couples who secreted themselves to the island for just this purpose.

17 I am not able to explain why this is so; today, women dominate residential real estate and are represented in most other areas of commercial real estate, but, with rare exceptions, not in investment sales.

18 At its peak, the land under the Emperor's Palace in Tokyo was assessed at a value greater than that of the state of California.

19 Scarcely a year later, Sonja thanked us for the tough love.

20 Years later, I reminisced on this transaction, which kicked off the commercial real estate response to the technology boom. Enamored by the move to LA, I failed to recognize the deal's significance. Subsequently, tech powered California's—and America's—economic growth into the twenty-first century.

21   I have rollerbladed in other locales, such as Central Park in
     Manhattan, on the banks of the Seine in Paris, and along the
     beaches of Ipanema and Leblon in Rio, but I rate even these
     experiences inferior to the Strand.

22   Fortunes largely amassed by the progeny of immigrant Jewish
     families who fled the pogroms in the Pale of Settlement in
     the late nineteenth century. These families built many of
     Manhattan's skyscrapers, which established the precedent for
     other US cities and for the world.

23   Statistics indicate that, on average, a drunk driver has driven
     drunk eighty times before finally being arrested, an assertion I
     would certainly not dispute.

24   Perhaps best described in Ephesians 6:12: "For we wrestle
     not against flesh and blood, but against principalities, against
     powers, against the rulers of darkness of this world, against
     spiritual wickedness in high places."

25   Probably America's most famous seer, Cayce read the entire
     Bible every year and taught Sunday school weekly while con-
     ducting readings and dispensing counsel in a sleep-like state
     until his death in 1945. Over 14,000 of his readings have been
     archived by the Association of Research and Enlightenment, a
     nonprofit dedicated to facilitating the study of his work.

26   In terms of the broader market, the tech-heavy NASDAQ
     composite index, launched in 1971, closed above the 1,000
     mark for the first time in 1995; by the summer of 1999, it had
     cleared 4,000. Nearly three years earlier, Alan Greenspan, then
     chairman of the Federal Reserve, had already declared the
     market subject to "irrational exuberance." The travel range of
     a hot internet stock in a single trading day would exceed the
     movement of a traditional stock over weeks and even months.

27   Now a faint memory of the pre-9/11 era.

28   In addition to base rent, retail tenants typically pay additional

rent, calculated as a negotiated percentage of gross sales, if they do well and their sales exceed a certain threshold.

29   Shorthand for the Year 2000 bug, Y2K referred to a computer coding problem whereby four-digit years had been abbreviated as two digits in most computer programs in order to save memory space. Thus, the computer would not know if it was the year 2000 or 1900. Although fixable ahead of time with updated software, the problem nonetheless created global panic, which left many feeling foolish in hindsight when nothing happened.

30   A translation produced by forty-seven eminent scholars at the direction of the King of England in 1611.

31   Posited in 1969 by the psychiatrist Elizabeth Kübler-Ross, the stages depict the alleged progression of emotional states experienced by the terminally ill after diagnosis, to wit: denial, anger, bargaining, depression, and acceptance.

32   In a further twist, Ken died from cancer a year later at the age of 60.

33   More than just a funeral home, it consists of a complex of historic structures including a mortuary, on-site crematory, mausoleum, and multiple chapels, redesigned by Julia Morgan in 1928 in a Moorish and Gothic style.

34   In this category I had not put Daniel, whom I regarded as intrinsically wise and who dealt with tangible, measurable problems such as substance addiction.

35   The award was announced, ironically, two months after he died from cancer at the age of 49.

36   The San Francisco Municipal Transportation Agency, which operates the cable cars, buses, and trolleys, as well as a light rail system that runs underground and vertically parallel to BART in downtown San Francisco.

37 Wanda's half brother Clarence Carnes, also known as the Choctaw Kid, had previously been incarcerated at Alcatraz as its youngest inmate at the age of 18. He was befriended in prison by organized crime figure James Joseph "Whitey" Bulger Jr. After Clarence died in 1988, Bulger paid for his body to be transported to Choctaw lands in Oklahoma and properly buried. Bulger later became a fugitive from justice and regularly made the FBI's Ten Most Wanted list until captured in 2011 at 81 years of age. Natalie wrote Bulger at the penitentiary to obtain more information on her uncle Clarence and received a very long letter in reply, the crime boss reminiscing about their days in the joint.

38 The Odyssey was composed in a Greek dialect and in dactylic hexameter. As part of my training with the Jesuits, I read the *Aeneid,* a comparable epic poem written by Virgil, in its original Latin, and also in dactylic hexameter, the "meter of epic."

39 Many years later, she called me out of the blue, declaring that she had been "emotionally unavailable" when we met and offering me another chance. I declined, although I did watch her movies and graded her acting.

40 Consisting of 3,400 eleven-watt incandescent lightbulbs strung on 126 lampposts that completely encircle the lake.

41 Glass that is printed with a ceramic frit and fired into a permanent, opaque coating. Fritted glass allows for intricate patterns and helps to reduce glare, cut cooling costs, and lower the danger to birds.

42 On the way, I offered to take him on a side trip to Prairie du Chien, Wisconsin, which he declined.

43 Among the New Atheists' more formidable opponents was David Wolpe, senior rabbi at Sinai Temple in Los Angeles, with whom, coincidentally, I would later study Torah.

44 John C. Caiazza, "Athens, Jerusalem, and the Arrival of Techno-Secularism," in *Zygon*, Volume 40, Number 1, March 2005, pp. 9–21.

45 As measured by the percentage of religiously unaffiliated residents when compared with other major metropolitan areas.

46 Or, more accurately, scientism, whereby the idea of science as a method for testing empirical hypotheses is inflated to an ideology positing that the entirety of reality and truth is reduced to claims falsifiable by this method.

47 According to historians, Hitler reviled the clergy and especially the Jesuits; they promptly resisted and hid the hunted until they themselves were captured by the Gestapo and deported to the camps.

48 And of others, including Steve Jobs, who gifted the book, post-demise, to attendees at his memorial service.

49 April Thompson, "Water from a Deeper Well: Huston Smith On Why Spirituality Without Religion Isn't Enough," The Sun, October 2002. Smith should know. Born the son of Methodist missionaries in China in 1919, he not only studied but also practiced Vedanta (Hinduism), Zen (Buddhism), and Sufism (Islam) for more than ten years *each.*

50 It was not unusual in the Union Square District for a ground floor retail tenant to generate more net income for the lessor than the net income of all the upper floors combined.

51 Our joint venture agreement provided for incentives based on the achievement of certain milestones, such as the issuance of specific permits, which were finally being actualized.

52 Among all states, California and Texas had the largest populations and economies, as well as being the major exporters. Both constituted "majority-minority" states, with a nearly identical percentage of Hispanic and Latino residents, and both were youthful, boasting among the lowest median ages.

53 The number of sworn officers in the Oakland Police Department had been reduced to a level that, on a per capita basis, was 35 percent less than in San Francisco or Los Angeles and 60 percent less than in New York or Chicago.

54 According to 2010 data from the Centers for Disease Control and Prevention (CDC), the number of abortions by black women roughly equaled the number of abortions by white women despite a nearly fivefold difference in population.

55 All criminal charges were later dismissed against the Reverend Hoye. Additionally, the Ninth Circuit Court of Appeals in a 3–0 opinion found "grave constitutional problems" in the City of Oakland's enforcement of its purported ordinance.

56 Born Karol Wojtyła 200 miles away in Poland, he is generally credited, after former president Ronald Reagan, as most instrumental in aiding the fall of communism.

57 I recalled the words of Anatoly Lunacharsky, Stalin's Commissar of Enlightenment. When asked by the dictator why the eradication of religion was proceeding more slowly than planned, he conceded, "Religion is like a nail: The harder you hit it, the deeper it goes."

58 The schism between the two offshoots of Christianity—Greek Catholic and Eastern Orthodox—mirrored the cultural and ideological differences between western and eastern Ukraine: the west historically under Polish rule, Catholic, and more liberal in thought; and the east ruled by the tsars and heavily influenced by Moscow. In Kyiv and the east, the Orthodox ruled.

59 According to the PEW Research Center, the percentage of Christians in most regions of the world is on the decline except in sub-Saharan Africa, where it is expected to grow by over 40 percent by 2060. Nigeria now has more than twice as many Protestants as Germany, the birthplace of the Protestant Reformation.

60 By comparison, approximately one million people died during the Great Hunger in Ireland from 1845–49.

61 The Church's namesake is Sophia the Martyr, an Italian widow who lived in the second century AD. Her daughters, Faith, Hope, and Agape—12, 10, and 9 years old—were tortured, mutilated, and murdered in front of their mother by the emperor Hadrian for refusing to denounce their Christian faith. Saint Sophia buried what was left of them with her own hands and perished three days later, lying atop their graves.

62 The Choctaw Nation encompasses some 220,000 enrolled members, of which over 40,000 reside in the tribal jurisdictional area of nearly 11,000 square miles in southeastern Oklahoma. The tribe is governed by a constitution with three branches of government and keeps its members current with *Biskinik*, a free printed monthly newspaper.

Acknowledgments

To those who helped turn the idea into a book: Corey Mandell and predecessor writing instructors; developmental editors Dawn Raffel and Kimmi Auerbach Berlin, who protected my voice; my beta readers, who willingly turned the page; and Ingrid, Alex, Georgie, and the team at Girl Friday Productions, who helped me with all the rest.

To Dave, Adrian, Jack, Gary, Phil, George, Peter, Ray, Sean, John, Tony, Dan, and all my other commercial real estate colleagues and the deals we closed and the times we had.

To Steve, Napata, and Gordon for their friendship and recollections.

To my living family and the principal characters: Ginger; Nat, Solis, Dasan, and Tenaya; Greg; David, Alice, Sonja, Napoleon, Tory, and Ross. For all the others in my extended families: my appreciation for being there and continually affirming that differences don't matter. Special thanks both to the interviewees and those who sagaciously left me to my own devices.

To God, who allowed me to pretend that I could be author of my own life, a great gift.

Permissions

Grateful acknowledgement is made to the following for permission to reprint previously published material:

About the Author

Martin Sawa is a commercial real estate entrepreneur with a diverse career as a broker, operator, and developer. He has negotiated numerous high-profile transactions in the San Francisco and Los Angeles markets.

Sawa received a BA from the University of Wisconsin and a Master of Urban Planning from San Jose State University. He currently writes and helps others execute both business and life strategies.

www.martinsawa.com